WORK,
IN PROGRESS

Bringing Human Values Back to the Workplace

Frank Mertens

ISBN: 978-1-4834-8934-6 (sc)
ISBN: 978-1-4834-8933-9 (e)

Library of Congress Control Number: 2018909683

Lulu Publishing Services rev. date: 08/31/2018

Dedicated to my daughter, Lia

Contents

Introduction

Why am I Doing This?

I have been working in global roles at companies for many years. In these positions, you often have to present to the various countries to get their buy-in for specific projects, strategies, campaigns, and so forth. These meetings can be instrumental, because they can make or break the efforts of weeks of work. Consequently, I like to have "dry run" meetings beforehand with my team so that we are sure to make a good impression and are best prepared for questions and challenges.

A few years back, my team and I had to present a campaign to all of our European colleagues. The team had worked really hard on the project and I was very proud of the work. Nonetheless, I was eager to be well prepared for the presentation, so I asked the team to get together the night before to run through our presentation and discuss potential challenges. This way, we would be able to respond accordingly and maintain trust and excitement among our European colleagues. After the "dry run", my team and I felt really good. We went home that night excited about the presentation the following day.

The official presentation started off fairly well. The team was confident, the story was clear, and the presentation was compelling. Then, something turned. First, the country head from France started to criticize the already approved strategy. Then, two other countries questioned the timing of the project, which had also already been approved. My team started to get nervous. The only person who seemed totally at ease was Julia. During the break, I quickly took her to one side and asked, "Did you know that this was going to happen?" She looked at me and replied, "No, of course not". However, when we went back into the presentation room, Julia walked to the country leads that were leading the "revolt" and somewhat sided with them. I was shocked. Somehow, she was in on it. How could she do this to the rest of the team, and to me? I acted quickly to neutralize the situation, and we were lucky to save our work.

Later, I discovered that Julia was interested in an open position in the French market. Therefore, to get brownie points, she had shared our work with the French colleague beforehand—full-well knowing that she was putting our work at risk. This market was notoriously combative with the global team, so Julia's actions literally sabotaged our work. The selfishness of one person threatened to undermine the work of many. Moreover, she had no problem blatantly lying. What kind of values are these? Is this where society is heading? These values are certainly not the ones that I was raised with and that I was taught to live by.

This is just one example of how unhealthy human values are allowed to poison workplace environments. However, there are many more. Some are less obvious, and others more so. We all experience them directly or indirectly and they shape the way that we see expected behaviours at work.

Fortunately, those not yet exposed and indoctrinated to the ways of the corporate world are championing entirely different values.

A young girl in India exemplifies this to perfection. Ananya Saluja, who is just 17 years old, spends her summer breaks teaching less fortunate children in Kashmir's Leh district. She also raises money to build playgrounds and libraries for the kids there. She was introduced to the plight of the children of Leh during a two-month volunteer program. Ananya was so taken by the experience, seeing the challenges that the local people faced day-in and day-out, that she felt an obligation to return and help. However, it was not just the act of caring that compelled her to action, it was also the joy, friendships, and unique experiences that she was privileged to experience in return for her actions that fuelled her motivation to return.

Ananya shared her feelings about her times in Leh, and why she benefits just as much as the children:

> "To us, a tablet is an everyday object. But to these children who rarely see a computer, a tablet is a little magic screen working without any cord! It took some time to get comfortable with the children, since our cultures, environment and the level of exposure to the outer world were completely different. But once we got past that initial unfamiliarity, we found a very special connection beyond all these differences. After returning, I realized that there was a strong bond between us that kept tugging at me."

This young woman's actions are driven by the healthy human values that surround us when we are young. Reciprocal kindness, caring, loyalty, and the benefit of hard work are the values that are wonderfully on display in this story. These are also the values, along with trustworthiness and honesty that are inherently part of most of us, and reinforced by our parents and our faith, when we are young.

The story of Ananya is remarkable, and I can relate to her motivations. When I was young, I also felt compelled to help those less fortunate than me. I was always eager to give change to those who were begging on the streets, I thoroughly enjoyed the occasional times I worked with my parents at a soup kitchen, and I remember with great fondness that one Christmas where we bought gifts, food, and a tree for a family down on its luck.

So, what happened? How could I go from a life profoundly motivated by strong, healthy human values, to one where calculation, deceit, and fear are the accepted values to adhere to in order to be able to do your job? This is the reality that many people the world over live with and it is utterly unhealthy and destructive. At home we teach our children healthy moral codes to live by, then table that philosophy in the workplace. We are living with split personalities.

Looking back, I do not believe that my journey in life has been so unique that my current values dilemma is an exceptional case. I had a great upbringing, where I was exposed to different cultures, different languages, and where I was encouraged to be curious. My parents were in creative professional fields and lived among the trendsetters, the culture-benders. So, my home was always filled with interesting people and great conversations. However, my parents were both grounded people with good values and extended this belief system into the household. I had a caring mom who was at home for a good part of my childhood until I was old enough where she could continue her career. My father was a fun guy, who loved playing with me on the weekends. He was away a great deal at work which was the common role that a man played in those times. Nonetheless, my home growing up was fun, caring, safe, and with good values that dictated our lives. This home life, and the values that guided it, seemed to be similar to that which many of my friends experienced at the time. Therefore, I do not believe that my evolution from one value system to a dual value system, differs from the experiences of others.

My friends and I grew up with a basic set of values that seamlessly integrated into our lives. We were taught to be honest, not just with your parents but to your family, friends, teachers, and acquaintances. We were taught to be trustworthy. We were also taught to care for others. The most common saying was that you should "do to others as you would like to be treated" After all, there is a good chance that you may stumble at some point and will need the help of someone else. It may be inconsequential such as spraining your ankle at the playground and need help getting home. It may also be more serious, like having a stranger come to your rescue from thugs who are about to hurt you. You were also reminded to work hard, because if you did, it would be noticed, and you would get ahead in life on the merits of your efforts. The last value that we were taught was to be loyal.

For a very long time in my life I saw no reason to question these values. They made sense to me. They were also brought to life in all aspects of life that I saw around me. Consequently, the rare occasions where these values were challenged affected me enormously. I remember how shocking it was when my BMX bike was stolen when I was nine. I had left it outside of the variety store while I got some candy. I never locked it up. Why should I? People would leave it where it was. It wasn't theirs after all! When I came out of the store eating my candy, somewhat rushing on a sugar high, I was perplexed that my bike was gone. Did my friends take it? Did I leave it around the corner? Nope, someone had taken it. This was clearly a very unusual occurrence. The fact that I remember this story in such detail today, reinforces the point that the event was an aberration from the expected behaviours at the time.

As soon as I entered the working world, the values that motivated these BMX thieves were introduced and encouraged. It wasn't overt and sudden; rather the importance in adhering to these new, darker, values gradually grew. As I became more immersed in the corporate world, greed, selfishness, deceit, fear, and so forth became expected values that governed actions and behaviours at work. I hated it and was never able to fully live by this corporate code. Nonetheless, I could not completely ignore it, or my career growth would suffer. Before I had children, I often wondered how parents could comfortably (or so it seemed) act on these destructive corporate values. Did they teach them to their kids? Did they simply "turn on" a new personality as soon as they put down their briefcases at home? It baffled me.

Today, the situation with a world torn apart by two conflicting values systems has gotten so bad that we are reaching a tipping point. The most glaring illustration of this came in 2016, when the world experienced two "biblical" political earthquakes: Brexit, and the U.S. presidential election. The values of trust, equality, mutual respect and harmony that underpin the European project were rejected by one of its largest member states—the United Kingdom. In the wings, other movements in several European countries are expressing the desire to equally reject these healthy values. In the United States, protectionism and populism are so rife, that a man who exemplifies the most barbaric and evil values was elected President. Since his time in office, Donald Trump has fuelled racism, hatred, sexism, and more. It really feels like "the dark side" is taking over.

Fortunately, there are signs that an alternative reality is also in play. The sheer scale of reaction to Brexit and Trump shows that people do not want to accept these decisions, nor the values that guide the actions being taken by Prime Minister Theresa May, or by the Trump administration. Another sign of disdain for the current status quo is that the interest in a corporate career is seriously waning, replaced by the allure of working independently or starting a company. Lastly, the strong desire among the next big generation, millennials, to have more purpose in their work and career, suggests that an environment fuelled by healthy human values would be incredibly appealing.

Since there seem to be equally strong polarizing forces bringing us to this tipping point, I felt compelled to write this book. It is simply impossible to live a split personality existence. A choice will need to be made eventually. We may turn completely to "the dark side", or we may begin to reverse the tides. If I can help sway the balance towards a world more overtly guided by healthy human values, even if it is just a little bit, then that would be fantastic.

I also feel that I have a responsibility to act. I have a young daughter who is just about to enter school, and her future concerns me. She is incredibly sensitive and is a good soul. If the corporate world continues in the trajectory that it is currently taking, my little girl will likely have a very miserable future working life. I also do not want to be like those parents that I referenced earlier on, who routinely switch in and out of their "work identity" and "home identity". The exhaustion of it all will affect my ability to be there at full strength throughout her life. More concerning is that all it takes is that one time when you are too battered by the workday that you forget to "take off" your office identity and treat your little one like an unkind work colleague. I would not be able to forgive myself. Therefore, I feel that I have to be active in helping society bring back healthy human values in the working world. If my small contribution helps create a healthy change, I will feel that little bit better about the father that I have been to my daughter. She simply deserves it.

Chapter 1

The Problem: The Incompatible Values That We Live With

I absolutely love evenings at my house. Everyone is home, everyone is moving around, and the energy is just fantastic. It is also the only time in the day where my daughter is allowed to watch a little bit of TV. Occasionally I allow myself to sit down with her so that we can enjoy her shows together. As I observe my daughter's attentiveness to the TV screen, I am amazed and how much she is influenced by the characters in her favourite shows and by the principles and messages that they communicate. At the moment, she is a big fan of *Dora the Explorer* as well as *My Little Pony*. Her entire world revolves around the characters in these shows. She has a huge collection of Dora books, a Dora wrist watch, a Dora backpack, My Little Pony clothing and bedding, and an enormous collection of stuffed animal characters from both shows. To a certain degree, Dora the Explorer and the Ponies, especially Pinkie Pie, are my daughter's role models. A natural consequence of this relationship with Dora and with the Ponies is that my daughter's daily thoughts are consumed by these characters and therefore by the values that they communicate.

Popular children's TV shows today further, by and large, healthy and good human values. Honesty, trustworthiness, caring, hard work, and loyalty are all ever-present themes that guide these shows and their storylines. As a consequence, these shows and their role model

1

characters play a foundational role in shaping the belief systems of our children in their formative years.

Just the other day, I was privy to the cutest example of caring that I have experienced in a very long time. A friend of my daughter was joining her same nursery. This little girl has a slight disability and consequently is a bit smaller than the rest of the kids. Naturally, she was a little shy going into the room with all these kids; all these new faces, and all these unfamiliar dynamics. My daughter took her friend arm in arm into the nursery, sat her in the middle of the room, and called the other kids to come around. Then she began to hold court:

"Everyone, this is Jenny and she's my friend, and so I want every one of you to be extra nice to her and be her friend too."

The behaviour completely warmed my heart. She wanted her friend to not feel uncomfortable or sad at all, so she used her popularity in the nursery to "force welcome" her little friend. When I asked her afterwards what had prompted her to take this action and care for her friend like she was her sister, she simply said,

"That's what Pinkie Pie would do."

When it comes to her idea of work, my daughter often refers to Dora. My wife and I are sort of softies when it comes to our daughter. We tend to pamper her a little bit too much, giving her "surprises" more often than is probably healthy. We just love her so much. However, we saw the error in our ways and decided to put in place a star system to reward our daughter when she completed a task. To our surprise, without missing a step, she told us exactly how the star system would work:

"Okay Mum, I'll finish three things just like Dora and then I'll get a prize, right?"

As adorable as both these examples are, the important fact is that our young kids are surrounded by pretty good role models who preach solid human values.

Now let's have a look at adult role models and understand the values that guide them. As we will see, the difference between the values that are taught by the role models of our young children is quite extreme.

To identify the people whom adults most look up to, and therefore are likely role models, I looked at various lists that measure popularity. According to Google in November 2016, the three most popular celebrities in the world, in order of importance, are Kim Kardashian, Donald Trump, and Justin Bieber. *Biography* looked at the most influential people from the nineteenth to the twenty-first century and concluded that Marilyn Monroe took the top spot. *Forbes* looked at the world's most powerful, and therefore most spoken about and often most admired, people in 2015 and concluded that Russia's Vladimir Putin was number one. *Time* magazine's most influential Titan of 2016 is Mark Zuckerberg. Selena Gomez is the most followed person on Instagram in 2016 with ninety-nine million followers, according to Statista. If we line up all these people in a row and compare them, we see a handful of similar traits among all of them. They are self-consumed, arrogant, lacking transparency, and calculating. A handful are even downright mean.

How is it that within a short few decades, we go from looking up to people and characters who champion caring, honesty, trustworthiness, loyalty, etc., to admiring people who live by the codes of arrogance, egotism, deceptiveness, and so on? Even more perplexing is that we don't simply shed one set of values and adopt a new set; it is that we live with both. This is especially pronounced among parents because we try to instil good, healthy human values in our children when they are young. We encourage them to be honest and trustworthy. We teach them to care for others, to share what we have with them, and to work hard in order to achieve success and acknowledgement. Simultaneously, many of us head to work on a Monday and plot to undermine a colleague whose team is threatening ours, lie to a distributor to get a more favourable cost, and withhold information from a boss to manoeuvre into his or her position.

The issue with this reality, is that there is no harmony between these two value systems; there is no yin yang dynamic that allows you to live with both and have balance in your life. In *Basic Human Values: An Overview*, S.H. Schwartz writes that "people everywhere experience conflict" when pursuing different value systems. According to Schwartz, there is real struggle between seeking change and seeking conservation, and real tension between pursuing self-transcendence or self-enhancement. In other words, it is impossible to live honestly with both value systems. We are lying to ourselves in some shape or form. Perhaps this is why we try and teach ourselves to have two faces: a personal face, and a professional face. This never-ending "acting job" cannot be healthy, neither physically nor mentally. If we think about it, we are asking people to have split personalities, and split-personality-disorder, or dissociative identity disorder (DID) as it's now called, has potentially life-threatening risks for those affected.

What is even more concerning about a society that claims to live with both a healthy "human value" system, and a more destructive "corporate value" system, is that one will most likely eventually prevail, and the odds are favouring the "corporate value" system. The proverb "one bad apple spoils the barrel" is fitting because it underscores how easy it is for destructive forces to influence their surroundings. If we factor in the absolute time spent at work compared to at home, the chance that the human value system can prevail looks even bleaker. According to the American Bureau of Labor Statistics in 2014, the average person spends just under 40 percent of each day working, 32 percent is spent sleeping, and the rest is spent on a collection of activities. In other words, we spend 25 percent more time at work compared to all of our waking free time. This means that we are spending a considerably greater amount of time practicing bad values versus good values. Therefore, there is a very good chance that we are progressively conditioning ourselves to fully adopt the corporate value system as our universal value system. Once this happens, it will be a very unpleasant world indeed.

One of the most striking and worrying consequences of a world driven by a corporate value system, is the number of psychopaths in leadership positions in companies around the world. I suspect that when most of us look for a reference to define what a psychopath behaves like, we think about the character that Christian Bale played in

American Psycho. He is intelligent, self-consumed, meticulous, lacks emotion, and enjoys killing. Much of this is true, but not all psychopaths are killers.

According to *Psychology Today*, which aggregated the research from a wide range of respected thinkers, the symptoms of psychopathy are the following: superficial charm and glibness; an inflated sense of self-worth; a constant need for stimulation; lying pathologically; being manipulative; a lack of remorse or guilt; shallow emotions; and lack of empathy. I have met a few people in my career who display these symptoms with abundance. What I find shocking is that these people find it easy to move ahead in organizations without accomplishing much.. One person in particular was thoroughly disliked by her team because she did very little aside from bullying them with orders. When it came to sharing results, not only did she take credit for them, but she also embellished the actual impact on the business. Somehow these corporate psychopaths are able to charm the right people, pull the right strings, and influence the right conversations so that they fluidly step up in rank and responsibility.

In 2010, a study of 203 managers across several companies conducted by Paul Babiak, Robert Hare and Craig Neumann concluded that the rate of psychopathy in corporate management was three times higher than that in the general population. These findings are further supported by data in a 2015 Inc.com article that states, that while just one out of a hundred people in the general population qualify as a psychopath, that rate rises to 3 or 4 percent among business leaders. While the absolute number of all psychopathic leaders is relatively small, the fact that they excel in corporate environments today is a testament to the absurdity of what we now accept as normal in our working lives.

Therefore, not only are the two value systems incompatible, not only is there a strong chance that the corporate value system will likely prevail over the human value system, but the degenerative effect on humanity can be significant. This is enormously concerning for the health of society.

This current societal reality has taken generations to develop, and has been influenced by many societal, economic, technological and political forces. It is therefore important, first and foremost, to understand the biological starting point. In other words, we need to understand the fundamental values that we are genetically predisposed to. For any parent, it will come as no surprise that babies are born with a basic moral code, in the same way that babies are born with the most obscure and random personality and behavioural traits. I found it so amusing, but also highly interesting, that my daughter, in her first year, displayed behaviours that she simply could not have learned by observing my wife or me. She would be so incredibly fidgety in her crib with movements that were all too familiar to me, or she would strike these momentary poses that were spitting images of my wife. Therefore, in the same way as certain attributes are handed down within a family, other attributes are handed down within a species.

It is also important to look back at recent history to understand the decisions that we have made resulting in our current world of conflicting value systems. Whether it is the financial deregulation that resulted in the meteoric rise of the financial services and banking industries, or the invention of social media that resulted in an increasingly vain and anxious daily way of living, or the heavy investment in reality TV that resulted in the introduction of a new type of role model, each decision has had an effect on the values that we deem important.

Finally, it is important to understand the milestone moments in every human being's life that can have a notable effect on that person's values. S.H. Schwartz writes: "It is common to speak of three systematic sources of value change in adulthood: historical events that impact on specific age cohorts (e.g., war, depression), physical ageing (e.g., loss of strength or memory), and life stage (e.g., child rearing, widowhood)." To this list I would add professional experiences (e.g., job loss, which is commonplace today), technology adoption (e.g., social media, mobility), and increased globalization (e.g., cultural interconnectedness, competition).

Clearly, there are many dynamics fuelling the divide between the human value system that we grew up with and the corporate value system that we grow into. Looking at the whole picture, the task to reverse the direction of any aspect of this growing divide seems daunting. However, given the growing dissatisfaction among people in all corners of the world with the direction in which society is going, the desire for change is ever growing.

Based on a survey conducted by *The Atlantic*, 70 percent of Americans believe that their values are getting worse, and 77 percent believe that people's actions are purely motivated by self-interest. The dissatisfaction with economic and societal leaders is even more alarming, with 66 percent of people believing that the economy is heading down the wrong direction and only 17 percent of people believing that Wall Street and bank executives share the same fundamental human values as the rest of society. The recent monumental voter rebellions, in the form of a Trump election win and a decision in the UK to "Brexit", coupled with growing populism in countries throughout Europe, suggests that we have reached a tipping point.

If there was ever a time in history to discuss the chasm that has developed between healthy human values and destructive corporate values and provide a point of view on where we can start to make healthy changes, it is now.

Chapter 2

The Values That We Are Born With

From the moment that she was born, my daughter has been a bundle of energy. She would kick frantically in her crib in bursts of excitement, let her presence be known wherever she was with a good cry here and there, and couldn't keep her hands still, grabbing at everything in sight. Yes, she was quite a handful, but my wife and I loved every bit of it. The only downside to having such an active child is that going out anywhere with her was one heck of a physically and emotionally draining task. So you can imagine how stressed out we were when we had to take our first transatlantic trip to Canada to visit our in-laws. Not only was the flight going to be a taxing affair but having to deal with all the social commitments was a daunting thought.

One of these commitments was visiting my wife's grandmother in her nursing home. She was very frail and the thought of having my little tornado offspring interact appropriately with this very old woman was worrying. My daughter was just over a year old at the time but actually already understood key things that were told to her. As such, we prepped her as best as we could.

We walked into the nursing home with our daughter being her active little self. Worry set in. Some of the nurses looked judgingly at us as we made our way down the halls. Eventually, the moment of truth arrived. We stepped into my wife's grandmother's room. As my daughter stepped closer to this older lady sitting hunched in her bed, her attitude and demeanour completely changed.

"Hello, my dear!", the old lady said.

My daughter calmly leaned forward, raised her left arm, and gently caressed her great-grandmother's face. She then slowly sat down beside her, looked up, and attentively listened to what this wise old lady had to say. As her great-grandmother spoke, she didn't move an inch. My wife and I were shocked. Our little girl displayed such empathy and care for this person that she barely knew. Somehow, she felt the vulnerability, remembered what we had told her beforehand, and demonstrated some authentic human emotions towards a stranger. It was absolutely beautiful.

Does this suggest that we are born with a basic set of human values? Are certain values hardwired into human beings, or at least into most human beings? Logically, the answer should be yes, because as a primate we should have some built-in tools that allow us to navigate the world around us from the very start of life. Many western philosophers did not believe so. Enlightenment philosopher Jean-Jacques Rousseau claimed that all babies are born "perfect idiots." Thomas Hobbes, who was a great English philosopher from the 17th century, argued that all new-borns enter the world as nothing more than "selfish brutes." They were both wrong.

Scientific Proof

A large body of work in recent times from a wide range of researchers and intellectuals has confirmed that human beings are indeed hardwired with a basic set of human values and morals. One of these recent pieces of work can be found in *The Happiness Hypothesis*, which was written by a psychologist named Jonathan Haidt in 2006. In this book, he writes that human beings are born with five inherent values. The first value is caring, specifically caring for other people and not doing anything to voluntarily harm them, be it physical or emotional. The second value is being fair and reciprocating kindness. In other words, creating common ground and establishing a foundation of trust. The third value is being loyal to those in your group and working with others to help them accomplish things and to succeed. So, in a very primitive way, protecting and assuring the future of your group or "clan." The fourth value is about respect, specifically respecting authority. Finally, the fifth value is about having self-control and having some restraint. In other words, being considerate to those around you.

So, when my daughter met her great-grandmother, she was tapping into her inherent value of caring and respect, which was manifesting itself in a very unique behavioural change that was surprising to both my wife and me.

An automatic, or natural, desire to help, and therefore to care for another human being was also proven by an experiment done by Harvard University. According to the Smithsonian, the Harvard experiment nicknamed "The Big Mother Study" (as in Big Mother Is Watching You), demonstrated that children naturally helped others irrespective of whether their mother, or parent, told them to do so, or whether the parent was even present with them.

Other research even concludes that we are born with a rudimentary moral compass. A group of researchers at Yale University's Infant Cognition Center conducted several years of research among children under twenty-four months of age to determine whether they could judge good from bad. The Baby Lab, as it is known, achieved its results through tests, including a very simple exercise. They set up an innocent puppet show that had a cat and a rabbit and presented it to these young babies. The puppet show was not elaborate but looked professional so that there was a sense of seriousness for the very young spectators. The show began with a big grey cat coming onstage to try and open a big plastic box. No matter how hard or how often he tried, the big grey cat could not open the lid all the way. He pushed and pulled in all directions. The cat was clearly frustrated, even sad. Before all was lost, a bunny wearing a green shirt came onstage to help. The bunny looked at the cat, then at the plastic box, and finally helped the grey cat open the box. Then, the same exercise was re-peated but with a twist. The big grey cat once again came onstage, looked at the plastic box, and tried to open it to no avail. However, this time a new bunny came onstage wearing an orange T-shirt, looked at the big grey cat, saw that he had trouble opening up the plastic box, and walked towards the cat. Instead of helping the cat open up the box, he forcefully slammed it shut. Then the bunny in the orange T-shirt quickly ran away. So, the message from this exercise is that the bunny with the green T-shirt is nice and helpful, whereas the bunny with the orange T-shirt is mean and unhelpful.

After the puppet show was over, the babies who had just viewed the show, were reintroduced to the two bunnies that they had seen. A member of the research team who had no prior knowledge of which bunny was mean or nice offered both bunnies simultaneously to each baby. If a baby's mother was present, which was usually the case, she was asked to close her eyes in order to not influence her baby's decision. The Yale research team defined a preference for good as a baby who either reached for the good bunny or stared at it with con-viction. To the surprise of the researchers, a significant amount of the babies chose the good bunny. On average 80 percent of all babies in the study chose the good bunny, and that percentage grew even higher to a staggering 87 percent among children who were three months old. The results were conclusive: children were able to differentiate between good and bad, and preferred good.

Paul Bloom, a professor of psychology at Yale University asso-ciated with the Baby Lab, concludes from these studies that babies are clearly born with a rudimentary sense of justice. He believes this because these babies are able to judge a good action from a bad action before they can even speak or walk. One of professor Bloom's peers from the University of California at Berkeley, reinforces his con-clusion through additionally conducted research but uses slightly more conservative language. This developmental psychologist states that, "there isn't a moral module that is there innately, but the elements that underpin morality – altruism, sympathy for others, the understanding of other people's goals – are in place much earlier than we thought and are clearly in place before children turn two years old."

Another two studies, outlined in an article by the Smithsonian Institute, reinforce these findings. The first study, called Giving Leads to Happiness in Young Children, concluded that children under the age of two years old "can tell, to a certain degree, what is good or bad, and act in an altruistic fashion." The second study, called Babies Know What's Fair, stated, according to the Smithsonian, that "toddlers are particularly equitable to judgment based on values. They are natural helpers who are keen to help others that are in distress, even if it is at a cost to themselves." This will manifest itself in the form of visible concern displayed if another child's painting is torn up, or sharing rewards, such as gummy bears, after the successful completion of a shared task.

Through all this recent scientific evidence, we can comfortably confirm that good human values and a basic sense of good and bad are part of our genetic makeup at the time that we are born. Thank goodness that the great thinkers of the past with all their great wisdom on many different topics were very naive when it came to children! New-borns are not "perfect idiots", and they are certainly not "selfish brutes". They have a solid foundation of good and justice.

In order for us to build on our foundation, it is important that we understand the reasons and motivations for why we have hard-wired human values and morals such as caring, loyalty, respect, and justice. We must, therefore, explore the two main historical inputs into our universal behaviour: Our anthropology, and our spirituality.

Anthropology and Values

In our evolution, we know that brain size increased, and with it so did behaviour. Analysing the different tools belonging to our early ancestors, we see a trend of greater craftsmanship as evidenced through their tools and weapons. Comparing tools from two million years ago with more recent ones of a hundred thousand years ago, it's clear that they've become smaller and much more ornate. They also move from pure utility to personal or communal indulgence. Early discoveries were solely for hunting, cutting or crushing, whereas later discoveries were also for painting and communicating.

When looking at some of the early cave paintings, we can see scenes where men seem to be hunting as a group, or we can see people sitting around campfires. These very basic settings suggest that community, and therefore social dynamics within the community, were being developed. However, to understand the values that dictate these social dynamics is impossible without a live specimen. The best place to look to find a comparable specimen that is alive today, is among the group of apes that is most closely related to our ancestors – chimpanzees.

A 2014 article, published in the National Center for Biotechnology Information (NCBI) by Anim Behav, states that:

> there is currently great interest in the phylogenetic origins of altruistic behaviour within the primate order. Considerable attention has been focused on chimpanzees, *Pan troglodytes*, because they are our closest living relatives and participate in a wide range of collective activities, including hunting and food sharing.

There are select activities that chimpanzees and humans share that no other primates participate in. Among male chimpanzees, these include grooming one another, forming coalitions and controlling the borders of their territories. Among female chimpanzees, these include creating lasting social bonds with other female chimpanzees and sharing food with their offspring that is difficult for the offspring to retain or process by themselves. In addition, both male and female chimpanzees are the only non-human primate species that share food among other adult chimpanzees in the wild on a regular basis.

The act of grooming shows that chimpanzees care for one another. Research suggests that the motivation for grooming is social bonding, and that it is learned by copying what the mother chimpanzee does to its child. In other words, the young chimpanzee experiences the nurturing care of its mother, then reciprocates this act of caring to those in his or her group to create social bonding. Additionally, it is the female chimpanzee that sustains the health of the group, so it is natural that select behaviours will be copied and passed on through the generations.

When chimpanzees create coalitions and protect their borders, it is for self-preservation. Only through this level of community organization can the chimpanzees fend off rivals who may be interested in taking their food. In order for this dynamic to succeed, it requires a basic sense of loyalty and trust. So, chimps develop a primitive need, or importance, in loyal behaviour to further the prosperity of the group.

Food sharing is motivated by group-preservation, which ultimately helps self-preservation. If food is shared among the group, then the group will be stronger and consequently will be able to protect its territory and care for the young. With food sharing comes the values of fairness (or honesty) and reciprocal kindness. Emory University primatologist Darby Proctor led a study that confirmed that chimpanzees have an evolved sense of fairness because, as he stated in an interview with LiveScience, "If you're involved in some cooperative act you need to be sure you're engaging in something that's beneficial to you." Therefore, by sharing its food, the individual chimpanzee will be assured that it too will receive food. Consequently, the chimpanzee is ensuring its livelihood.

We can conclude from our analysis of chimpanzees that the root reasons why they have these core values of caring, honesty, fairness, loyalty, and trustworthiness, all boil down to self-preservation. That self-preservation can be in the form of social acceptance (via bonding and mating), or in the form of pure physical survival (via food guarantee and protection against rivals or predators).

Religion and Values

Our spirituality also significantly influences the base values that we pursue from very early on in life. The main reason for this is because many parents follow the core values of their faith when raising their children. Therefore religion, to a certain degree, is the main outside influence that shapes our early value system.

Research conducted across the world's religions such as Christianity, Judaism, Islam, Confucianism, Hinduism, Buddhism and others, has proven that they all share similar foundational values. These include a deep caring for all life, compassion and kindness, honesty and integrity, commitment and responsibility, and generosity and sharing. Since the great religions have been with humanity for many generations, it is likely that their base value systems were developed from the human needs identified through human observation. Consequently, it seems understandable that all religions should be based on the same core human values. Naturally, each has evolved to include thinking from each period of its history, as well as thinking from key figureheads within that faith. However, the evolved thinking has added more values versus having stripped away the core values mentioned above.

The reasons that the world religions continue to push their values is to create a sense of purpose and to assert control. Human beings across the globe are in desperate need for meaning to propel them through life. The jobs that they do and the passions that they enjoy provide superficial meaning, but there is always a deep-rooted desire to be driven by something more profound. According to Pew research, over 50 percent of Americans believe that religion plays an important role in their lives, which suggests that in the world's most capitalist society, the place where there are the most distractions, there remains a huge desire within the population to find meaning beyond these distractions.

Consequently, the core human values of caring, honesty, fairness, loyalty, and trustworthiness that are shared by the world's religions are the endorsed behaviours that people follow to live a meaningful life.

By combining the insights from human anthropology and humanity's history with religion, we can understand that these core human values play an existential role, both functionally but also emotionally.

On the functional side it is about self-preservation, both socially and physically, and on the emotional side it is about purpose and meaning. The importance of these values to our well-being is clear. What is not clear, is the relative importance of each of the values. If we could understand this relative importance, we may be able to hypothesize which human values are more easily shed over time compared to others. Therefore, we should explore the scientifically recognized hierarchy of needs to be able to rank the human values accordingly.

Human Values and Our Hierarchy of Needs

The most universally acknowledged thinking on human needs is by Abraham Maslow. His theory on the hierarchy of needs was fully expressed in his 1954 book *Motivation and Personality*. Maslow's hierarchy is illustrated in the form of a pyramid where fundamental needs form the base and exceptional needs are at the top. From bottom to top, the needs are as follows, "physiological", "safety", "belongingness" and "love", "esteem", "self-actualization", and "self-transcendence." The four bottom layers of the pyramid represent the needs that Maslow described as "deficiency needs", which means if these needs are not met, an individual can feel anxious and tense.

The base need is physiological, which includes the primitive requirements for survival such as air, water, and food. Achieving this need is paramount for any human being and requires a certain degree of collaboration with other human beings so that the air, water and food is shared. This behaviour was also observed among chimpanzees. As such, the human values of reciprocity and fairness are likely not easily shed. Their definition may evolve over time, person by person, but their existence will always be there.

The need for safety is second in Maslow's hierarchy. It includes things such as personal and financial security, health and well-being, and safety against external factors such as accidents or illness. In the same way that chimpanzees created coalitions to protect their borders and create safety for the group, humans also need to build coalitions to create safety for themselves and for their families. As such, the human values of loyalty and trust will be important to most people throughout their lives and will therefore not easily be shed by many people. However, as society shifts to work environments that are more about the individual (driven by a growth in self-employment, freelancing, start-ups, etc.), the need for the values of loyalty and trust may be changing. Instead of being deep-rooted, these values may evolve to being opportunistic and therefore superficial.

The third need in Maslow's hierarchy is more intimate because it involves feelings such as love and belongingness. This need is very important to children and can even supersede the need for safety, as evidenced by the many examples of abused children that continue to cling to their violent and tormenting parents. According to Maslow, humans need to feel a sense of belonging and acceptance among their social groups. Deficiencies of these needs affect a human being's ability to maintain an emotionally healthy relationship with others. If we consider that the divorce rate has gone up by 40 percent since the 1980s, based on an article published by *The Washington Post*, we can believe that the need for love and belonging is not fully being met for many in society. Consequently, the associated human value of caring for another human being is weakening in society at large. Therefore, while the human value of caring may be vital to children, it can be less important in adulthood.

The fourth level need in Maslow's pyramid is esteem. Esteem is the common human desire to be valued and accepted by others. Deep down inside we all want to be better than others in some aspect of life because that makes us desired and valued. This superiority allows us to demand respect from others. Given that respect is a core human value, to nourish it requires that we dish it out but also that we receive it. Consequently, most people engage in a wide variety of activities outside of work where they obtain a certain level of mastery. These hobbies become the means by which they get respect from others and subsequently their source of esteem. The problem is that respect or acknowledgement is rarely granted. Instead, it is a lot more common to be disrespected. Additionally, since the rules of respect are very much shifting with the millennial generation, it can be expected that this human value is easily ignored.

The highest level of Maslow's hierarchy of needs is self-actualization. It refers to a state when a person realizes her or his full potential. Therefore, it is a state where a person's life has full meaning. This level is rarely achieved, and it is unlikely to have happened without a person having embraced and followed the core human values outlined in the above paragraphs.

Human Values and Adulthood

The information outlined in this chapter is both encouraging and concerning. What is encouraging is that we enter this world with good, genetically built-in human values that allow us to survive both physically and socially. These are the values of caring, fairness and reciprocal kindness, trustworthiness, loyalty, and being considerate and respectful. What is equally encouraging, is that we are also born with a rudimentary moral compass, allowing us to know good from bad.

What is concerning is that as we grow into adulthood, many of these values can be discarded or redefined. By looking at what human values are fundamental to each level of Maslow's hierarchy of needs, we see that even the base values of fairness and reciprocal kindness can change their definition as we get older. Loyalty and trust become more opportunistic than life-guiding, caring can fade away, and respect will likely be ignored altogether or completely redefined.

While it is natural for values to change as you get older due to changing influences around you, it is not natural that the changes have to be negative. We have the opportunity to evolve the core human values in a very positive and constructive way. Currently, it seems that this is not happening in the world at large. Quite the opposite is happening. Therefore, we need to look at the different influences in our lives that are shaping the shifts in values to determine where the most damage is being done, and from there explore reform.

The main influences in our lives that will influence our change in values are the home, school, work, and culture. Out of these four influences, there is one that has an impact on the other three: work, or more specifically, the corporate world. The corporate world has influence in the home because the parents work in the corporate world and bring home the habits that they have learned at work. The corporate world also impacts schools because curriculums and teaching methods are influenced by what students need in order to be prepared for the workplace. Finally, culture is clearly informed by the corporate world because it is more or less funded by the corporate world.

Consequently, creating reform in how values should evolve as we get older needs to start in the corporate world. To do this, it is important to understand how the corporate world itself has evolved over time. This will provide clarity on which events and influences have shaped the values that are adhered to today in the workplace.

Chapter 3

The Evolution of The Workplace and The Values in The Corporate World

The workplace has changed enormously over the past decades. The "job for life" career has long faded away. Walled offices have given way to open plan workspaces. The appeal of big companies has dissolved in favour of start-ups. Fixed hours have evolved to more flex schedules. Two-hour Martini lunches have been replaced with eating at your desk (where you try and finish off that presentation, while simultaneously shovelling down that mixed salad you bought at the closest deli outside of your office). Even hierarchical structures have been binned to make way for chaotic and complex matrix organizations.

We will look at some film and television references to illustrate these points. One of the most respected television series of the past few years took place in corporate New York City in the 1960s. *Mad Men* focused on the hip lifestyle of the advertising business of the mid-twentieth century, but also touched on the corporate philosophy of that era. The show, especially the first few seasons, was so entertaining because of its attention to detail in all aspects of the storytelling—the sets, the wardrobe, the props, the situations, the expressions, the relationships, and the authenticity of the stories themselves were meticulously crafted. As a result, it accurately reflects the past.

One recurring theme in *Mad Men* is about employees' connection to the workplace. There was a sense of loyalty and stability. Even the client accounts tended to stick around for a while at agencies in those days, which is completely different in the advertising business today. A film that shows how far removed loyalty and stability is in the office environment today is *Office Space*, a brilliant comedy set in the late 1990s. The whole storyline revolves around corporate downsizing. Even before the announcement that consultants were coming in to help with restructuring, the atmosphere in the office was poor. There was no connection to the company, no sense of loyalty or appreciation, and there was certainly little stability. The tension was horrible, as best brought to life by the "red stapler man" who would eventually blow a gasket at the end of the film.

Another theme that was consistently brought to life in *Mad Men* was separation in organizational structures. The lavish office of Don Draper, or even the plush rooms of his subordinates, were decorated with couches and chairs, whiskey glasses and decanters, mood lighting, and proper artwork. There was stature and sophistication. Fast forward to the present time into the world of the hit HBO series *Silicon Valley*, a comedy that exaggerates the world of the start-up scene. However, the humour comes from scenarios anchored in elements of reality. Does the concept of the office exist in this world? Not really. Is there any sophistication? Hardly. It feels more like college fraternity living gone bad. Is there stature? Sort of, but more based on smoke and mirrors, versus one that is built through experience earned through hard-work and paying your dues.

A final theme brought to life in many scenes of *Mad Men* is the casual, "work-lite," lunchtime ritual. The "Two Martini lunch" was common, although disguised as a business lunch. However, it was universally understood that it was a lot more play than work. The approach to work did not entertain the thought of having your head down all day and late into the evening. There was a different rhythm to work culture. A film that references the old way of working but is set in a contemporary setting is *The Intern*. In this movie, Robert De Niro plays Ben Whittaker, a seventy-year-old intern at an eCommerce start-up. The fact that this young company has an in-house cafeteria is new to

Ben. He quickly realizes that it forces people to stay at work for longer periods of time, so there are less distractions from their daily jobs. When he is made aware that they also have an in-house masseuse, he is surprised in ways he could not have imagined!

The changes in the workplace over the past sixty to seventy years are clearly staggering. Accompanying these organizational and behavioural changes are equally big changes to what people deem important and what they are no longer concerned with. In other words, there has been a notable change in corporate values. To best understand the influences that got us to where we are today, we should dig into each decade and explore the triggers that have pushed corporate life in new directions.

Life in the 1950s

It is important to understand the backdrop to work life in the 1950s. Europe was aggressively rebuilding after World War II. Many cities were still partly rubble. The war had depleted resources. In the book *History of Europe and the Middle East* the authors state that Britain had lost a quarter of its national wealth and gold reserves were nearly exhausted. If it were not for American loans, the country may have suffered economic collapse. Germany was busy building political and economic bridges after years of destroying them.

It was a time of enormous integration among many European states. NATO was in its infancy, the European Coal and Steel Community was established in 1951, the European Economic Community was kicked-off with the Treaty of Rome in 1957, and the great Franco-German partnership that would be the thrust for European prosperity, was birthed. However, even as some countries got closer, others remained weary and weren't ready for integration. Britain had an insular sense of security based on standing apart, and Spain, under Franco, viewed the EEC as a "fief of freemasons, liberal, and Christian-Democrats." In other words, Europe was moving forward, but had many distractions.

In the United States, the 1950s were considered "good life" years. It was a decade of substantial economic boom. Consequently, consumers were spending more readily, taking advantage of a growth in available goods that were scarce during World War II. The federal government was spending aggressively, creating jobs in the process. Their focus on foreign aid via the Marshall Plan stimulated demand for American goods and services. Old and new industries blossomed; steel, automotive, electronics, plastics, and computers were all thriving industries. With a growing economy, the labour market was bustling and content. Consequently, workers seldom challenged employers as wages and benefits grew.

Suburbia became a big part of American society during the 1950s on the back of the baby boom, which was in full swing during this decade. This, in turn, further spurred on the economy because of its positive impact on the construction business. The term "keeping up with the Joneses" came from this growth in suburbia, where families didn't want to be outdone by their neighbours.

With prosperity came new forms of consumer expression. The teenage voice was increasingly being heard, influencing television networks, movie studios, record labels, and comic book companies. Most importantly, the 1950s was when rock 'n' roll was born. It was propelled to the center of culture by none other than Elvis Presley. His rebellious attitude lit a flame inside the younger generation. This flame would turn into a raging inferno in the decade that followed.

The 1950s also saw the official start of the civil rights movement in the US, which would go on to have a huge social and political influence.

It was a time when the manufacturing sector dominated, especially in Europe. In America, jobs in the service sector grew enormously on the back of greater consumer spending and growing international demand for all things American. These were truly golden years for America, where its economy was leap-frogging that of its European colleagues. The United States was shaping what the corporate world, globally, would look like. Therefore, it makes sense to focus on America when exploring which corporate values were rife in the 1950s.

One way to get a sense of corporate life, and its values, in the 1950s, is via the entertainment medium that was sweeping the American nation—television. Over 80 percent of households in America had TVs by 1957, totalling roughly 40 million television sets.

Popular Culture in the 1950s

A very popular television series in the 1950s was *I Love Lucy*. This sitcom was about the average life of a young couple living in an apartment in New York City. The husband (Ricky) is a singer and bandleader, and his wife (Lucy) is an aspiring performer. Lucy doesn't quite have the skills required to make it in show business, but relentlessly tries to find her place under the spotlight, leading to highly entertaining situations. In between her attempts at becoming a star, she plays the role of a dedicated housewife and attentive mother, and occasionally works. One such job was at a chocolate factory. A very memorable episode shows Lucy and her friend Ethel struggling to find a suitable position at the factory, getting pushed from one department to the next, after failing to adequately do the various jobs. They end up at the chocolate wrapping assembly line. A very demanding boss puts them through the wringer. Hilarity ensues as the two ladies try desperately to shovel chocolates down their mouths in order to keep up with the ever-accelerating conveyor belt.

In addition to the eye-watering comedy, the skit highlights two interesting aspects of work life in the 1950s. The first observation is that people worked very hard. This scenario speaks about the blue-collar labour market, but it also reflects the manual and exhausting working environment of that era. The second observation is that there was a sense of loyalty. Lucy and Ethel were clearly not great workers, but they were given many chances to find their place in the company. That is certainly not a common philosophy shared today!

The attitude of the day in American work life was championed by the President, Dwight D. Eisenhower. Known as "Ike" by the people, he was the perfect father-figure for the 1950s. He had the age to carry wisdom, but also had the modern outlook to carry the country through growth in the post-war era. Personally, he was like everyone else, which made him incredibly relatable and someone to whom the people listened. His philosophy was one of harmonious teamwork, and this thinking seeped into the workplace. The values of hard work, loyalty, and caring were a result of Ike's merchandised moral code and the bountiful work opportunities.

Labour historians say that workplaces in the 1950s were very harmonious, even between the different generations. According to an article by Todd Henneman in Workforce.com, "young workers in the 1950s gained the reputation for following rules and obeying authority." The respect for authority manifested itself in all aspects of life. If we look at the types of television programming that were universally popular in the decade, we see two types of authority figures dominating the airwaves. Popular shows such as *Dragnet* or *The Lone Ranger* centered on good, law abiding heroes. They always prevailed over the "baddies."

The other format that was enormously popular was the variety show. The one person that reigned supreme was Ed Sullivan. His weekly Sunday night show, *Toast of the Town*, was admired by families across America, bringing them the best of entertainment at the time and educating the nation on everything from comedy, to opera, to dance and music, to acrobatics, and so on. He was the authority on culture. In hindsight, his stature was amusing because he did not have enormous charisma. *Time* magazine wrote about Mr. Sullivan in 1955 that he was:

a cigar-store Indian, the Cardiff Giant and a stone-faced monument just off the boat from Easter Island. He moves like a sleepwalker; his smile is that of a man sucking a lemon; his speech is frequently lost in a thicket of syntax; his eyes pop from their sockets or sink so deep in their bags that they seem to be peering up at the camera from the bottom of twin wells. Yet, instead of frightening children, Ed Sullivan charms the whole family.

I suppose his drabness was actually a reflection of the reliable and trusted, "grey suit," working man of the time. There was comfort in uniformity after a period of intense emotions and turmoil associated with the war.

Work Culture in the 1950s

It is interesting that with an era of enormous growth, comes a movement that seeks sameness. Whether it was the "white picket fence" suburban architecture, the grey flannel suit office uniform, or the "keeping up with the Joneses" mentality, there was a hunger to advance, but that all advance at the same pace and in the same way. The young working-class spearheaded this movement. Todd Henneman refers to a *Fortune* article that referenced this group's uniformity in dress, and their contentment in following the status quo. There was no desire to take chances because things were moving along just fine. Moreover, there was a confidence in big brother. Neil Howe from LifeCourse Associates, a consulting firm, states: "The idea was that you trust these big institutions because they were built by all these people who sacrificed so much and the way that you get ahead is by following the rules. So, people did exactly that." The result of this mind-set was that people stayed in one workplace, one company, for their entire careers.

Companies took a paternalistic view of their workforces. Melvyn Dubofsky, from the Binghamton University in New York City, claims that "there were a lot of incentives for employees to remain with the company at which they started". There was financial security and social stability. It was understandable that work colleagues became "family." If you did not leave your company, chances were that your social network was made up, in large part, of colleagues from your job. Consequently, there was a universe created around the husband's (since it was a decade that saw the role of the woman as being a homemaker) work. With this social reality, it was natural to do what was necessary to keep the status quo. As a result, loyalty to the company and care for your fellow office colleagues was expected. The label that was put on workers of this decade was "The Organization Man." This was coined by William Whyte in his 1956 study of the same name. In it, Whyte speaks to the worker as a rigid conformist, who was happy to put the corporation ahead of himself.

The 1950s were also the years where the retirement age of sixty-five was institutionalized. Why? There was a common belief at the time, that performance decreased as age increased. This artificial "end point" reinforced the corporate philosophy that it was important to take care of the employee financially and socially because, after sixty-five, they were on their own.

In summary, the decade of 1950s was an era where corporate values truly mirrored human values. The two worlds were so closely intertwined that it was natural for the value systems to be the same. The enormous economic growth that fuelled the 1950s meant that there was security and stability. As a result, the values of loyalty and caring were strong. Longevity with an employer meant that there was enormous respect for the company. Consequently, the values of trust and honesty were extremely important. Finally, the value of hard work was admired because it showed appreciation for the company that was providing a stable and secure financial and social future for you and your family. However, out of stability and conformity comes curiosity. In the decade that followed, this would have a significant influence on society and the workplace.

Life in the 1960s

The 1960s were arguably the most transformational years in modern times. Literally every aspect of society went through seismic changes. The political landscape shifted to the left, which shook governments the world over. Wars raged that would monumentally impact the global geopolitical landscape. The Cold War went into overdrive. Landmark assassinations rocked the foundations of the countries in which they took place. The Space Race galvanized the greatest minds in America and Russia and helped thrust science forward in ways not previously imagined.

Social movements transpired that forever changed humanity, society, and culture. Big music revolutions happened, whose leading artists and musical styles continue to influence musicians today. Some of the most iconic films of all time were created, and television shows that are admired to this day were made.

Clearly, the corporate world, and the values that anchor it, could not help but also go through change. Interestingly, these changes, while very healthy at the time, would evolve into negative forces in the decades ahead.

Economic and Political Life in the 1960s

As in the previous decade, America's hegemonic stature in the world was unchallenged. However, after many years of steady growth, cracks began to appear. This was evidenced by two noticeable, but short, recessions. The first happened in at the tail end of the 1950s. Known as the Eisenhower Recession, this recession started in 1958 and lasted for eight months. It had a notable impact on America, Europe and Canada because it profoundly impacted many businesses, some terminally. An example, according to Wikipedia, was part of the mining industry in the United States, which was forced to shut down. The second recession took place during the dawn of the new decade, and solely impacted America. Lasting only ten months, the recession of 1960 to 1961 would cause unemployment to rise to 7.1 percent. Moreover, the unhealthy unemployment levels would last for months after the recession had officially ended. Therefore, these mini economic earthquakes forced economic and political discussions.

The back-to-back recessions and the resulting high unemployment rate ushered in a demand for change. This came in the form of President John F. Kennedy, who won the 1961 American election on a campaign promise to "get America moving again." Immediately upon taking office, he focused his administration on economic recovery. His target was to achieve economic growth of four percent 4 percent to 6 percent per year and lower the unemployment rate to below 4 percent. To do this he initiated two key initiatives. The first was to institute a 7 percent tax credit for businesses that invested in new plants and equipment, which would in turn fuel employment. The second was to stabilize the dollar to ensure continued foreign demand for American goods and services, which would also ensure a growth in US jobs.

To do this, Kennedy's Secretary of Treasury, Robert Roosa, initiated the London Gold Pool. In short, this proposal pooled the gold reserves of Britain, West Germany, France, Italy, Holland, Luxembourg, and Switzerland, with those in Fort Knox. Therefore, each time that a bullion of gold threatened to hit US$35.20, American and Western European banks would sell gold. Reversely, if a bullion of gold fell below US$35, the group of allied banks would buy gold. As such, the value of the US dollar was kept stable. The London Gold Pool forced European nations to be joined at the hip with the United States, thus firmly connected their economies. Consequently, America was assured a steady stream of foreign consumer demand. The US economy would jolt into a boom-like growth.

The economy reacted with great innovation and entrepreneurialism, forming new businesses that would reshape industries, or create them altogether. Pioneering companies that are still admired to this day were born in the 1960s. Giants in sports (e.g. Nike, Vans, and K-Swiss), in entertainment (e.g. Universal Studios Hollywood), in food (e.g. Domino's, Frito-Lay, and Haagen Dazs), and in nutrition (e.g. Weight Watchers) came out of the bold new thinking fuelled by government economic growth initiatives in this decade. Additionally, median family income would almost double between 1961 and 1969. There was excitement in the workplace and the value of creativity was now very much applauded and admired.

A third factor contributing to economic growth in America was increased competition with the Soviet Union. There were two key thrusts to this competition: The Space Race, and a stronger commitment to the Cold War.

President John F. Kennedy had a huge impact on heightening the Space Race by announcing a bold target to Congress on May 25, 1961. During that speech, he announced his ambitious goal of safely sending an American to the Moon by the end of the decade. This galvanized the nation, and by 1969 the United States had sent Neil Armstrong, "Buzz" Aldrin, and Michael Collins to the Moon in Apollo 11.

Clearly, the impact on the scientific community was noteworthy. However, the impact on culture was equally substantial. We need only look at the most popular television shows and movies of the decade to see that the fascination with space was all-consuming. "Star Trek", "The Jetsons", "Lost in Space", and "I Dream of Jeannie," are television shows that were all launched in the Sixties, whose settings or topics were about space. These shows were produced with such passion and brilliant storylines that they are still entertaining audiences today. In film, two of the all-time masterpieces produced in the 1960s centered on space exploration: "2001: A Space Odyssey", and "Planet of The Apes." Two consistent values in all these television and movie gems are adventure and bravery. Since the airwaves were flooded with these shows, it was unavoidable for these values to not impact the population at large, and thus also the corporate world.

Innovation was on the rise. The number of submitted patents in America noticeably grew across industries in the 1960s, compared to previous decades. Another aspect of the workplace that was also on the rise was labour revolt. Sharon Smith wrote an article in *The Socialist Worker* that stated, "strike levels began to climb as early as 1965, and from the years 1967 to 1971, the average number of workers involved in strikes doubled." In 1962, all nine New York City newspapers went on the longest strike in U.S. history. Most of this was due to misrepresentation of their union leaders. However, there was also a deterioration of working conditions, brought about by the need for greater output due to growing consumer demand. Bravery and fairness were now firmly part of the corporate value system.

Competition with the U.S.S.R. was also dialled up under the guise of the Cold War. The United States engaged in conflicts around the world that would test its might against the Soviet Union. Consequently, military spending would be kept high, which resulted in a steady growth in jobs. Naturally, the government as an employer had an impact on corporate values in America. Loyalty and hard work were expected. These were values that anchored the corporate landscape in the 1950s and, thanks to government control of a big part of the labour market, continued to be pertinent in this sector of the economy during the 1960s.

War and Strife in the 1960s

There was one big negative impact of increased military spending—real war. The two big escalations of the Cold War in the 1960s would impact humanity forever. The first was the Cuban Missile Crisis in 1962. This conflict literally brought the world to the brink of nuclear war, or "the abyss of destruction" as Kennedy would call it. The fear that it created was palpable. Europeans, especially West Germans who would have been at the front line of the war, shivered. They were seriously wondering whether their annihilation was days, then hours, then minutes away. There was no place to run. Once it all ended, there was certainly a huge relief. However, the closeness of it all rocked all those affected to their core. The sense of total powerlessness seeped into the European public consciousness. This kept people grounded and aware, even as the economy grew and lives became more prosperous. The values of resourcefulness were very much set in motion, affecting both personal and professional lives.

The second big war of the 1960s was the Vietnam War. During its peak in 1969, five hundred thousand American troops were on active duty in Vietnam. While the war started in 1954, it was under the Kennedy and Johnson administrations in the 1960s that the war escalated. The draft was a big part of the war. It is often assumed that

31

a large percentage of the troops sent to Vietnam were drafted. That is false. Only around one third of the troops were drafted, but due to the sheer volume of men, the debate around the draft process became a big social discussion point.

The media fuelled negative discussions around the war because, for the first time, the reality of war was broadcast right into the living rooms of all Americans. Night after night, the news showed countless body bags being loaded onto military planes. Why so many young American men were dying in a jungle half a world away, for a cause that wasn't fully understood, gripped the nation—especially the youth. This triggered a huge anti-war movement in university and college campuses across the United States. The majority of these activists were white, middle class, and well educated. The combination of being educated and having financial stability provided the freedom to question authority. This would eventually break a paradigm that existed in the workplace—blind obedience.

The shift in the cultural mindset was beautifully brought to life in film. Several of the most culturally relevant movies of all time that were produced in the sixties, questioned authority. *Easy Rider* is perhaps the most obvious example as it spoke directly to the counterculture of the day. According to Calvin Wilson in his book about the film, *Easy Rider* was a "touchstone for a new view of society was fully brought to life. The beauty of this new perspective was then shattered by representatives of the establishment at the end of the film.

Bonnie & Clyde is another iconic film of the decade that questions authority. Frank Miller from Turner Classic Movies wrote:

> For many members of the American counterculture, Bonnie & Clyde was a rallying cry. The main characters' bank robbing was seen as a form of revolution, while the film's paradox, in which the criminals were more sympathetic than their law-abiding killers, seemed to legitimize the violence against the establishment.

In other words, Bonnie & Clyde championed the fight against authority, and the need to debate a new world order.

The many high-profile assassinations in the 1960s suggest that the establishment had a strong aversion to its authority being debated, let alone challenged. The bloodshed started with the assassination of John F. Kennedy in 1963. He was the embodiment of change and a departure from the old-world order. Visually he was young—philosophically he was bold. He championed individual responsibility and thus individual thinking. The famous words from his inauguration speech touch on this sentiment: "Ask not what your country can do for you, but what you can do for your country." His death was a blow to progress, and the sadness spread the world over. His brother, Bobby Kennedy, would make a run at the White House in 1968 and would also lose his life by gunshot.

In the civil rights movement, two prominent figureheads would also be assassinated. The first was Malcolm X in 1965, and the second was Martin Luther King in 1968. Both men were instrumental in changing policy and in forcing the plight of the black man into a national discussion. The peaceful nature of Dr. King's movement, the humanity of his approach, and the optimism of his message, made his killing all the more horrific. Evil had dealt a crushing blow to society. Outside of America, the killings continued. A revolutionary who fought the exploitation by the United States of South American economies was also murdered in 1967. His name was Che Guevara. He firmly believed that America was an authoritarian country. Cuba provided the perfect platform to exercise his convictions. However, a CIA-backed group ended his life. The "authority" prevailed.

Popular Culture and Social Change in the 1960s

Living through these extraordinarily violent years, it was impossible that values would not be affected. Trust in the system was being questioned because the lack of societal freedom was being exposed. Although the economy was booming, there was labour unrest in pockets of America due to lack of trust with union representatives. As such, the decade saw the value of trust being redefined. It continued to be important to both human and corporate value systems but putting your faith in bigger institutions was being questioned. The preference for individuality (i.e. trust in oneself) was germinating.

This sentiment was most evident in the various movements for individual rights that mushroomed in the 1960s. The civil rights movement was by far the most prominent, culminating in the landmark march on Washington, where Dr. Martin Luther King gave his historic "I have a dream" speech. According to the National Archives, the March on Washington for Jobs and Freedom on August 28, 1963, was the largest gathering for human rights in American history. It gave rise to the Black Power Movement later in the decade. Individual rights for black Americans were firmly demanded, and resistance to the contrary would never again be silenced.

The fight for women's rights would also go into high gear. The subservient family role that was thrust upon women after the war had no more place in society. The National Organization for Women was founded in the mid-sixties, and by 1968 "Women's Liberation" was a household term. The gay rights movement was also set in motion late in the decade. In 1969, a police raid on a renowned gay establishment, the Stonewall Inn, in New York City, was met with firm resistance. The act of police defiance had not happened before and made a public statement that gay men and women deserved individual rights. In all three movements, the common thread was that trust in the establishment to be fair no longer existed. Trust in the individual, or the "clan", was an increasingly appealing value.

Music fuelled individual thinking, and championed new perspectives on the existing world order. Legendary guitarist Carlos Santana commented on the artists of the sixties, saying "The Beatles, The Doors, Jimi Hendrix created revolution and evolution themes." Literally all corners of the musical landscape were contributing to what Santana said. The rise in folk music, led by great thinkers and true poets such as Bob Dylan, provoked discussions on a wide range of topics affecting society. Some of his songs, such as "The Times They Are A-Changin'," were anthems for the civil rights and anti-war movements.

The San Francisco sound, blossoming out of the Haight-Ashbury scene, projected many anti-establishment themes. A comment by Janis Joplin explaining why she was viewed as an outcast encapsulates the anti-establishment spirit of the scene: "I was a misfit. I read. I painted. I thought. I didn't hate niggers." The values of unity, love, and compassion were core to the San Francisco musical movement, culminating in the 1967 "Summer of Love" and an epic gathering two years later in Woodstock.

These same values were also written about by bands and musicians propelling the worldwide domination of the British Invasion. Although so many iconic bands such as The Rolling Stones, The Byrds, The Kinks, Cream, and The Who were part of this "invasion," no other band is more associated with the movement than The Beatles. Their 1967 album *St. Pepper's Lonely Hearts Club Band* was even nicknamed, according to Wikipedia, "The soundtrack of the Summer of Love." The spirit of acceptance was galvanizing society.

It would not have been imaginable in previous decades, that a record label dedicated to black artists could be so loved that it would achieve 79 top ten hits in the Billboard 100. Motown accomplished exactly this in the sixties. The music business was clearly disrupting the thinking of the time and influencing millions. The values of individuality, inclusion, and compassion were embraced by young people across the world. The corporate world did so as well, since it needed to target younger consumers for many products that fuelled growth in various industries.

Carlos Santana made a fitting statement to the impact of the 1960s on society, saying "the sixties were a leap in human consciousness." Naturally, both human and corporate values evolved. While the personal and professional worlds became less intertwined than they had been in the 1950s, they continued to share similar values. The value of caring grew in importance as a consequence of the various movements of the decade that encouraged compassion.

Corporate Life in the 1960s

Loyalty also continued to be an important human and corporate value. The key difference was that blind obedience to the company, which was prevalent in the 1950s, seriously weakened. Since union leaders weren't always reliable, and some work environments deteriorated, the need for workers to be resourceful to get treated fairly was a widespread reality. The fact that union leaders and managers were not always being forthright meant that the value of honesty within the corporate value system began to weaken.

Clearly, the value of trust was also affected. Workers who had poor work experiences began to shift their trust away from their company towards smaller like-minded groups. Obviously, they were taking inspiration from the human rights movements that were thriving all around them. However, looking at the broader picture, the value of trust continued to be strong in both human and corporate value systems. The economic boom meant that there was health across most industries. Therefore, most workers trusted their employers, and those companies trusted their employees.

The new values ushered in during the 1960s were creativity and self-expression. A more politically and socially active youth, coupled with an economy that was thriving off of the creation of new businesses, meant that creativity was going to galvanize society. As we know today, many of those creative undertakings were so brilliant that they are still around today. A great focus on self-expressions also meant that the seeds of selfishness were planted, which would yield problems in the decades to come.

Life in the 1970s

The 1970s marked a turning point for the relationship between human values and corporate values. It was during this decade that these two value systems began to drift away from one another. In an essay published by the *New York* magazine in the mid-seventies, the author

Tom Wolfe wrote that the 1970s were the "Me" decade. He argued that this ten-year period saw the shift away from communitarianism, which was common in the 1960s, to the more "atomized individualism" where self-interest ruled. This was understandable given the economic backdrop, which saw the worst economic performance in most industrialized countries since the Great Depression. Consequently, the "opportunity for all" cultural belief that reigned supreme in the previous decades, no longer existed in the 1970s.

A telling way to capture the angst of the seventies is by looking at how music evolved. The start of the decade saw a group that embodied the love generation, The Beatles, disband. This created a profound sadness among millions of adoring fans the world over. The Beatles were such beacons of optimism that when they called it quits in 1970, it ended a movement. A lot of upbeat music with lyrics that spoke about love, championed by big Motown artists such as the Jackson 5 or folk artists such as Carole King, continued in the early part of the decade. However, there were also topics of tension in many influential artists of the early 1970s. Stevie Wonder released *Where I'm Coming From* in 1971 in partnership with his new wife, Syreeta Wright. As stated in his biography written by Sharon Davis, he and his wife wanted to "touch on the social problems of the world," and have the lyrics "mean something." Wonder quickly followed up this album with *Superstition* in 1972, whose songs were written to "deal with the negative effects superstitious beliefs can bring," according to Wikipedia.

One of the best-selling albums of all time, *Dark Side of the Moon* by Pink Floyd was released in 1973 and dealt with topics that "made people mad," according to founding band-member Roger Waters. Glam rock pioneer, David Bowie, also wrote about more socially provocative topics in his album *Diamond Dogs*. The theme of the record took inspiration from George Orwell's *1984* book, speaking of a post-apocalyptic world. Even a soon-to-be respected mega-star, Bruce Springsteen, spoke about the troubles of a blue collar working life and the shifting moral codes.

These sparks of rebellion and despair were understandable, given the big cultural happenings of the early Seventies. The decade began with a landmark event in the United States that seriously fractured American citizens' relationship with their government. The Kent State massacre on May 4, 1970, saw the Ohio National Guard shoot on un-armed students who were protesting the bombing of Cambodia by the United States military. Four people were killed and nine were seriously injured. This act sparked a massive national student strike, over four million people strong, and consumed the media headlines.

In 1972, the world was rocked by several big events. The first was the terrorist attack that killed eleven Israeli Olympians at the Summer Games in Munich. Safety was no longer an expected part of everyday life. Even more chilling was the symbolism of this act. The fact that innocent Jews were massacred on German soil, not that long after the end of World War II, tore open barely healing wounds. Terror attacks were rampant during this time, notably hijackings. The cover of the August 11, 1972 edition of *Life Magazine*, captured the scale of this epidemic. The picture showed a plane in mid-flight with the rear exit hatch open (which was a common way for hijackers to escape) and the headline simply stating "Skyjacking" in capital letters. Flying was a legitimate hazard during this time.

The other big event in 1972, was the Watergate scandal in the United States. President Nixon was caught ordering an "array of clan-destine activities, many of them highly illegal, such as bugging the offices of political opponents." Nixon's blatant abuse of power led to his resignation in 1974. The message that it sent to the world at large was that those on the highest rungs of power were cheating. Trust in the system was rattled.

The final big cultural event of the early Seventies was the 1973 oil crisis. The Organization of Arab Petroleum Exporting Countries (OPEC) issued an oil embargo that resulted in the cost of a barrel of oil rising from US$3 dollars to US$12 dollars per barrel. Consequently, gasoline was rationed in many countries. This significantly impacted the workforce. The unemployment rate in the economic engine of the world, the U.S., went from 3.5 percent in 1969 to 5.6 percent in 1974.

This marked the start of a series of large, highly publicized labour disputes, according to Albert E. Schwenk in his article *Compensation in the 1970s*. For example, in 1970 "almost 210,000 postal workers walked off their jobs in the first mass work stoppage in the history of the U.S. Postal Service." A year later, four railroad unions also had strikes. Workers were angry, and no longer trusted their employers. In the United Kingdom, a staunch American ally, the situation was also bad. Labour minister Jim Callaghan summed up his nation's situation perfectly: "Our economic comparisons with the world grow worse. If I were a young man, I should emigrate." The value of self-interest over loyalty in the workplace of many countries was growing.

As we moved into the mid-1970s, the honest, straightforward, and sometimes dark song writing of the early decade was replaced by the escapism of disco and stadium rock. People no longer wanted songs that spoke about "false realities," as many of the love songs did. Songs that put a mirror in-front of their lives or forced reflection about the issues facing society, they wanted even less. Instead, they craved distraction. They needed to step away from their real worlds. Disco distracted people through the party-vibe that surrounded the scene, while stadium rock distracted people through theatrics.

Disco gave people a high that they could not get in other parts of their lives, especially not at work. The party atmosphere and hedonistic dance culture that surrounded the scene was a nice distraction from the hardships facing society. The 1975 hit single from the Bee Gees, "You Should Be Dancing," embodied the "forget it all" attitude. The song was beautifully put to picture in one memorable scene in the film *Saturday Night Fever*. Travolta's character had just had a long week at work, so he headed to the dance club. There, he danced away his weekday woes, while being admired by the patrons of the club. Unfortunately, the disco genre went into intense overdrive, where even CBGB (NYC club that birthed the US punk scene) acts such as Blondie and stadium rockers Kiss found themselves developing disco songs. The artificiality of the scene was its downfall because it simply was so at odds with the reality of everyday life, which for many was miserable. Eventually, disco self-destructed.

Stadium rock was also a movement that allowed for escapism. Huge bands such as Kiss and Aerosmith put on dazzling shows with elaborate outfits, and spectacular visual effects. They created worlds that their fans could inhabit. Kiss went all in to create escapism. Their live performances were legendary; filled with extravagant theatrics such as blood spitting, fire breathing, never-before-seen pyrotechnics, and levitating drum kits. It was an all-out assault on the senses. Their movement was so strong that their followers became known as the "Kiss Army" and by 1977 Gallup rated them the most popular band in America.

Aerosmith, on the other hand, created escapism by championing the same kind of hedonistic indulgence present in the disco scene. Vocalist and key songwriter of the band, Steven Tyler, made sex the main topic of his lyrics, and the drug consumption that surrounded the band's lifestyle was well documented. They too had a fanatical fan-base, known as the "Blue Army" based on the blue denim jeans and denim jackets that were commonly worn by their followers. These blue collar "troops" idolized Aerosmith's messages and lifestyles. While these are just two noteworthy examples of bands from this genre, many others deployed similar escapist "tactics" that strongly resonated at the time.

Interestingly, the hunger for distraction was also reflected in the types of television shows that were developed and gained notoriety in the mid-seventies. Whether it was *Happy Days* or *Three's Company* or *The Love Boat*, the themes in popular television shows were incredibly light-hearted and most were comedies. They allowed viewers to escape to a simpler world, one without real problems. Comedy also uplifted. According to Ranker.com, seven out of the ten best television shows of the 1970s were comedies. Some prolific comedic writing took place at this time. The iconic *Saturday Night Live* was first aired in 1975, and the cult film *Animal House* hit theatres in 1978. Writers knew people needed distraction, and creating laughter was a perfect way to achieve it.

Hardship and Upheaval in the mid-1970s

The profound desire to escape the real world was to be expected, if we consider the societal reality that surrounded most people through the mid-seventies. In the United States unemployment grew to a staggering 8.5 percent in 1975, and inflation mushroomed. In fact, the inflation rate during the 1970s was roughly three times higher than in any other period since the start of the 1900s. This enormous rise led to "stagflation", causing interest rates to rise to unprecedented levels every year. Prices tripled while wages did not. Economic stability seemed like a thing of the past in many countries. Consequently, the value of trust in the corporate world continued to weaken.

These economic hardships meant that retaliation was inevitable. During the mid-Seventies, there were several "I've had it" events that further impacted the zeitgeist. The example most directly correlated with the economic situation, was the mass riot that ensued during the 1977 blackout in New York City. When the city fell into darkness, citizens did not come together. Instead, they took advantage of the chaos to engage in city-wide looting and releasing their anger through disorderly acts including large scale arson. Thirty-five blocks of Broadway were destroyed, and the damage was estimated at over $300 million dollars, according to a Congressional study.

Other examples of retaliation were the bold attempts to fight the government by the Weather Underground, or "Weathermen" as they were eventually called. This group was a clandestine revolutionary party, whose core purpose was to overthrow the U.S. government. In 1975, they bombed the United States Department of State in Washington D.C., causing panic in an already turbulent time.

A less destructive anti-establishment movement was for women's rights. By 1977, feminists had gotten Congress to approve the Equal Rights Amendment. However, the fear by many conservatives created a successful drive in government to ensure that the Amendment would not pass. Belief in the fairness of government was significantly shaken.

41

In Europe, the far-left movements were ever present. The most notorious was the Red Army Faction in West Germany. This militant group was responsible for over thirty-four deaths. In 1977, their terror activities peaked leading to a national crisis known as the "German Autumn".

In other parts of the world, there were also movements against the status quo. In Cambodia, Pol Pot's Khmer Rouge overthrew the government, and forced citizens to embrace a radical agrarian way of living. In South Africa, students protested the conditions in the Soweto township, which led to the 1976 uprising where seven hundred black school children were killed by police. The images covered newspapers around the world, underscoring the darkness of the times.

All these uprisings fuelled a clear lack of caring towards governments and business, since these institutions did not seem to care for their people. Consequently, in the workplace, the distance that employees began to feel towards their employers would echo the broader cultural sentiment. As a result, there was an erosion of the value of caring in the corporate world.

Popular Culture Self Expression in the 1970s

The motion-picture industry seemed to echo this fearful mood, unlike the television business which tried to make people forget it. Popular films that are still admired to this day, such as *Jaws*, *The Exorcist*, and *The Omen* played on the unknown. They fed on fear that was already part of the cultural subconscious. Other films amplified the struggle against "big power." *Star Wars* was a masterpiece of good versus evil, perfectly reflecting the "battle against the man" that seemed to be brewing in many corners of society.

By the end of the decade the desire for rebellion was growing. Disenchantment with "the system" was universal—and no other industry manifested this tension better than the music industry. The vacuum created by the implosion of disco and the growing boredom of stadium rock was filled by more truthful and much more aggressive new music styles. Punk, heavy metal, and hip hop were born. Gaining real momentum by the end of the decade, these incredible music innovations came out of frustration and despair. Unemployment was rising, trust in governments was eroding and living conditions in certain places were horrible. Citizens needed an outlet, a voice with whom they could identify. All three of these different musical sounds did exactly that. Punk, hip hop, and metal had an aggression, an anger, and an energy, that created a community that was needed to fill the void that existed in society.

In heavy metal, musical giants such as Led Zeppelin, AC/DC and Black Sabbath were voices for the industrial towns where factory work was shrinking. In hip hop, Kool Herc, Grandmaster Flash, and Afrika Bambaataa provided a new outlet for the gang-filled, crumbling Bronx in New York City where there was staggering unemployment. In punk, the Ramones and The Sex Pistols were allies of disenfranchised urban white youth who did not see a role or future for themselves in the current society. Punk was arguably the most rebellious scene, seeking to provoke the establishment outright. As Sex Pistols' guitarist Steve Jones proclaimed in an interview, "actually we're not into music. We're into chaos."

The desire to speak out was to be expected, since society seemed to be getting worse. Simply ignoring it or escaping from it seemed fruitless. In the United Kingdom, the end of the decade saw the "Winter of Discontent," which consisted of a series of strikes throughout the public sector that affected all parts of the nation. Power cuts were common and basic sanitation was in dire straits. A BBC reader, Mr. S. McIntyre, wrote, "As a 10-year-old in 1978, I remember the piles of garbage piled up in our local recreation ground in Stanmore, Winchester (a council estate in a well-off part of the U.K.). The piles of rotten waste became our playground."

Not only did unemployment continue to be high in many countries, and living standards continue to deteriorate, but political upheavals seemed to be on the rise. The end of the seventies saw a re-escalation of the Cold War, triggered by Soviet provocation in several "critical political theatres" in the world at that time. The U.S.S.R. was able to overthrow two pro-American regimes, one in Iran, and the other in Nicaragua. It also aggressively engaged in Afghanistan, ignoring vocal U.S. opposition. President Jimmy Carter responded to these actions by withdrawing from a key armament control treaty (SALT II), imposing embargoes on the Soviet Union and significantly raising military spending. Carter even initiated a boycott of the Moscow Olympics. This increased insecurity the world over, and in all parts of society.

Clearly, with strikes, immense unemployment rises, and existential fear brought on by an escalating Cold War, values in the corporate world changed. The value of trust that employees firmly had in the fifties, and mostly in the sixties, was no longer prevalent. Instead, employees became more independent because they realized that they could only depend on themselves. The value of caring also weakened. As lies piled up from companies and governments, and actions did not reflect words, workers felt that the work environment no longer had the family dynamic which was enjoyed in previous decades. Loyalty also became a frail value in the corporate world. The reciprocal kindness necessary to nourish loyalty was no longer universal. Employers fought with unions, unions didn't always speak for the workers, and governments didn't act on the people's behalf. Naturally, people began to value selfishness over loyalty because it was a better choice for personal survival. In short, there was a clean split between many human and corporate values that would never come together again.

Innovation in Technology in the 1970s

Fortunately, not all was bad in the 1970s. The values of creativity, self-expression, and resourcefulness notably grew. Inventions that changed the world came out of the seventies. In aviation, both the Jumbo Jet and the Concorde saw their maiden flights. In medicine, the MRI scanner and liposuction were invented.

In electronics, the innovation was staggering. The first video cassette tape and the Sony Walkman changed the way visual and audio content would forever be consumed. The creation of the bar code would revolutionize retail. The introduction of video games would create an industry that generated $99.6 billion dollars in worldwide revenue in 2016.

Topping off all these life-changing inventions were two introductions that would accelerate human progress like no other: the microprocessor and the personal computer. Two companies that would be instrumental in the computer business were founded, one year apart, in this decade. They would create hardware and software that would make the personal computing industry ubiquitous. Microsoft and Apple, and their founders, were perfect examples of the independent thinking that spurred on the creativity of the decade.

The inventors of most of these remarkable introductions listed above were free thinkers. Whether it was Ralph Baer, who invented Pong in isolation from his regular corporate job, or Raymond Damadian, who invented the MRI scanner and was labelled "an underdog physician who showed chemists and physicists a new way to look inside the human body" by PBS, they embodied the values of self-reliance and independence that emerged from the withering reliability in the "established" corporate world. In their cases, pursuing these values benefited all of humanity. In the coming decades, this behaviour would create businesses that and people who would enormously hurt society.

Life in the 1980s

The 1980s was a decade of enormous prosperity, which ushered in cultural dynamics that would propel humanity to new heights. Technology made a huge leap forward: Computing became a ubiquitous part of corporate life; mobility was introduced to the masses; and the mass penetration of the VCR, or Video Cassette Recorder, empowered everyone to watch television shows whenever they pleased.

Economic liberalization also profoundly impacted how big corporations would run their operations, seeing manufacturing relocate to less costly countries outside of the developed world. This would set in motion a workforce shift in America and Europe towards a knowledge- and service-based economy. The eighties would also put in motion the accelerating disparity in income distribution, which would have a seismic influence on corporate values. The value of selfishness that grew in the 1970s out of distrust, blossomed in the 1980s out of greed. The "yuppie" was born out of this economic shift, and the "greed is good" mantra, made famous by the 1987 film *Wall Street* starring Michael Douglas, would summarize the mind-set that was firmly part of this period and would dictate culture for several decades thereafter. Extravagance and indulgence grew in importance, as was evidenced by the growth of the movie blockbuster and the meteoric rise of MTV and its lighthouse stars.

The decade did not start off positively. Unemployment was high and growing in many countries around the world. Germany, France, Italy, Australia and Korea all saw notable rises in their unemployment rates. In the United States, the situation was exceptionally bad. According to History.com, "by early 1982, the United States was experiencing its worst recession since the Great Depression. Nine million people were unemployed in November of that year. Businesses closed, families lost their homes and farmers lost their land." Fear took hold of society.

Not only was the economy in many countries in a frightening state, safety from human and natural predators was also a concern. In December of 1980, Beatles icon John Lennon was gunned down outside of his Central Park apartment in New York City. A few months later, the U.S. president, Ronald Reagan, was shot in an assassination attempt, only sixty-nine days after taking office. A short time after that, the IRA attempted to kill the British Prime Minister, Margaret Thatcher, in a seaside hotel in Brighton. The unexpectedness of these acts rattled the world, especially throughout American and European society. This chilling statement by the IRA further instilled fear in the broader population because it suggested that more terror was on the horizon: "Today we were unlucky, but remember we only have to be lucky once – you will have to be lucky always."

Then in 1981, the deadly disease known as AIDS was discovered as it began to ravage small communities of drug users and homosexual men. While there was no immediate concern towards the broader population, the ruthlessness of the disease coupled with the cluelessness of the scientific community about its origins and potential treatment left a chill in society at large. It was therefore no surprise that millions of people around the world sought escape by watching the wedding of Prince Charles and Lady Diana on television in 1981.

Economics and the Rise of the Yuppie

The darkness that kicked-off the decade was attacked head-on by the leaders of key developed countries. In the United States and the United Kingdom, economic policies would be initiated that would propel prosperity. Better known as "Reaganomics," since it was spearheaded by the Reagan Administration, this economic policy increased government spending, significantly removed government regulation and reduced federal income tax and capital gains tax. Another name given to this economic approach was "trickle-down economics," suggesting that greater prosperity at the top would encourage spending, thus benefiting those at the bottom.

Germany also sought to reduce the government's role in the economy through a policy called "Wende" (reversal). It sold shares of state owned companies such as Volkswagen and Lufthansa, with the goal of improving the performance and flexibility of the labour market. Even in France, the socialist desire for greater government control called "dirigisme" was abandoned for an approach called "rigueur", or corporatization. The European Community also expanded to further trade and collaboration, taking on Greece in 1981, and Portugal and Spain in 1986.

The results of these economic initiatives were mixed. In the United States there was enormous growth, where both small and large companies hired millions of new workers. In Europe, the French economy grew, the German economy remained more or less flat, and the British economy initially went down. In the U.K. unemployment actually rose to 11.9 percent by 1984. However, a growth in newer industries and the service sector helped the British economy rebound in the later part of the decade.

In the United States, these initiatives created record budget deficits, where the federal government would rack up more debt in eight years than it had in its entire history. The most striking result from these initiatives, was the imbalance that was created in the workforce. Some people got enormously wealthy during this period, while others did not enjoy the same gains. At the start of the decade, the total workforce income share of the top one percent was approximately 10 percent. By the end of the decade, this percentage hovered around 15 percent. Since "all boats were rising," the disparity was not a concern.

A new type of professional was born out of his era, the "yuppie" (young urban professional). The growth of this group was so noteworthy that *Newsweek* named 1984, "The Year of the Yuppie." What was very noticeable about this group, was their value system. Two famous quotes highlight what made these people tick. The first is from the respected news commentator and political analyst, William Kristol, who said "Yuppies don't have loyalty. They have useful relationships and meaningful encounters." The second is by renowned novelist, Douglas Coupland, who said:

> Yuppies never gamble, they calculate. They have no aura: ever been to a yuppie party? It's like being in an empty room: empty hologram people walking around peeking at themselves in mirrors and surreptitiously misting their tonsils with Bianca spray, just in case they have to kiss another ghost like themselves. There's just nothing there.

Yuppies introduced incredible selfishness and a "cosmetic existence" into the workforce. Key human values would be shattered by these "new professionals." Caring, loyalty, honesty, were all brushed aside. Instead, arrogance, egotism, and deceptiveness were prioritized. While this group only represented a fraction of the working population, they tended to populate high profile industries such as finance, tech, law, advertising and others. As such, their influence on corporate culture was significant. Subsequently, the values that they forcefully introduced, would not only infiltrate the broader workforce, they would thrive. This would set in motion a shift in corporate values that would never again course-correct.

Popular Culture and the Rise of Decadence in the 1980s

The self-absorbed mindset of the yuppie and unhealthy obsession with materialism were championed by the music industry. One of the soundtracks of the decade by Madonna, proudly spoke of her sole pursuit of money, "...'Cause the boy with the cold hard cash is always Mister Right. 'Cause we are living in a material world and I am a material girl." In singing these lyrics in "Material Girl", she made countless fans around the globe feel that this ambition was something that they should take on as well. Madonna was by no means the main artist championing this superficial mindset. With the launch and immediate popularity of MTV in 1981, artists quickly realized that image was key, so they went in full force. Since record labels didn't know what to make of this new marketing vehicle, they let their artists go wild. This allowed musicians to unleash their indulgences on-screen.

The mega-group of the eighties, Duran Duran, showcased sexual indulgence, lifestyle indulgence, and experience indulgence in their videos. These videos were played in very heavy rotation on MTV. Whether they were singing in some exotic destination surrounded by tropical creatures or singing in front of scantily-clad women provocatively moving in a boxing ring, Duran Duran promoted superficiality to the extreme. As a consequence, their on-screen existence became the aspiration of millions of fans.

Glam metal bands such as Mötley Crüe, Def Leppard, Poison, Bon Jovi, and Guns n' Roses, who dominated the decade, were just as bad. Their makeup, over-the-top outfits, and "eye for the camera" behaviour shouted materialism and self-absorbed ideals. Even Michael Jackson screamed excessiveness with his videos. This was not because of what was narrated on-screen, but because of the budget extravagance of his films. The video for "Thriller" cost a half-million dollars, which created as much news as the content that made up the epic fourteen-minute masterpiece. For perspective, one of the blockbuster films of the 1980s, *Crocodile Dundee*, which generated $328 million dollars in revenue in its year of release, only cost $8.8 million to produce.

While music has always had an impact on corporate society and the values that guide it, the ubiquity of the music video made contemporary music artists an instrumental part of corporate culture. Since these artists could now significantly help sell products and services, they were readily used. Pepsi alone sought the endorsement of Michael Jackson, Madonna, Lionel Richie, Tina Turner, and David Bowie throughout the eighties. As a consequence, the values that these artists embodied would have a more pronounced effect on corporate values. Materialism, indulgence, and superficiality seeped into the fabric of the business world.

Society was slowly becoming conditioned to viewing selfishness as a natural part of everyday life. In addition to influences in the workforce (via the yuppie) and in culture (via the MTV obsessed musician), people were being taught to get what they wanted, when they wanted it. There were two big technologies which became mainstream in the 1980s that fuelled this expectation. The first was the VCR. Television viewers could now record their favourite shows and watch them at the time that they pleased. They could also rent a movie whenever they wanted. This total control would nourish people's selfish viewing desires. The industry exploded in the eighties, creating a huge video rental business. Giants such as Blockbuster Video were founded in this decade. According to Wikipedia, "by mid-1985 the United States had 15,000 video rental stores, and many record, grocery, and drug stores also rented tapes."

The second technology that influenced the rise of selfish behaviour was the Walkman, or portable music cassette player. People could listen to music where and when they wanted. No longer did you have to sit at home or listen to the radio and wait until your favourite song came on. The music industry was revolutionized. Meaghan Haire from *Time* magazine wrote, "the cassette tape would outsell vinyl records for the first time in 1983. By 1986 the word 'Walkman' had entered the Oxford English Dictionary." A famous advertisement for the Sony Walkman from 1981 showed people dancing in the street all listening to their music, consumed by their own feelings and indifferent to the feelings of the other people around them.

In addition to furthering selfishness, the VCR and Walkman set in motion two other dynamics that would have negative effects on value systems: the addiction to instant gratification, and desired isolation. Having full control of your listening and viewing time meant that you could completely cater to your moods. So, if you had just broken up with a girl that you loved a great deal and wanted to listen to songs that would indulge your feelings, then you'd pop that perfect mixed tape into your Walkman. If you were lounging around at home on a rainy Sunday and felt like binging on action films, you could pull out your Bruce Lee collection and be entertained for hours. In short, you could gratify your desires immediately. Often these desires were fuelled by powerful emotions, so satiating them quickly could become quite addictive.

The other dynamic that was being propelled by these technologies was isolation. The growth of the video game console, via the NES (or Nintendo Entertainment System), during this period contributed to this as well. All three of these entertainment options were not social by design. The VCR and gaming console were meant for at-home consumption, where you were fixated to a screen as opposed to communicating with others. The Walkman, that may have advertised freedom in the community at large, was really just offering up a means to shut yourself out from the world around you. While the advertisements of the time tried to show that the Walkman was social, the settings were just ridiculous. The 1981 Sony Walkman ad mentioned above, actually showed people dancing in harmony with their headphones on and Walkmans plugged in. How is that even possible? They must all have synced their Duran Duran tapes to perfection! Joking aside, these technologies truly encouraged separation from the world around you. Consequently, these technologies were beginning to teach the population at large to be less considerate of others, be it by feeding your own emotions first, or by not interacting with others to begin with.

The departure from human values at home and in the workplace throughout the 1980s was also influenced by a changing family structure and a growing hunger for adventure. It was quite common by then to have both parents working. Along with greater empowerment of women and each parent living their own professional lives, divorce rates among younger families rose. The desire to move beyond the comforts of your family surroundings also grew during this time. People sought adventure. A quick review of the most loved films and television shows of the decade reflects this hunger for adventure. Seven out of the ten highest grossing movies of the decade are about adventure: *E.T the Extra Terrestrial*, *Return of the Jedi*, *The Empire Strikes Back*, *Indiana Jones and the Last Crusade*, *Raiders of the Lost Ark*, *Back to the Future*, and *Top Gun*.

Adventure was also available in the workplace. Aside from more money being accessible, international working opportunities grew off the back of growing global trade and foreign direct investment (FDI). The second half of the decade saw global merchandise trade volume almost double, and global FDI surged to US$630 billion dollars (according to IMF data).

The 1980s represented the true tipping point in the separation of human and corporate values. Selfishness and materialism trumped loyalty and substance. Adventure and the pursuit of wealth marginalized family and the satisfaction of fair compensation for hard work.

However, compassion would be salvaged through big political movements that would set roots at the end of the decade. The most notable was Perestroika in the Soviet Union. This policy brought an end to the Cold War, led to the opening of many East European nations, and was the catalyst to the fall of the Berlin Wall in 1989. By the end of the decade we not only saw the reunification of Germany, but the wheels were in motion to rid South Africa of apartheid. Consequently, people were beginning to comfortably live with values that were quite opposite from one another. The era of a life with conflicting values, the era of "societal split-personality-disorder" had begun.

Life in the 1990s

The 1990s represented a seismic shift in workplace dynamics the world over, driven by several landmark introductions into society. The first was the rapid growth of technology and how it integrated into professional environments across all businesses and categories. The second was the entrance of the next big generation into the workforce—Generation X.

The nineties also saw the rise of several movements that would impact all aspects of society, including the workforce. Feminism, which had been growing in momentum, made huge strides during the decade, resulting in 1992 being officially named "The Year of The Woman". Off the back of greater global connectivity through technology, and corporate globalization, multiculturalism mushroomed during this period. Entrepreneurialism also grew, due to shifts in traditional go-to-market capabilities across many sectors, as well as a growing desire for self-directed versus conformist professional philosophies.

The discussion of work-life balance took hold in this decade, as companies grew and demanded increasingly more from their employees. While many of these dynamics bore fruit in previous decades, their significant growth, coupled with the big technology surge, resulted in the 1990s being a true change between "traditional" working paradigms, and "new world" workplace realities.

Technology advancement in the 1990s was transformational on multiple levels. Computing became ubiquitous in the workplace, but also significantly penetrated the home. According to U.S. Department of Labor, in seven short years personal computer ownership in the United States grew from 15 percent to 35 percent. Alongside this integration of technology into home life, Internet penetration exploded. The first web browser went online in 1993, and by the end of the decade roughly 50 percent of Western countries had Internet access. The ability to gather vast amounts of information, and having the computing power to aggregate it, redefined what was possible. The growth in knowledge and the freedom to express it was uncanny.

New industries grew out of this new world that would reshape the business world. Amazon and Ebay were founded in 1994 and 1995 respectively, and drastically altered retail. Google was founded in 1998, disrupting the current thinking on access to information and advertising. Netflix was founded in 1997 and would eventually turn the television industry on its head. Napster was founded in 1999, permanently reshaping the music industry. Millions jumped onto this bandwagon, exploring new work opportunities. Jobs grew, and money to experiment was also readily available.

During this decade the mobile phone industry exploded. At the start of the nineties, cell phones were very uncommon. Few people had them; they were very clunky, and had limited features making them more of a novelty than a utility. However, by the end of the decade in the U.S. alone, over 25 percent of people had cell phones. Worldwide the growth was incredible. A statistic from the ITU World Telecommunications Database shows that in 1990 the number of mobile subscribers worldwide was only 11 million, and by 1998 the number had exploded to 318 million.

Richard Goodwin wrote for KnowYourMobile that the period from "1990 to 1995 represented the upward swerve in design and portability, with mobile devices gradually starting to appear in the hands of average consumers for the first time. By the late 1990s, mobile devices fast became the norm thanks to models such as the Nokia 6110 (the iconic curved phone with the stubby antenna), and the Motorola StarTAC (the flip phone that looked like it came right out of a Star Trek episode)."

The growing availability of cell phones were reflected in pop-culture: James Bond first used a cell phone in 1997's *Tomorrow Never Dies*, showcasing fictional extras that are now realities, such as scanning and a car remote. Mobile handset ownership was not just becoming a convenient utility to own, it was becoming a must-have social status symbol and fashion accessory.

The quick penetration of these three technological thrusts meant that companies invested more, creating even newer and better products. The speed of change that is now part of daily life, was birthed during this decade. People embraced this momentum, but also didn't want to be left behind.

Values were noticeably impacted in two powerful ways. The first was that impatience grew enormously. Instant access to information and people, coupled with the already established ability to be instantly gratified in music (via the portable music player), and in film (via the VCR), meant that people were increasingly unwilling to wait for what they wanted. The idea of working for what you get, to truly earn something, was being re-defined. The growth in credit card debt during the nineties reinforces this point. During the decade, credit card debt as a percent of total household debt from consumer loans almost tripled and grew to represent just shy of 60 percent of all outstanding household debt from consumer loans. The accumulation of "stuff" at all costs was truly underway.

In addition to impatience, people were becoming much more self-absorbed. The new types of popular television genres support this point. The most notable was reality television. In 1992 MTV launched the smash hit *The Real World*, a show that focused on the lives of a group of strangers who lived together for a few months in a house while cameras recorded their every move, interpersonal

55

relationships, and everyday drama. It celebrated the actions and intrigues of self-consumed individuals. The producers actually sought out narcissistic people because it made for great entertainment. Indirectly, it began to "teach" its viewers that egotism, and making the world revolve around you, was acceptable. The popularity of the show is unquestionable. To date, it has run more than 600 episodes.

Another globally loved reality show franchise that started in the nineties was *Survivor,* a contest where everyday people were put into "survival" situations and were eliminated one-by-one after each episode. The show had a "win at all costs" philosophy at its core (a theme very much championed in sports marketing at the time, via the darling brand Nike, with its iconic "Just Do It" campaign). As such, it promoted the importance of self, versus the broader good. Originally launched in Sweden in 1997, it later became a global phenomenon when adapted for U.S. audiences in 2000.

Another television genre that consumed culture in the 1990s was the "fictional everyday life drama", spearheaded by such iconic shows such as *Friends, Beverly Hills 90210,* and *Sex and the City.* They all centered on groups of people living in modern society, trying to find their way through the trials and tribulations of life. The characters in these shows were completely self-absorbed, and audiences loved them because they could see their thoughts reflected in these characters. As these new television genres became central to pop-culture, and their values were broadly consumed, they were influencing people to become less considerate of others, preferring to cater to their needs first.

In the workplace, the importance of self, and being able to do things when you wanted and where you wanted to, was also becoming a reality. Once again, mobile technologies and personal computers facilitated this change. A great quote from a November 2000 article in *The Journal of Marriage and Family* (Perry-Jenkins et al.) shows the impact that this new technological reality had on people at work: "The growing use of computers, pagers, and cell phones, for example, meant that, for some employees, work could be performed almost anywhere: at home, on the highway, or in an airplane". Clearly, the separation between working hours and personal hours began to blur. At first, this was very liberating. You could finish off that report at home and avoid a very stressful morning the following day. However, as the penetration of these devices grew, so did the expectation of being more available for work.

Real tension was being created by a growing unhealthy work life balance. This did not necessarily mean that there was more time spent at work, but that work was consuming the thoughts of people when they were at home. A study by Robinson and Godbey in 1997 argued that people didn't always spend more time at work, rather the pace had changed so drastically due to technology that people felt overworked. Another study by Mischel et al. in 1999 said that certain groups within the workforce actually did experience an increase in work hours. So, whether it was a faster pace or more hours, people felt stressed.

The impact on the home was significant. An article by Ayse Idil Aybars in *The Industrial Relations Journal* states "that mothers and fathers who described more pressure at work also reported greater role overload and a feeling of being overwhelmed by multiple commitments." This issue was severe enough in Europe that a European Employment Strategy was conceived in 1997 to tackle the matter. Looking at this from a values perspective, it is clear that loyalty was further weakening. The anger that was being generated by this life-consuming work reality, coupled with the self-consumed attitude mentioned above, made people less committed to their employers.

World, Meet Generation X

The discussion around work-life balance was enormously influenced by the introduction of Generation X into the workforce. Many had grown up in households where both parents worked. As a result, this group was often home alone. They had a nickname that reflected this reality—"latchkey kids", which referred to the home key that was tied to a string and carried around their neck so that they could get into the home after school. This generation wore a chip on their shoulders. Sometimes they were viewed as lazy. However, this was an over-simplification of the underlying perceived issue that they faced: they saw their parents prosper at work and realized that achieving the same level of upward mobility was going to be difficult, since work environments had changed. Job security was no longer guaranteed.

In North America, the nineties may have been associated with enormous job creation due to select initiatives put in place by President Bill Clinton (e.g. NAFTA, increase in minimum wage, tax reform, etc.), as well as the growth of the technology sector, but in Europe unemployment was rising across the board. Overall, the new workforce generation did not necessarily feel insecure, but they definitely felt that surpassing what their parents had accomplished was not a fait accompli. The bar was already set very high by their parents' achievements, and loyalty and reliability of employers was no longer to be expected. An advertisement by Travelocity in the United Kingdom from the era, summarizes this sentiment beautifully with its headline "Your life is meaningless and you will die having achieved comparatively little. You need a holiday."

Gen Xers reacted to this "existential dilemma" in a few ways. First, they sought to create truly authentic and real experiences, to get that energy uplift from life. Huge cultural revolutions in music, sport, and art emerged as a result. Second, they became a lot more independent, taking control of their professional and personal lives. This fuelled both the start-up scene of the decade and the surge in the feminist movement.

The pursuit of authentic, rich, and real experiences was very important to Generation X. They did not believe in following the status quo. Key trends in pop-culture during this decade are a testament to this. The big music revolutions of the time radically departed from the paradigms that dictated the industry in the decades before. For example, the rave scene took off during this decade. This movement allowed fans to congregate with like-minded people in secret locations and indulge in activities that the world at large viewed as reckless.

Grunge also emerged and thrived in the 90s. It was a direct retaliation to the over-choreographed and overly commercial music movements of the past. There was real angst, and grunge provided a release from the pent-up anger and frustration. A big trend in sports also reflected this move towards independence, fuelled by uncontained energy: extreme sports. Several anchor sports of this new sport genre blossomed in the 90s, be it the resurgence of skateboarding, the explosion of snowboarding, or the birth of mixed martial arts. The interest grew so rapidly that the first X-Games were held in 1995, known as the "Extreme Games". This generation definitely sought intense emotions. After decades of "overly-produced" culture, this made sense. What did this mean for the workplace?

Essentially, many Gen Xers worked to live, they did not live to work. There was clearly some apathy towards existing work cultures. This did not mean that Gen Xers slacked off, which was a common label given at the time. In actual fact, they worked very hard and continue to do so today. A study by Workfront in 2016 of 2500 workers in the United Kingdom, found that Gen Xers are the hardest working cohort (chosen by 60 percent of the people surveyed).

Generation X was also instrumental in the growing start-up scene of the decade, which contributed to the upswing in the North American economy. Since they believed that established companies and categories were no longer reliable, they started their own. The entrepreneurial spirit was truly awakened by this cohort. In fact, a *Time* magazine article titled "Gen Xers Aren't Slackers After All", reported that four out of every five new businesses of this time were at the hands of Gen Xers. The scale of this entrepreneurial environment was staggering. According to the World Bank, the number of registered companies globally almost doubled in the 1990s. This generation was actually given another nickname by The New York Times in 1999, when the newspaper called Gen Xers "Generation 1099", referring to the form used by self-employed professionals when submitting their income to the Internal Revenue Service, versus the typical W-2 form used by regular employed workers. Looking at this from a values perspective, the belief in hard work was rekindled, but primarily with scenarios where they had full control.

Beyond spurring self-employment and the entrepreneurial spirit, Gen Xers also redefined workplace cultures. Since many of these start-up company bosses were barely out of university, they brought their "fraternity" living culture to their new company environments. Netscape co-founder and the internet whiz-kid of the decade, Marc Andreessen, was a poster child for this new corporate executive and the culture that he championed. An article by *Wired* magazine in January 2015 describes him perfectly, writing "he was less than two years out of college and had not shed all the trappings and eccentricities of undergraduate life. He worked late and got up late. His taste in clothes, it was said, ran to frat-party ready." Marc and many like him, introduced "loft interior design", bean bag chairs, and "playful" open-plan office living to the working world, permanently changing the expected personalities of the corporate environment. Structure and hierarchy was replaced with a matrix working approach.

Gen Xers also manifested their independence in the nineties through important social movements, notably feminism. They were following on from their parents who spearheaded the second wave of feminism in the previous decades. According to the Encyclopaedia Britannica, the women leading the third wave of feminism "grew up with the expectation of achievement and examples of female success as well as an awareness of the barriers presented by sexism, racism, and classism." They tackled these issues with greater energy and confidence.

Women, War and End-of-the-World Worries in the 1990s

Culturally, the girl power movement kicked into gear through the music industry, where icons such as the Spice Girls and No Doubt front woman Gwen Stefani, championed the cause with vigour. Academically, women sought higher learning, and the decade marked the moment in history where women surpassed men in both university or college enrolment rates as well as completion rates, based on a Pew Research study. Professionally, women jumped into the workforce and by the end of the decade 60 percent of women aged sixteen and older were in the labour force (based on the same Pew study).

The shift towards a way of living that focused more on the individual was further encouraged by some of the big global events of the decade. Three big wars consumed the media for the first part of the decade and put a spotlight on the volatility of society. The first big war was in 1991. The mighty Iraq invaded the tiny country of Kuwait, kicking off the Gulf War and an American engagement in the region that remains today. The second big battleground took place in Europe. The Yugoslav Wars, which began in 1991, ended up breaking apart Yugoslavia and perpetuated war crime atrocities that hadn't been seen in Europe since World War II. The last was the Rwandan genocide of 1994, a horrifying event lasting just over one hundred days where between five hundred thousand to one million Tutsis were killed in brutal and barbaric attacks by the Hutu people. These various wars made people realize that the value of focusing on the individual versus the community or country, may be a better strategy for personal security and well-being.

Another big event, the death of Princess Diana, showed that caring for your fellow human being was being skirted if financial gain could be achieved. The unexpected death of the princess aided by the relentless pursuit of the Paparazzi, rocked the world since she was truly the "the people's princess". Diana was literally killed by the suffocation of the establishment. Therefore, people indirectly were being taught to rely on themselves, to be selfish, because the institutional powers (be they governments or corporations) did not have their best interests in mind.

A final event that influenced people's relationship with the established order, was Y2K. The Year 2000 bug scare predicted that there would be massive computer malfunctions on January 1, 2000. Paranoia consumed the world for the late part of the decade. Catastrophic scenarios were readily discussed in the media, suggesting possibilities of

61

planes falling out of the sky, entire networks breaking down, and so on. The assistant managing editor of *Time* at the time, Howard Chua-Eoan, spoke about the panic at the publisher saying:

> Time Magazine and Time Inc. information-technology staff set up a generator-powered "war room" in the basement of the Time Life Building in New York City, filled with computers and equipment ready to produce the magazine in case of a catastrophic breakdown of electricity and communications.

People were horrified that the new computer age would mark the end of the world as they knew it and voiced their anger at governments and multinational corporations for letting this happen. It marked another key moment where citizens recognized that they could no longer trust the established institutions and should solely rely on themselves.

The decade may have been very dynamic and progressive, both socially and economically; it may have been the only decade where we had "just the right amount of technology", according to Kurt Andersen of *The New York Times* (because we weren't yet fully tyrannized by our devices); it may have been a decade that had enormous cultural innovations that continue to be praised to this day; it may have been the decade where many aspects of society were for the first time becoming democratized. However, it was also a decade that saw the gap between rich and poor widen, as evidenced by the launch of the housing boom, which has made homeownership impossible for many today.

It was also the decade that introduced the "always on, always available" way of living, both personally and professionally. It was also the decade that made the expectation of instant gratification ubiquitous. As a result, the nineties profoundly impacted values. Trust in the status quo further eroded, leading to even less loyalty (since it was already fairly bruised from previous decades) towards governments and corporations. People became a lot more self-absorbed and self-directed. They primarily cared for themselves and their personal interests. Kindness often had an agenda, especially in the workplace. Respect your employer? Forget it. Impatience grew, and thus the appreciation for "working for your fair share" seriously declined. People also became increasingly addicted to extreme experiences to give them the base pleasures of life. The world of the "artificial existence" commenced, and thus the permanent departure from real human values went into full gear.

Life in the 2000s

The 2000s were a decade of enormous anxiety, where the world order was properly questioned. In all aspects of society, things seemed to be falling apart. The economy suffered two momentous blows that turned the business world on its head and caused the closure of many big companies. Globalization went into overdrive with the rise of China and India opening up a new era of competition and rattling workforces in the West. Terrorism took on a frightening new role in global politics. Epic wars were raged that created unease the world over. New diseases were introduced that rivalled the fear of AIDS in the 80s. Even the environment was unpredictably ferocious, unleashing catastrophes that rocked humankind. In this atmosphere, people turned towards themselves.

In culture, this manifested itself in the form of a growing emphasis on extrinsic values such as fame, money, and image as opposed to intrinsic values such as community, self-acceptance, and so on. Celebrity and multi-media fuelled this dynamic.

In the workplace, selfishness reigned, driven by the need for survival. Jobs were disappearing, and as a consequence people became very protective of their areas of responsibility. Kindness and collaboration drastically weakened. The world became a colder place. The age of trust and reliability was now permanently gone. A moment of optimism peeped out from the darkness in 2008, when Barack Obama was elected to the presidency of the United States on the back of his message of hope. However, further setbacks at the end of the decade quieted any rise of optimism.

A Positive Start, and Then...

The decade could not have started with greater contrast. In the year 2000, the momentum of the 90s and the dot-com bubble were still in effect. Global annual GDP growth, according to the World Bank, was 4.34 percent. In the United States alone, there was an increase of 3 million workers between 1999 and 2000. On March 10, 2000, the NASDAQ composite actually peaked at 5,132.5 (a level only again reached in 2016). The mood was very bullish. Respectable financial publications, such as *Forbes* and the *Wall Street Journal*, actually encouraged investors to explore high risk companies.

At the same time, pop culture consumption reached record levels. For example, the book *Harry Potter and The Goblet of Fire* became the fastest selling book ever, and Eminem's *The Marshall Mathers LP* became the fastest selling solo album ever.

However, in 2001 it all crumbled. First, the dot-com bubble burst in March, wiping out "US$5 trillion dollars in market value for tech companies. More than half of the Internet companies created since 1995 were gone before the middle of the decade, and hundreds of thousands of skilled technology workers were out of jobs" (according to David Gewirtz on CNN.com). Even the tech giants that we admire today took enormous hits: Amazon stock prices fell from $107 per share to just US$7 per share.

If that was not bad enough, in September of that same year, the attack on the World Trade Center in New York City forever changed the world. The evil in the world, the hatred that bubbled beneath the surface of so many parts of society, was made so public, so evident, that it could not be ignored. Humanity, and all the values that guide it, was brutally shaken.

For a brief moment, people came together, and great human values took over. I can remember how hordes of people in my neighbourhood in Jersey City clocked unthinkable hours at the pier to help boats ferry supplies and people over to Ground Zero. Throughout the city, there was great kindness and compassion. The devastation brought people together. However, there wasn't a stable economic backbone that allowed this positive spirit to thrive. Countless seemingly unbreakable companies folded at lightning speed. Worldcom (a huge telecommunications company), Enron (an energy and commodities service company), and Pets.com (an online pet store), all disappeared. It was hard to make sense of it all. As a result, people turned to themselves. It became universally understood that looking out for number one was the way that the world would run from this day forth. Fear quickly seeped into the fabric of society.

This sentiment never had a chance to weaken, because the onslaught of disturbing news simply would not cease. One of the main contributors was war. Off the back of 911, several wars in the Middle East commenced. Disturbance in the region was not uncommon at the time, but the scale of international involvement that would kick-off during this decade had not been seen for generations. This meant that the emotional proximity of these battles was much closer, since many family members and friends were directly affected. Countless young men and women from across North America, Europe, Asia, and even Africa joined the "coalition of the willing" or "Operation Enduring Freedom". The coalition death toll in the decade in both the Afghan and the Iraq war (excluding local fighters), amounted to just shy of ten thousand (according to iCasualties.org and the U.S. Department of Defence). The stories that circulated through communities at home were horrifying. One such story of a U.S. serviceman, was shared by Charlie Shaw on Thought Catalogue:

> I was deployed to Iraq in 2004. A few months into our
> tour my friend gets two weeks leave, he was assigned
> as the gunner on my Lt's Humvee. A couple of hours

before we go on mission the Lt asks me if I'd like to fill in for my friend and be his gunner. I have a bad habit of running my mouth and I didn't think spending a lot of time with the Lt was a good idea so I declined saying, "I would sir, but I hear your driver is so bad that he voids my life insurance policy and my folks would really need the money." He laughed and walked away. That mission, his vehicle was hit by an IED and the blast killed the gunner, a SPC from HQC who volunteered for the mission.

The culture of fear was also provoked by the Bush Administration to rally support for the war. President Bush's declaration of "an axis of evil" during a January 2002 speech cemented the darkness that would be part of the political discourse for the decade ahead.

If a rattled economy and a war-mongering international political environment were not stressful enough, mother nature felt the need to inflame emotions a bit further. Two major natural disasters happened in the 2000s. The first was the 2004 earthquake in the Indian Ocean that created a series of deadly tsunamis that killed up to 280,000 people in fourteen countries. The scenes of devastation were broadcast the world over and were horrifying. Beyond the wreckage and the loss of life, the sheer helplessness that survivors felt was shocking. One such survivor, Lou Harrand, wrote about her ordeal in Stylist in December 2014, saying:

I didn't see the wave come in. But it hit me from behind with such colossal force I was immediately separated from Greg (her newly married husband) and dragged under ten feet of water. I couldn't see anything. I could just sense a tangle of bodies above me, crushing me as I battled for breath. The strength of the water was unbelievable. I was thrust about, as if in a huge washing machine, colliding violently with the other debris in the water – furniture, suitcases, huge pieces of wood, bodies.

66

Before viewers around the world had time to move on from this calamity, another disaster struck a year later in the United States. Hurricane Katrina hit the Gulf states on August 29, 2005, breaching levees across the coastline. The loss of life was approximately 1,245 people, according to Wikipedia. A majority of the deaths were in New Orleans, where there were countless storm surge breaches. Once again, the media covered the devastation in great detail, sending horror around the world. Images of people stranded on rooftops, bodies floating in the water, and entire neighbourhoods underwater were terrifying to look at.

In both disasters, the various governments were not prepared, and their ineptitude caused an enormous loss of life. The message that this inability to protect citizens had on the population at large, was that your own well-being, your own safety, was truly entirely in your own hands. The institutions that were built to provide some of these basic civic benefits, were incompetent or were not paying attention. Either way, the confidence in these bodies hit a new low. It was another sign that the age of self-reliance, and egotism, was firmly here.

Confidence and trust were hit a terminal blow when the subprime housing crisis led to the global financial meltdown of 2007 and 2008. Mark Adelson, the former chief credit officer at Standard & Poor's, is quoted in the *Wall Street Journal* saying that total estimated losses from the crisis could be as much as US$15 trillion. Countless companies perished. The most public ones were Lehman Brothers and Washington Mutual. Together they held assets worth roughly one trillion US dollars. In addition, both General Motors and Chrysler filed for bankruptcy, but were later saved by bailouts.

The blow to the global workforce was immense. The banking industry, the heartbeat of the financial world, the community that everyday people relied on to keep them safe and secure, let the people of the world down in a horrendous manner. The values of confidence, reliability, trust, and honesty in the workplace were destroyed. From that moment on, the philosophy of defensiveness and protectionism began to reign among employees at large.

Technology and the Power of Distraction in the 2000s

To deal with the pain that kept on pummelling people around the world throughout the decade, society provided countless distractions. The four big drivers of distraction were technology, social media, consumerism, and television media.

Technology exploded during the 2000s. Web 2.0 ushered in a whole series of tools that allowed people access to relevant information more quickly. Arguably the biggest of these were Google PageRank and Adwords. The latter tool, Adwords, was launched in 2000 and birthed new industries that dominate online marketing today, notably Search Engine Marketing (SEM) and Search Engine Optimization (SEO). These allow the right webpage or advertisement to find consumers with greater relevance. As such, consumers became more easily "distracted" by the personalization of this new information source.

Wireless technology mushroomed during this decade, allowing people to connect to an "alternate world" with greater ease. Again, this allowed people to get distracted from the real world. Along with greater mobility came the widespread adoption of the smartphone. Led by the introduction of the iPhone in 2007, smartphones allowed people to escape to things that interested them versus facing the realities right in front of them. The simplicity of the iPhone interface democratized this technology and spearheaded the "third hand" revolution we view as normal today. Even the technology that delivered television programming evolved to give greater control to consumers. The Video on Demand service allowed people to watch what they wanted, when they wanted it, which ultimately gave people more opportunities to fulfill their desire for distraction.

The decade also saw the introduction of social media. The platforms that really kicked off this movement were Friendster, MySpace, and LinkedIn. Social Media as we know it today was really pioneered by Friendster who built their platform on a "six degrees of separation" principle. Founder, Jonathan Abrams, believed that a community could only be built with people who have common bonds. He even went so far to describe his platform as a "dating site without the dating". Friendster grew quickly, collecting three million users within a year of inception. However, MySpace was the giant of the decade. It was so popular that it actually overtook Google in 2006 as the most visited website in the United States. Later in the decade, Facebook would overtake MySpace in unique visitors. The desire for leading a "virtual life" was so strong that a platform called "Second Life" was created in 2003, and quickly grew an audience.

Overall, the popularity of social networking was astounding, but not surprising. The appetite for voyeurism was already firmly established through the reality show phenomenon, and social media allowed this to be done with those that you knew. It was the ultimate distraction platform. You could focus on your small circle, compare how you measured up to those around you, collect apps (so, collect "stuff"), and pay less attention to the less pleasant things going on in society at large.

The collection of "stuff" became almost universally accessible during this decade. The rise of China and India as the "factories of the world" accelerated this phenomenon. China's exports alone grew by a multiplier of ten during the decade, surpassing the trillion-dollar mark in 2008. The appetite in the Western world for more and more "things" only grew as prices were very palatable due to the cheap labour costs offered by these rising powers. In other words, both China and India were allowing consumer markets to thrive.

Interestingly, the desire to consume is actually a subconscious manifestation of our innate impulse for "survival, domination and expansion", according to professors William Rees and Warren Hern. Combine this primate need with the ability to satiate it repeatedly, and we had a perfect environment for the "retail therapy" distraction in the 2000s.

Television programming also favoured formats that provided distraction. The one format that skyrocketed in popularity throughout the decade, was the reality show. The spectrum of concepts on offer was broad, ranging from talent shows such as *American Idol* and *Dancing with the Stars*, competition-type shows such as *Survivor* and *The*

69

Apprentice, or voyeuristic shows such as *Big Brother* and *The Real Housewives*. All of these shows allowed viewers to live vicariously through characters who were "real". Somehow, this allowed the audiences at home to feel better about themselves or feel that a better reality was actually attainable (because the "real" person on-screen was actually living it).

Interestingly, the desire to feel good about oneself, and to be motivated to overcome daunting odds, was a recurring theme in many of the top dramas of the decade. Two stand out examples were *Lost* and *Breaking Bad*. Both titles were fitting for the spirit of the decade. Both had themes that were extreme enough to make viewers feel that "this could never really happen to me", but relatable enough for viewers to draw parallels to their lives. *Lost* centered around the survivors of a plane crash on an obscure island, and their trials and tribulations finding ways to return back home. *Breaking Bad* focused on a science teacher who was diagnosed with cancer, turning to illegal meth production to finance his medical bills and protect his family for the future. These shows, and many popular films of the decade, such as *The Lord of the Rings* trilogy or the Harry Potter movies or *Gladiator*, acknowledged the fear gripping society, but found a way to deal with it, to narrate a possibility to prevail over the fear. This approach provided an ideal distraction from the truths of reality, through imagined or "false" hope.

To further compound the destructive effects of distraction from reality, society began to "teach" citizens to consume more abbreviated information. The biggest manifestation of this was texting. As mobile penetration grew, coupled with the popularity of social media, so did the appetite to continuously keep in touch. In North America alone, according to Statistica, handset penetration grew from 39 percent in the year 2000, to 90 percent in the year 2009.

In other parts of the world the growth was equally astonishing. Unlimited texting plans were not as ubiquitous as they are today, so people had to be more selective with the volume of their sends. As such, there was still a bit of sanity, but the change in how people would communicate was in full swing.

Another way that mobile adoption shaped our desire for abbreviated information was through texting language. In order to send information more quickly, and with greater ease, the mobile "nomenclature" that we habitually use today was born.

Beyond mobility, newspaper publishing was also evolving, introducing formats that provided commuters more bite-sized information versus the long-form articles that had been the norm in the business for decades. Throughout this decade, we saw the popular roll-out of many free daily newspapers such as *Metro* and *20 Minuten*. Their concept was simple: just enough information to entertain and inform you during your commute. Whether it was forced reading, or ongoing access to friends, family, and co-workers, an environment that would allow people time to focus was rapidly diminishing.

A Decade of Unrest

The decade that marked the start of the new century was turbulent, ushering in a new relationship that people around the world had towards society and the governments and companies that guided it. Security was perpetually questioned, be it through natural, economic, or political events that repeatedly hammered the decade. Governments and many companies either triggered these events, or poorly reacted to them, destroying any remaining beliefs in the values of confidence, reliability, trust, and honesty that were associated with the corporate world. Work environments became soulless, where people were constantly watching their backs and readily manoeuvring to protect their areas of responsibility or jobs. Loyalty towards oneself began to reign supreme, since few other entities could be counted on. Layer on the rise in personalized technology usage, social media, and the ability to gift oneself repeatedly (through the rise of cheap goods available thanks to the "China Phenomenon"), and the values of selfishness, self-centeredness and egotism clearly took dominant positions in decision-making.

The ability to create joy for oneself was increasingly delivered through artificial and materialistic means, and through sheer distraction. However, this could not address the deep-rooted anxiety that was prevalent within society. As an illustration of this, in the United Kingdom, antidepressants prescribed by the National Health Service (the NHS), nearly doubled throughout the decade.

The deep-rooted anxiety blanketing society during this decade is the reason why there was enormous support for movements that championed healthy human values. President Barack Obama's campaign for hope galvanized not just the United States, but the world at large. Coca-Cola's focus on championing happiness was met with enormous support, propelling the brand's stature and affinity to new heights. While these two examples meant that people felt that these inherent human values were no longer readily displayed in society at large, they unfortunately did not create societal change. This was because the values guiding corporate life were forcing people to live by different codes in their work life compared to their personal life. The split-personality-disorder way of living was now firmly established, and breaking from it was proving incredibly difficult, even impossible.

Life in the 2010s

The current decade, which is nearly complete, has continued pushing the themes and challenges of the previous decade. The key difference is that everything has accelerated. The global domination of online living, and all the technology and business development that has mushroomed on the back of this, has impacted business life-cycles, employment trends, corporate attitudes, and so forth. The inability of governments and corporations to keep up with change, to help provide stability on the back of change, has caused a growing number of political movements to erupt across continents. Miscalculations by governments, both internationally and locally, have allowed hatred to flourish. Whether it is international terror, or police brutality in the

United States, the result has been a growing cloud of fear that has permeated through all levels of society. Even the frameworks that guide government institutions, are being put into question by society, resulting in the potential breakup of long-standing processes, partnerships, and agreements.

Fear has been fuelled by another threat, cyber security. The age of the hacker has been properly introduced during this decade, threatening all parts of society—personal security, corporate security, and national security.

Last, but not least, the 2010s have seen a changing of the guard in respect to the dominant cohort in the workforce. Millennials, who began seeping into the workforce in the 2000s, properly entered in this decade. Some research suggests that they have taken over boomers in 2015 as the biggest group in the workforce. In PwC's research "Millennials at Work", they state that millennials will make up 50 percent of the global workforce by 2020. Regardless of the various statistics, their sheer volume combined with their unique attitudes towards life and work, shaped by all the turmoil of the past few decades, are fundamentally redefining society. When it comes to values, millennials are fighting the decay of human values in the workforce, looking to create environments with greater purpose. As such, the 2010s (and most likely the upcoming decade) will create enormous turbulence in the workforce as corporate values are questioned and established companies look at ways to evolve in order to remain attractive to their future workforce.

Tech Take-over and Human Values in the 2010s

Technology has been the driving force of change throughout the decade thus far. Every part of life is impacted. Socially, we live through our technology. Culturally, we are informed and entertained by our technology. Politically, we are informed and communicate via our technology. Professionally, everything around us is influenced by technology. While it has given our lives a greater amount of freedom and has provided access to so much that would have seemed unimaginable in the past, we have also become imprisoned by technology.

This dynamic has gone into overdrive during this decade. Today, our mobile phone is as important as air and water. A study conducted by Pew Research, states that 67 percent of smartphone owners admit that that they check their phones for missed calls or messages even if their phone did not ring or vibrate. Even worse, *Psychology Today* released an article stating that 40 percent of Americans are officially addicted to the smartphones.

Social media, another technology that has become a ubiquitous part of life, is fuelling this dependency. In 2016, one third of the global population used a social media site every month, according to We Are Social's "Digital in 2017" annual report. This represents a growth of 20 percent year over year. Facebook alone had 1.86 billion monthly active users, which is roughly 23 percent of the global population. Clearly, the need, versus solely the desire, to stay connected is unstoppable. However, this need is driven by a hunger for voyeurism, and the urge to compare oneself to those around you. As a result, we live life with constant anxiety. This anxiety is, on judgment, a bit silly, because it is anxiety formed by the fear of missing out, or the fear of not being connected. Nonetheless, it is very real.

Add onto this self-absorption-driven anxiety with the anxiety created by job insecurity and day-to-day security fears (which have been elevated throughout this decade as a result of cybercrime, most evidenced by the account hacking scandal of Yahoo, the Sony email hacking catastrophe and the 2016 U.S. election rigging debate), and you have a society that is continually living on the edge. As a result, attitudes and values have permanently shifted inwards. The radical adoption of selfish values has accelerated, and the demand for personal control is firmly established.

The meteoric growth and advancement of technology throughout this decade, coupled with a growing desire for control, has furthered the desire, and necessity, to pursue dreams and break conventions. As a result, some truly noteworthy professional undertakings have emerged. Google has made self-driving cars a scalable reality, ushering in a new development era where both new and established manufacturers are energetically investing. Since 2010, Tesla has shown how to make electric cars a commercially viable possibility, opening the floodgates to countless new electric or hybrid model releases by goliaths such as General Motors, Nissan, Renault, Ford, Mercedes-Benz and BMW. Uber, who beta launched in 2010, then officially launched their app in 2011, fundamentally changing the taxi and transportation world. Airbnb permanently disrupted the hotel business by pioneering a new perspective on travel, and inspiring countless new businesses that are changing how people vacation. WeWork, founded in 2010, has redefined the concept of the office space by offering thousands of entrepreneurs unique benefits that they would not get conducting business at local coffee houses.

Most of these companies are driven by a hunger to change the world, and to leave a real legacy. In other words, they are making human values part of the corporate culture once again. They are leading the charge in reversing the current negative corporate value reality that exists in most companies today.

The urgency to bring about a shift in values has also been driven by the global rise in terrorism and hate. The rise of the Islamic State (also known as ISIS or ISIL), since the outbreak of the Syrian civil war in 2011 is astounding. In a few short years, this rogue organization was able to push out Iraqi government forces from key cities across the country including the large city of Mosul, inject bone-chilling fear into communities across many Western countries through the terror attacks conducted by its followers, and shock the world through its brutal beheadings of innocent people publicly shown on social media.

Social and Political Upheaval in the 2010s

The randomness and enormity of the attacks in Paris, Brussels, Munich, Berlin, Nice, and Istanbul, made people in all corners of the world realize that the assumed safety in their cities was a thing of the past, and that unimaginable hate exists right in their communities. Further hate was brought to life across the world in several other manifestations.

The first was the ongoing aggression in the United States of police against blacks. In 2015, police killed at least 258 black people, and by September 2016 the number of black deaths for that year was 173 (according to *The Washington Post*). While the numbers are under a third of the total killings by police, the publicly documented examples (through bystander cell phone video footage) often show clear abuses of power.

The second was the election of Donald Trump off the back of a racially charged, misogynistic, and protectionist campaign that rattled people in all corners of the world. Given the power of the United States on actions and policies the world over, Mr. Trump's predisposition for hate and anger has created enormous uncertainty.

The third was the rise of populism, spurred on by right wing political parties popping up in countless countries. The growth was so significant that a Far-Right "counter summit" was held in January 2017 in Koblenz, Germany, where party leaders from as many as nine countries participated, including France, Italy, Netherlands, and Germany. The most vocal of these are in France and the Netherlands, where their followers are so numerous that their ability to change the political direction of their respective countries has been noteworthy.

Activism has been growing in response to all this hatred. Sizeable movements ushered in the decade. The first was the Arab Spring that kicked-off in December 2010 in Tunisia. Multiple uprisings followed across the region, with the most noteworthy occurring in Egypt, Libya, and Syria. They fought the oppression and violence of their leaders, wanting to create healthier and less corrupt political systems within their countries. Unfortunately, there was no structure to these movements, and chaos ensued that resulted in equally corrupt and destructive groups settling into power.

In 2013, the #BlackLivesMatter movement was set in motion after the acquittal of the policeman responsible for the death of the

African-American teenager Trayvon Martin. People across America rose up to fight the broken system, which they believed was being allowed to continue operating unchecked. The movement was very vocal during the 2016 United States presidential election, motivated into action by Donald Trump's apparent disregard for policing reform, economic inequality, and other issues that disproportionately affect African Americans.

The administration of Donald Trump, and its policies regarding human rights, women's rights, LGBTQ rights, and so forth, also triggered the Women's March in January of 2017. The Women's March on Washington drew close to 500,000 people, and similar marches around the world grew the total amount of demonstrators to roughly five million, according to several sources.

Clearly, all of these movements show that this decade represents the most turbulent time in modern history since the civil rights era. The difference though is that this time it is global. People are fed up with the powers that be, with their apparent disregard for people's well-being. The corporate world is very much part of the problem, as it is seen as influencing governments, and being responsible for the inequality and hatred that exists in the world today. The Occupy Wall Street movement in 2011 made this point abundantly clear.

Occupy Wall Street was created to fight the perceived influence of corporations (particularly in financial services) on governments that helped drive social and economic inequality through greed and corruption. It gained international recognition through its slogan "We are the 99 percent", which highlighted the huge income inequality between the top one percent of the workforce and the rest. This divide had been growing for decades, but countless distractions throughout that time, be they technological development, entertainment evolution, social media, war, or an economic upswing, had blinded the masses from what was happening right under their noses. In fact, the main event that initiated the growth in income inequality was the financial de-regulation of the 1980s. Now, the situation is quite severe. According to the Marjorie S. Wheeler's book *Divided We Stand*, income inequality in the OECD countries is at its highest level for the past half century. In a report on July 22, 2014, the *New York Times* wrote that "the richest one percent of people in the United States now own more wealth than the bottom ninety percent". A more recent report from Oxfam, stated that the wealthiest one percent in the world own more than half of the world's wealth in 2016. Whichever way you look at it, the speed at which inequality has grown is staggering. Add to this reality the devastating reports about the financial crises in countries such as Greece, Russia, and Brazil, the Chinese stock market scare, as well as other ongoing negative financial news, and the fear and anger of the masses is understandable and is growing.

A Generational Shift in Work-life Attitudes in the 2010s

Trust in corporations is at an all-time low, and the governing belief among most working people is that human values have almost entirely vanished within the traditional workforce. As a result, people are aggressively exploring different employment options, or are planning their exit strategy. In the United States and the United Kingdom, new forms of employment structures are taking over the workplace. Self-employment, freelancing, zero-hour contracts, on-call scheduling, are becoming the norm. This makes the workplace a lot more dynamic, but also creates risk for the well-being of the national workforce. The reason is that these types of employment do not have the financial stability of permanent and full-time jobs, and therefore this section of the workforce can easily slip into poverty. Consequently, it is not surprising that with shaky economic environments, many people are choosing to remain with their full-time employers. However, since they are not satisfied at their current job, they will leave at the earliest opportunity (according to a PwC report).

Corporations are very concerned by this reality because this decade has marked a graduation of one cohort out of the workforce, and the introduction of another. Baby boomers are leaving the workforce en masse. This "loyal" workforce, that allowed company values to shift over time, is retiring. In the United States alone, there is a "silver tsunami of retirees", according to Dan North (chief economist at trade credit insurance company Euler Hermes North America), where it is estimated that roughly ten thousand baby boomers are leaving the workforce every day. Millennials, on the other hand, are streaming in. By the end of this decade more than half of the global workforce will be filled with millennials. Generation Xers will still make up a sizeable amount of the other 50 percent, given the accelerating retirement of baby boomers, but millennials will reign.

Consequently, there is a growing demand of companies to deliver the values that this new cohort hold dear. They are looking for meaning and purpose and aren't consumed by the desire to make money, as was the case with previous cohorts. As such, the broken value-system that guides many companies today, especially publicly traded companies, is increasingly frowned upon. These companies have been creating this "non-human" value system over many decades, as has been documented in this chapter. Reversing the trend is proving very challenging. Half-baked actions or dishonest actions are quickly exposed. For example, during the run up to the 2017 National Football League's annual extravaganza, the Superbowl, consumer products company Heinz rolled out a campaign proudly stating that they would give all their employees the day off work following the big game. The company initiated this because they wanted their staff to fully enjoy the game. However, this declaration was half true. Factory workers were not given this "day off" benefit. So, this "meaningful" corporate initiative was just a nice public relations stunt. Social media quickly exposed this.

Another example of blatant disregard for a declared purpose came from Volkswagen in 2015, via their emissions scandal. The company's publicly declared purpose is "to offer. Clearly, this purpose was properly not adhered to, since they developed software that allowed thousands of cars to cheat emissions tests. The media coverage was enormous and reputation to the company was significantly tarnished. Fans voiced their anger on the company's Facebook page. Gary Oliver, one such fan, wrote "As someone who has owned, driven and loved Volkswagens for more than 40 years, because of your criminal actions, I will probably NEVER buy another. #BoycottVW Shame on you."

Consumers didn't just complain, they acted. *The Guardian* claims that profits were down 20 percent after the emissions scandal. Add onto dishonest initiatives by corporations to be "more human", to the fact that it has been widely documented that automation will affect an enormous percentage of the workforce in the next fifteen to twenty years (Harvard study "The Future of Employment", suggests that 47 percent of job categories will be affected by automation), and demands by the new cohort taking over the workforce will be increasingly severe. The pressure for corporations to act is clearly gaining momentum in this decade.

In the 2010s, corporate leaders are awakening to the fact that a failure to authentically champion healthy human values is simply no longer tolerated by the general public. Consumers and employees are becoming increasingly vocal about their demands of corporations. The 2016 Edelman Trust Barometer shows that a staggering 80 percent of the public at large expect that businesses should improve the economic and social conditions in the communities that they serve. This same report also showed that people understand that profits need to be made but did not believe that one needs to be at the expense of the other. These demands result in action taken with people's wallets, but also in the ability to attract talent. The 2016 PwC Annual CEO survey showed that 82 percent of CEOs recognize that the best talent will choose to work for companies that share their own values. As such, these same CEOs should be realizing that more human values are going to be required in the way that their organizations operate and behave if they are to attract the best and the brightest in the years ahead. Interesting, but rocky, days are ahead for the global workplace as corporations try and untangle the soulless and "dark values driven" process, structures, and beliefs that govern their current companies and the people that work within them.

Summary of the Evolution of Values in Work Life Across the Decades

Work life has gone through staggering changes since the 1950s. The harmonious and healthy relationship that existed between home life and work life has sadly vanished. Instead, a split-personality-esque relationship now governs these two worlds. However, the status quo is not sustainable, and there are signs that a demand for change will quickly begin to be unavoidable. So, what can we draw from the home and work life relationships from the past to inform the health of our future?

The golden age of work and home life harmony was clearly the 50s and 60s. The charming scenes of the famous "Bewitched" television show, where Darrin's boss would be a common fixture in the Stephens' "magic-ridden" household, exemplified the connectivity and harmony of the world of work and home. The values that governed work life truly mirrored those that guided personal and home life: caring, trust, honesty, kindness, the expectation of hard work in exchange for guaranteed loyalty, reigned. A core reason for this was that employers took an almost paternalistic view of their workforce—as Darrin's boss did (although he did find himself in some hilarious situations when magic was carelessly deployed by Samantha, her mother, or even little daughter Tabitha). Even as blind obedience was dislodged with the introduction of self-expression and creativity, off the back of the anti-war, civil rights, and women's movements, these did more to add to the health-versus-disrupt-the-health of the values that governed the relationship between home and work life. Bottom line, the family approach to employment assured trust and acceptance.

This harmony was permanently broken in the 70s and 80s as selfishness began to be prioritized when people experienced a true economic roller-coaster. Oil crises and a turbulent political environment caused a notable rise in unemployment across the Western world. Add onto the fear of financial insecurity, the fear of personal security, propagated by a rise in terrorism and an escalation of the Cold

War, and people's belief in the strength of the system was shattered. Therefore, when the economic tide turned in the 80s, it was natural for people to want to take full advantage. They did not trust that ongoing prosperity was assured, hence there was a strong motivation to get as much as they could while the going was good. Instinctively, people were compelled to "beat the system". The adoption of this mentality represented the tipping point between a union of home and corporate values. Greed kicked in, which fuelled selfishness. As a result, honesty, trustworthiness, and reciprocal kindness in the workplace began to dissolve.

Michael Douglas' character in the 1987 movie, *Wall Street*, exemplified this to perfection. He cared little about others, only his personal gain. His character would be a model for many professionals for decades that followed. Fortunately, the Silicon Valley tech world that blossomed in this era, together with its hippie-minded pioneers, went against the corporate grain and created work environments where employees weren't encouraged to "beat the system". Instead, their employees were part of a clan that would "steer the system". These cultures have birthed admired workplace philosophies that drove the growth of that tech scene, and some of the most iconic companies that guide it today.

In the 90s, the broadly adopted self-absorbed mindset was given more energy by the introduction of technologies that not only allowed opportunities for personal wealth gain, but also started to create an addiction to instant gratification. This meant that people viewed work as a means to accumulate stuff; to feed their hunger for wealth and material possessions. Colleagues that got in the way would be out-manoeuvred. Companies that didn't facilitate this materialistic drive were exchanged for those that did. There was little loyalty, caring, or trust. However, there was clearly a desire among parts of society for a different way to achieve instant gratification and perceived wealth. Several cultural movements of the decade fulfilled people's desires for instant gratification but did so while furthering the values of caring and reciprocal kindness. The most noteworthy was the rave scene, which eventually grew into Electronic Dance Music (EDM) that dominates the music world today. The collection of experiences versus stuff was what drove the scene, and only through community was this achievable.

Interestingly, companies that attract the best talent today are ones that do exactly that. These companies, such as Google or Airbnb, create a strong sense of community among their employees, and provide means by which this community can regularly have novel experiences that feed employees inherent desire for instant gratification. Additionally, these experiences are anchored in the company values, which are purpose-driven. This assures that the experiences are meaningful, and thus powerful.

Throughout the 2000s and this decade to date, similar patterns from the past decades, combined with the technology that has become essential to most parts of our lives, have furthered protectionist and selfish values. The stock market crashes of the 2000s brought about employment upheaval similar to that seen in the eighties. As was the case in that decade, there was heightened concern about personal financial well-being. This fear has only grown throughout the 2000s and 2010s as technology has evolved at an unbelievable pace, threatening to affect the workers of close to half of industries today.

Companies are facing competition that didn't exist a few decades ago and are wrestling to find ways to deal with their new reality. Naturally, workforces are among the first parts of the businesses to be affected. Within this new economic reality, there is a combination of a "get it before it's gone" mentality among employees, and an anger and distrust towards corporations.

At the same time, social media and the change in news media delivery, have taken the expectation and need for instant gratification to new heights. A perverse "comparison way of living" has grown, influenced by a distorted expectation of life informed by celebrity and reality show culture, and has made people even more aggravated with what they expect from their jobs and employers. Add onto this boiling fear the rise of China and India, and the perceived threat to job security for many in the Western world, and the protectionist behaviours that exist among employees in the corporate world today are unlike anything seen in modern history.

However, the current working cohort, millennials, that will dominate the working world in the years ahead, are showing the corporate world that they want better values to be part of the places in which they work. They are demanding the type of harmony that existed between home and work life in the 1950s. Beyond looking for a family-feel in their work environments, they are also seeking real purpose in their professional lives. Interestingly, the companies that consistently rank at the top of the annual "Glassdoor Best Places to Work" deliver to these needs. These companies have great cultures, empower their employees, create true families by putting great emphasis on team-building, and have strong values that are honestly and thoroughly reinforced in everything they do. Many also have thorough recruiting practices to ensure that the right people join their "clan".

Overall, it is clear that there is a current backlash to the split-personality-disorder reality that has been created by an evolution of the values system in the corporate world. Variables that have fuelled the current negative values reality in the corporate world will regularly re-appear, perhaps even with greater frequency. However, it is important that these moments of turbulence don't act as catalysts for companies to lose the values that connect them to their workers. As it was in the 1950s and 1960s, and is the case in the most loved companies today, alignment with human values and creating a true family-feel are important to be able to overcome adversity, and to heal some of the "illnesses" that are rife in society today. The lack of harmony, or balance, in the values that we are living with has created social ills that risk permanently damaging the dynamics that allow for a functioning society. Left unchecked, discontent will most certainly rise, and civil unrest will likely consume countries and societies in the not-so-distant future.

Chapter 4

The Influence of Business Values on the Current Health of Society

In April 2015, several leading thinkers on global socio-economic and political matters provided their perspectives on the current health of society in an interview for the 25th anniversary of the Lionel Gelber Prize, a prestigious prize given to the best book, of that given year, on international affairs. They were asked whether they believed that the world today was in better shape than it was in 1990. They unanimously said "yes". According to a report by Reuters which covered the event, "the questioned experts noted that the world has seen extraordinary declines in poverty and child mortality (in fact, the World Bank stated that the rate of poverty fell from 37 percent in 1990 to 10 percent in 2015), there have been epic rises in global trade and investment, human rights have improved, and there has been a continuous spread of democracy. Even threats such as loose nuclear weapons from collapsing nations, or a war between India and Pakistan, or debt crises in struggling regions such as Latin America, Southeast Asia or Russia, and many other global pandemics, have been avoided."

Why was this event and the perspectives of its participants so interesting to a leading international news agency? There is a general misconception that the health of society is getting worse. In fact, the main indicators of societal well-being, according to Eurostat and the

OECD, such as income and wealth, personal security, general health, governance, education, and so forth, are improving.

A strong gauge of this was when President Obama, the leader of the world's biggest and most powerful economy, took stock of his accomplishments. When Barack Obama left office in January 2017, he proudly listed his accomplishments in making American society healthier than when he took office.

- He improved the economy and added 11 million more jobs (improving income and wealth),
- He gave 20 million Americans insurance coverage through the Affordable Care Act (improving financial and personal security),
- He led an international effort to cut carbon pollution, resulting in the Paris Climate Agreement (improving environmental health which should impact personal health),
- He improved schooling resulting in a record-setting 83 percent high-school graduation rate (so, improving knowledge and education), he repealed Don't Ask, Don't Tell, and advanced the cause of civil, women's, and LGBT rights (improving societal well-being), and he negotiated several landmark trade deals (improving economic health).

Nonetheless, the population at large does not necessarily judge societal health by these indicators, nor does it feel or see the improvements that experts and government leaders proudly celebrate. Quite the opposite is actually felt by the people. A 2015 YouGov survey revealed that a staggering 71 percent of people said that they believed that the world was getting a lot worse, and only 5 percent responded that the world was getting better. Ipsos Mori, a leading international research company, did a survey in November 2016 among sixteen thousand people across twenty-two countries, which found that a majority of people believe that their country is in decline. Interestingly, the United States ranks among them even though the facts, outlined in the above paragraph, show otherwise.

There are countless reasons that people are feeling this way. War seems to be continuously raging and is claiming innocent lives across the Middle East, in pockets throughout Asia, in the Ukraine, in Somalia, in South Sudan, and so forth. Hate is bubbling all over the world through groups such as the Islamic State, Boko Haram, al Shabaab, and far right groups across Europe and America. Police brutality towards blacks is seen to be on the rise in America. Racism and populism is seeing a renaissance in countries around the world, and especially in perceived "civilized and harmonious" nations throughout Europe and in the United States. Migrant flows seem never ending, and debates rage among leaders and intellectuals in countries on whether local communities can deal with the influx of people. Cyber security and cyber terrorism are ongoing threats based on the importance that the media is giving them. Governments can't seem to get their houses in order. Corruption scandals seem routine, fuelled by broken corporate values systems. Even the discontent with the current work life is a universal topic of discussion, as was thoroughly discussed in the previous chapter.

Which of these influences are contributing more heavily to the sentiment of societal decay, or "declinism" as it is labelled, can be debated. It will likely vary by person given their situation, location, media preferences, and a host of other factors. One relatively consistent variable is work life, and the influences that guide it, since it is a part of most people's lives. This is even more likely if we consider the sheer amount of waking time spent at work. The unhealthy split-personality-disorder way of living that is forced upon most people by the working world, as detailed in Chapter 3, must therefore play a significant role. Interestingly, there are some notable parallels between select medically proven symptoms and behaviours of split-personality-disorder, and two big illnesses prevalent throughout global society—depression and substance abuse. This suggests that the split-personality-disorder way of living is weighing heavily on society.

At their core, people suffering from opposing values, and thus somewhat split personalities, are not in harmony with themselves. As previously mentioned, actual medical symptoms of split-personality-disorder are depression and substance abuse. These are significant illnesses plaguing society, as will be discussed shortly. However, we need only scratch the surface of society a little bit more to uncover a plethora of other social ailments driven by a lack of personal harmony. They are ailments that are often driven by a need to fill the void of unhappiness. These societal illnesses are obesity, rage, marital distress, and even child abuse.

Depression in Society

Depression is a commonly occurring symptom in split personality disorder. This is because split personalities are usually triggered by some form of abuse. Interestingly, dual-values-living is often forced upon individuals by corporations in what can be viewed as a form of abuse. If select behaviours are not adhered to in work environments, the workers will get punished in the form of side-lining, or even firing. As a result, workers adopt these values to cope with the situation.

Depression is incredibly prevalent in communities across the world. According to the World Health Organization (WHO), approximately three hundred and fifty million people suffer from depression around the world. Depression is also the leading cause of disability worldwide. In his book, *Learned Optimism*, Martin Seligman outlines that depression is growing in every community, affecting all age groups, with pronounced penetration among teenagers. In fact, the WHO states that 11 percent of teens under the age of eighteen, globally, have a depressive disorder. Seligman also argues that if the current rate of growth of the illness continues, depression will be the second most disabling condition in the world by the year 2020, right after heart disease. In the United States alone, the amount of people diagnosed with depression is growing approximately 20 percent annually. Interestingly, the growth in depression follows a similar curve as the breakdown in corporate values, with a notable uptick since the 1980s.

Depression is extremely concerning because if left unmanaged, it can lead to a decline in psychosocial functioning which frequently leads to suicide. Depression-led suicide is a frequent result of split-personality-disorder. Coming to grips with the un-managed abuse, the seemingly "out of whack" world around you that preoccupies your thoughts and feelings, is simply too much for many. There is a chilling parallel to the competing values that people have to painfully live with day in, day out, in most working environments. People are being pulled so far in opposite directions that a breaking point is unavoidable. It is therefore not surprising that the suicide rate in society as a whole has grown 60 percent in the past 45 years, and that 90 percent of the claimed suicidal deaths are from mental illness, most commonly from depression.

Another fact that could suggest that the breakdown in values in the work environment is impacting depression-led suicide, comes from the demographic data from work-related suicide deaths. An article in *The Atlantic* in May 2015 referenced a study conducted by the American Journal of Preventative Health that looked at the global upward-trend of workplace suicide. The research found "that men and women between the ages of 65 and 74 were almost three times more likely to kill themselves at work as people of other ages." In other words, the baby-boomer generation is more affected than Generation X or millennials. The baby-boomer generation is also the age cohort that has seen what healthy work environments look like, because they were around when things were different. They are the only workforce group that has seen, first hand, the complete demise of the corporate value system. They have, on judgement, fewer delusions that "this is just how it has to be".

Substance Abuse in Society

Substance abuse is common among people suffering from split personality disorder. This is not surprising, considering that turning to drugs or alcohol can dull the pain of dealing with a world that seems crazy, or not running "normally". Furthermore, substance abuse helps bury the pain that has led an individual to develop a split personality disorder in the first place. This rationale can be easily applied to people who are living with two sets of opposing values. Just like people who have two different personalities, it is unnatural to be living with two very different value systems. Much like there is an internal battle for "supremacy" among different personalities, there is an internal battle for "supremacy" among different value systems. Therefore, living with two different value systems creates emotional pain, where self-medication is a natural response.

Interestingly, there has been a rise in substance abuse in society over the past few decades. According the 2016 World Drug Report by the UNODC (United Nations Office on Drugs and Crime), the global trend of people using drugs has steadily risen since 2006. In fact, the growth between 2006 and 2014 has been just under 19 percent. The demographic sample selected by the UNODC was people aged between 16 and 65 years old. In other words, these were people that fell, for the most part, in the cohort of working women and men. The drugs most on the rise are cannabis and pharmaceuticals (and other similar ones). These are often associated with dulling pain.

Another, more common form of substance abuse, has also risen since the days when human and corporate values where more aligned. Global per capita alcohol consumption has risen by roughly 20 percent since the 1960s, according to the WHO. This rise is off the back of growth in spirits and beer consumption, which are more commonly associated with binge drinking. Additionally, binge drinking is often associated with depression, caused by, among other things, workplace stress. To reinforce the point that workplace issues have a serious effect on alcohol abuse, we can look at alcohol poisoning deaths. In the United States alone, a whopping 76 percent of alcohol poisoning deaths are among adults aged between 35 and 64 years old, based on 2015 CDC data. In other words, the prime working age group is most affected by lethal alcohol abuse. A report by Katherine Keyes, assistant professor at Columbia University, reinforces the connection between workplace stress and alcohol abuse even further. In her analysis of several international studies, Keyes shows that there is a "global epidemic in women's drinking", brought on in great part by the pressures of working in "high-status, male-oriented environments" where alcohol serves as an escape, and feeds a desire for entitlement and empowerment.

Clearly, there are many reasons for substance abuse. However, since the gradual rise in alcohol abuse mirrors the gradual decline in the corporate values since the 1960s, and the rise in drug abuse began at the time of the economic recession in the late 2000s, when negative values were reinforced in the corporate world as people did what they had to in order to protect their employment, it can be said that the negative values that have been forced upon people in the working world play a big part. After all, the core reasons for substance abuse are discontent and pain. Therefore, a life where one is forced to behave against one's core values to keep the job, or to "fit in", is clearly a life filled with discontent and pain.

Obesity in Society

The obesity epidemic has been a regular topic of discussion in the media in most Western countries. According to the WHO, more than 1.9 billion adults aged 18 years and older are overweight. This represents 39 percent of adults 18 and over, worldwide (based on 2014 data). Out of these, 13 percent, or 600 million, were obese. If we look further into only the OECD countries (which are most of the countries in Europe, North America, Japan, Korea, Australia, New Zealand, Israel, and Chile), the percentage rises to 18 percent.

What is startling, is that before 1980 only one in ten people were obese in the OECD countries. Since then, the rates have doubled—or even tripled—and continue to grow. Worldwide obesity rates have doubled since 1980. What happened in that decade that could have propelled such a change? The eighties were the turning point for the rise of income inequality. Financial deregulation ushered in a corporate

91

mind-set fuelled by greed. Corporate values, and society, would be forever changed. Many would prosper, but others would not. Additionally, the "rat race" was properly set in motion. There was a constant desire to "get your fair share". This clearly created enormous stress for many. In other words, this era accelerated an existence where people were not in harmony with themselves. One of the ways to cope with psychological strain is to overeat.

A study by the University of Rochester in 2010 further demonstrated the relationship between workplace stress and overeating. The study, conducted with 2,782 employees, observed that chronic stress and lack of physical activity are strongly associated with being overweight or obese. Head researcher Diana Fernandez, M.D., M.P.H., Ph.D., and her team, noticed the same behavioural pattern among many of the people in the study: "They had worked all day curled over their computers or sitting in stressful meetings, and at the end of the day they looked forward to going home and "vegging out" in front of their television sets." This study reflects the view from The American Psychological Association, which states that stress or "emotionally draining events" can lead to acts that help satiate the tension, which can manifest itself as overeating, or eating the wrong foods. This can, if not dealt with early on, lead to a habitual behaviour which is hard to break and can lead to weight gain and even obesity.

Overall, there is a proven relationship between workplace stress and obesity, and this dynamic was properly set in motion in the 1980s, which was the turning point decade of the introduction of unhealthy values in the workplace. As such, it can be concluded that the tension created by this split-personality lifestyle has been contributing to the obesity epidemic.

Rage in Society

Is the world getting angrier? Most of us will have witnessed road rage, which seems to be an expected part of the driving experience.

Arguments in the street, or in bars among strangers are not uncommon. Political debates across countries are not always civilized, bench-clearing fights or vicious attacks are par for the course. People seem to be snapping in all parts of society with increasing frequency. Often, workplace stress is the culprit.

An article by Bruce Ritter of *The Real Truth*, collected several real-life stories of rage in society. One stood out to me because of its connection to workplace stress:

> In the San Francisco Bay Area, a 51-year-old father of eight worked two jobs to care for his family. Due to an irregular work schedule, and a stressful commute from his Antioch home, he slept in his car between shifts, home only on weekends. The pressures of being away from his family, marital troubles, and working two jobs to make ends meet, led to an emotional meltdown. Driving his SUV across the Bay Bridge, he called 911 on his cell phone and threatened to commit suicide with a pipe bomb. The threat shut down traffic and held the bridge hostage for hours.

The genetic makeup of humans makes us prone to anger and violence if confronted with a threat to our fundamental needs—security, food, and so forth, according to an article by Heather Whipps of the University of McGill. Through evolution, these fundamental needs have morphed into less "black and white" scenarios. Feeling disrespected, or feeling threatened, or feeling cheated, can trigger our primate impulse for anger or rage. In the corporate world today, having these feelings is to be expected since competition is fierce, loyalty is for the most part absent, and pressure is enormous. As a result, our "primate instinct" can kick in. A humorous illustration of this breaking point can be seen in a handful of YouTube videos where security cameras catch employees unleashing on their computers. One of my favourite ones can be seen here, where the build-up to the man's boiling point is very relatable: *https://www.youtube.com/ watch?v=Lj4UvCxNWww.*

These types of episodes are on the rise according to an article by *The Chicago Tribune* in 2001. The tensions created by these unhealthy values in the workplace play a significant part. For many working people around the world, there is simply no perceived harmony in their workplace environments, and the situation has worsened over the past decades. The author of *The Chicago Tribune* article, Lisa Anderson, reinforced this point beautifully: "A decade ago, they seemed like isolated incidents that made the headlines because of their bizarre nature." Yes, and today they may not even make the headlines because they are so commonplace.

Anderson writes that working people today live with unrealistic expectations thrust upon them. Everything is a battle, which manifests itself in all parts of our lives. How often do you see people jostling for position in a McDonald's line, or at the airplane gate? Anderson goes on to say, "the causes are myriad, including the round-the-clock, 365-day pace afforded by new communications technology; increased pressure for productivity; impatience; and the changing nature of such traditional rule-setting structures as home and church." The last point is interesting because it refers to the rift in values that pull people in uncomfortable directions.

The Health of Marriage in Society

To determine the health of marriage in society, I looked at divorce and marriage rates as well as happiness ratings among married couples. The data suggests that marriage has hit some hurdles since the 1960s. University of Maryland Sociologist Philip N. Cohen did a brilliant piece of research on the topic in 2013, where he analysed several robust sources, such as Eurostat demographics, United Nations data on marriage rates, demographic quantitative survey information from the USAID, and IPUMs microdata from global censuses. The summary of his work suggests that marriage is in decline across the world, with notable effects in Western countries. Interestingly, these are the countries most impacted by the breakdown of values in the corporate world. Cohen also suggests that marriage decline has not been driven by age or education changes. As such, it is not a cohort that is driving these global numbers, which is in line with the observation that the decline in corporate values is affecting all age cohorts.

Marriage rates are definitely dropping the world over, and there are many suggested reasons for this: income inequality, rising debt, rise in education, loosening of tradition, work pressures, etc. Many of these are related, to a certain degree, to the breakdown of healthy human values in the corporate world, and the egotistical mind-set that has gradually seeped into the consciousness of society at large. As a result of this, many countries are facing aging populations that are putting a strain on the social system. There are simply not enough people entering the workforce to generate tax revenues to help those leaving the workforce. This is a significant worry for many governments around the world.

Beyond the fact that people don't want to get married, those that are, are choosing to end their unions, or are just waiting until the right time comes along for them to be able to break free. A Eurostat report in 2016 showed that divorce rates have gone up across most countries since the 1960s, and a December 2014 article in *The Daily Mail* in the United Kingdom suggested that one in four married couples only stay together for their children. This same article also stated that a fifth of the couples surveyed plan to split after a final family Christmas. If you think about it, these striking claims are not that surprising. The strength of family lies in spending time together, communicating, and working on the relationships. As people are increasingly being forced to work later and harder, are under increased stress, the physical and mental ability to spend quality time with spouses or children is jeopardized.

With marriage rates dropping, and divorce rates high, you'd expect those still in marriages to be happy, or reasonably happy. The article mentioned above suggests this is not the case, and there is further research out of the United States that suggests that marital happiness is slowly declining. The National Opinion Research Center conducted surveys asking respondents simple questions on the state of their marital happiness. The question was worded in the following manner: "Taking things all together, would you say that your marriage is very happy, pretty happy, or not too happy?" When plotting on a graph the number of responses who claimed "very happy", to those that were less favourable, the line curved gently downwards.

Fortunately, there is evidence that millennials are beginning to reverse this trend. Literature suggests that this is likely due to the fact that they are choosing to wait a while before they get married, and that couples are living with one another for a longer period of time, so they are "seeing if this makes sense". However, it may also be because millennials are putting more value in family and want more purpose in their lives. These same millennials are also the group that is taking on the fight to reverse the current unhealthy values situation in the workplace.

Child Abuse in Society

Child abuse is a serious problem around the globe, and studies suggest that it is on the rise. A report published by the IPSCAN International Congress on Child Abuse and Neglect, states that a staggering 25 to 50 percent of children around the world suffer from physical abuse, and that 20 percent of girls and between 5 and 10 percent of boys suffer from sexual abuse. The sheer volume of these numbers suggests that the problem is truly global, and not an issue predominantly found in less developed countries and regions. In fact, the issues are very problematic in "civilized" countries the world over. Even more concerning is that the issues may be on the rise in the countries we would least expect.

A 2015 article in *The Japan Times* wrote that child abuse cases have consistently risen, resulting in the authorities becoming more involved in the issue. The year-over-year rise was a shocking 32 percent. In the United States, the 2015 Child Maltreatment Report from the Children's Bureau showed that the number of children subject to child abuse grew from 6.6 million to 7.2 million. Finally, in the United Kingdom, the NSPCC recently claimed that the reports of sexual abuse against children has risen sharply, and the number of children is the child protection system is increasing. These are just three examples, but there are countless more.

Michael Freeman, of the *International Journal of Children's Rights*, claims that a big cause of child abuse lies in the prejudice against children, which is compounded by the fact that human rights laws do not apply equally to children and adults. However, he also claims, along with other studies, that socio-economic influences have played a big factor in the issue of child abuse. A huge contributor to child abuse is neglect. In the United States alone, The National and State Child Abuse and Neglect Statistics claims that 78 percent of child abuse cases are due to neglect. The reasons for neglect are not surprising: financial difficulty, unemployment, and substance abuse are among the dominant factors. These factors have a direct relationship with the workplace and the values that guide it.

We've already discussed and confirmed the correlation between substance abuse and the workplace earlier on in the chapter. When it comes to unemployment and financial difficulty, clearly both are workplace driven. More importantly, they have been brought on by an increasingly selfish and calculating corporate environment where employees are less valued, and where loyalty has evaporated. In other words, both of these influences on child abuse are fuelled, in part, by the destructive values in the corporate world.

Final Thoughts on the Influence of Corporate Values on the Poor Health of Society

The base metrics of societal health, such as poverty decline, child mortality rates improvement, human rights adherence, rise in education, the spread of democracy, and so forth may be improving, but society is by no means healthier than it was several decades ago. Other, equally harmful, illnesses and issues have steadily grown in impact and reach since the 1960s, some consuming great parts of society. These new societal health problems are depression, substance abuse, obesity, rage, marital distress, and child abuse. At their core, these problems are fuelled by a disharmony that consumes the lives of those that are affected.

Each of these new societal health epidemics have countless reasons for their rise and spread across communities. Many of these drivers are unique to a specific epidemic, but there are some drivers that are shared among the different epidemics. This chapter has shown that the demise of healthy human values in the corporate world factors into these universal drivers. Whether it is the rise of a certain illnesses, or issues happening at the same time as the demise of values in the corporate world, or whether it is the fact that workplace environments are where select illnesses manifest themselves, it is clear that our working lives are creating substantial physical, mental, and social issues that are making society less healthy.

With many of these new health epidemics, society tends to look elsewhere to place blame instead of taking a good look at itself. The discussions about obesity have blamed fast food companies, soda companies, candy makers, and so forth. The debates around substance abuse have blamed cartels, poor policing, and countries' inabilities to protect their borders. Some discussions around depression have blamed the medical industry or public services for not helping citizens identify depression early on so that treatment can be given. Gosh, soon we may see that the church will be blamed for marital distress, or that the automotive industry will be blamed for increases in road rage! Our society is conditioned to lay blame elsewhere, instead of taking a look in the mirror and honestly assessing what society is to be blamed for. The fact that there is such disharmony in most workplace environments, and that people have been forced to adopt value systems that are not natural, is simply not tackled. The issue is too big, and the corporate system runs on this unhealthy value system. It is far easier for the system to divert attention to more manageable problem areas versus embarking on fundamental structural change.

Society is unfortunately excellent at creating distraction, and humans are easily susceptible to its effects. These distractions provide moments of perceived happiness, so that the real issues are left to fester. Over the course of the last few decades, this dynamic has mushroomed. Indirectly, these distractions are actually contributing to the rift in value systems. The most glaring example of this is with celebrity culture.

Chapter 5

The Expanding Cult of Celebrity and its Role in Furthering Unhealthy Values

C elebrity culture is nothing new. From the early days of the movie and music business, key figures have been merchandised by their "owners". After all, people love to admire others who are admired. Somehow, human beings are compelled to look up to something or somebody, to either create an aspirational goal, or to forget their real, uninspired existence. What differentiates the celebrity culture of the early twentieth century from the one of today, is the unhealthy moral code that guides it, and its sheer scale.

The culprit in fuelling this degenerative trend is the corporate world. After all, business has supported this cultural phenomenon from the very start because it helps sell their products or services. As media has mushroomed, so too has the volume of celebrity. Consequently, the means by which celebrities stand out has become more and more perverse. Right alongside these "stars" are big companies eager to take advantage of the fame to draw more attention to their products or services. Therefore, the corporate world is financing the one-upmanship that is turning to increasingly shocking and barbaric, even primitive, tactics to stand out. It is a vicious circle that is powered by two overarching values: self-centeredness and greed.

The desire, or even need, to have a hero to admire is not unhealthy or bad. In fact, it can be incredibly positive for a person's development.

Take religion as an example. Many of the characters in the stories of religious texts are looked up to and educate their followers about constructive values that should govern their lives. However, as the influence of religion waned over the last century, and its role in providing heroes to look up to weakened, something needed to fill the void. Celebrity has done this.

The issue is that traditional "idols" were admired and followed for their achievements or great deeds, but celebrities today are admired for their appearance or social stature. They rarely are looked up to because they are the embodiment of healthy human values. Most are admired for what they wear, where they were last night, who they are dating, how much weight they've lost or gained, how drunk they were, and so on. Scrolling through the various celebrity blogs and online magazines brings nothing of substance. Here are two from today that summarize the tone of all the rest: "Stephan Belafonte's brother claims his sibling punched ex Mel B's beloved dog and flirted with their nanny before filing for divorce", or "Va va voom! Kim Kardashian showcases hourglass figure in super sexy beige knit dress" (both quotes are from *The Daily Mail*). The types of topics surrounding celebrities today couldn't be further apart from the topics that surrounded religious heroes. There is no healthy human value that is merchandised, just superficiality and vanity.

A brilliant interview in 2012 of Russell Brand by Jeremy Paxman from the BBC, discussed this shift from religious admiration to celebrity admiration. To be clear, Mr. Brand is by no means a leading thought figure, but he certainly has experience with the cult of celebrity, and during this interview he made some compelling arguments. His central point about celebrity today was that it is readily accessible to everyone. As a consequence, people truly crave it for themselves, or are consumed by those that have it.

This is fundamentally different from the religious celebrity figures of the past. Celebrity today feels so much closer to people's reality. Therefore, there is a perceived right to have it. Why is this? Because the attributes of celebrity today are utterly meaningless and trivial, which

101

means that displaying them can be quite easy done by anyone. Russell goes on to say that when religion was marginalized in the 1960s, it marked the death of the era of grand ideas. Healthy, human ideologies that created movements, such as women's liberation, Dr. Martin Luther King's "dream", or John Lennon's "imagination" were also marginalized. Mr. Brand stated that "people's brains simply don't want to work that hard anymore. Instead, people find it a lot easier, and a lot more exciting, to consume nicely packaged, branded, and PRed stories".

Russell Brand reminds us that these celebrities and their stories are created to market and to sell. They are not made to further a healthy message or value. The most powerful part of Mr. Brand's argument is that the corporate apparatus that creates and nourishes today's celebrity culture is utilizing lowest common denominator messaging and content because it is easy to digest and can powerfully generate emotions. It really seems as though the corporate world is engaged in a type of cultural brainwashing.

The tipping point after which celebrity culture took a moral nose dive, happened in the 1990s and early 2000s. The advent of the reality show not only revolutionized television, it also redefined what it meant to be a celebrity. The age of the carefully groomed stars from the golden age of Hollywood was long over, but there remained a certain allure about celebrity. The reality show destroyed this last layer of sophistication. From that point on, celebrity culture went down a very self-indulgent path where selfishness and "me" behaviour was brought to the masses with gusto. The new breed of celebrity did not have any outstanding talent, they did not have exceptional genes—they just had outlandish behaviour. Therefore, the popularity of reality show characters was based on how selfish they were and how much they focused on merchandising their own brand to the world. This has led to some truly deplorable headlines over the years.

From the very start of the reality show era, the characters were allowed to showcase some morally horrific behaviours. In 1998, during the seventh season of *The Real World*, cast member Stephen Williams was filmed slapping castmate Irene McGee, after she called him gay.

The display of violence shocked audiences and led to viewer backlash. The show, nonetheless, decided to allow Stephen to remain for the remainder of the season. It seemed that ratings were more important than making a point about furthering healthy human values. Another example of nasty moral behaviour happened in 2007, on the set of *Celebrity Big Brother* in the United Kingdom. Three contestants of the show, model Danielle Lloyd, reality-show veteran Jade Goody, and singer Jo O'Meara, routinely bullied fellow contestant and Indian actress Shilpa Shetty. The taunts were seen as being racist, and, as a result, the television regulatory body, Ofcom, received a huge volume of complaints. The behaviour was truly despicable.

The violence on *The Real World* and the racism on *Celebrity Big Brother* were not uncommon. There are countless other examples of morally corrupt behaviour that seemed to be encouraged by the shows and the networks that aired them. The main reason? Ratings grew. The companies didn't budge because their advertising revenue increased as the popularity of the shows grew. As such, the selfishness and greed of the corporate world was encouraging this type of behaviour among celebrities. Consequently, viewers began to demand it. Granted, the fact that consumers loved it, and thus demanded it, made producers, networks, and advertisers encourage it. The whole thing is a vicious circle.

Corporations would likely say that they are just following cultural and consumer demand. However, this attitude shows no desire to take responsibility. In other words, this attitude suggests that corporations believe that this behaviour is completely acceptable, and that the values that govern these corporations are also acceptable, even though these values are very unhealthy.

The moment where the primitiveness of celebrity was taken to even lower levels was when the socialite celebrity was introduced in the 2000s. The party escapades of Lindsay Lohan, Paris Hilton and Nicole Richie marked a dark turning point for the definition of celebrity. No longer did celebrities have to be chosen, people could now become famous by simply being at parties, being pretty, and acting silly.

The hunger for voyeurism introduced by the reality show went into overdrive. Interestingly, it seemed to coincide with a hardening of the economic situations for the general population. The stock market crash of 2007 wiped out fortunes for many, and permanently changed the employment reality in the world. By this stage, income inequality had already accelerated, but the market crash drove this divide to earth-shattering levels. People were angry, scared, and desperately seeking solutions. Since they weren't finding them in the employment sector, they looked to other sources to dull their pain. Entertainment, specifically the new cult of celebrity, provided this. The fact that people could peek into the real lives of people living the highlife, that they could peek behind the curtain of Hollywood life, beautifully distracted them from their daily hardships. The fact that these celebrity socialites would fall on their faces due to acts of recklessness, made the average person feel good. It showed that even those without financial burdens, got sucker-punched by society from time to time. Whether it was Paris Hilton's 45-day jail sentence, or Lindsay Lohan's regular in and out of rehab soap opera, the tabloids and entertainment media covered every second. Corporations also fuelled the fire by legitimizing this behaviour through endorsements. Paris Hilton, for example, was signed by Guess, and launched a fragrance with Parlux.

There was no better acknowledgement that producers were feeding off this desire for voyeurism, than when the reality show *The Simple Life*, starring Paris and Nicole, was aired. The premise of this show was to place these two Hollywood rich girls into the daily lives of average Americans, deprive them of their money and privileges, and see how they got on. Every single episode allowed ordinary Americans to see celebrities make asses out of themselves. It allowed these same viewers to ignore their own issues because they could see the "more fortunate" struggle doing things that they could likely do with ease. It made viewers feel good about themselves. Aside from being soul-sucking and mind-decaying, the show also highlighted the self-centeredness that consumed these two young women and that was consequently being vividly marketed to viewers. A generation of young people were being groomed to be superficial, self-consumed, and materialistic. And who was pushing this along with fanfare? Corporations through their advertising endorsement that allowed the show to prosper.

If the role of greed-motivated corporations wasn't concerning enough in pushing this new "values void" celebrity to popularity levels rivalling that of rock stars, the advent of social media made their popularity unstoppable. The rise in social media popularity came at the perfect time to help fuel this new celebrity. It was in 2007 when Facebook began to become incredibly trendy, and Twitter was a year old, but already gaining in popularity. This was the exact time that the socialite celebrity became ubiquitous.

Celebrities were quick to jump onto social media because it allowed them to grab even more of the "limelight". Many became seriously addicted. Rihanna, Miley Cyrus, Justin Bieber, Selena Gomez and countless others were unrelenting with their posts, writing updates close to ten times per day. The constant stream of instant feedback is very powerful. The attention that they get is simply incredibly ego-stroking, which furthers their addictive social media behaviour. In some cases, the addiction is so strong that it actually affects their lives in seriously unhealthy ways. Musician John Mayer famously admitted that he had to go "cold turkey on social media" because his intense usage of Twitter made him unable to write songs. How crazy is that!

Celebrity addiction to social media has also resulted in some unwanted legal issues. A famous example is from Paris Hilton in 2010. She had been arrested for cocaine possession where the evidence was found in her Chanel bag. She tried to wiggle out of the arrest by claiming that the bag belonged to a friend but had forgotten that she had tweeted about her Chanel bag first thing that morning before leaving the house. Oops.

This never-ending stream of celebrity content has two concerning repercussions. The first is that the celebrities themselves feel obliged to post, otherwise they may fall behind on other celebrities' activities, or in the expectations of their audiences. They are only too aware that a decline in relevance means a decline in potential corporate endorsements. Consequently, the content will suffer. Regardless of who you are, no one's life is exciting twenty-four seven! Therefore, it is likely that posts from even the most notorious celebrity become either boring or forced.

A common example of forced commentary is during tragic global events. Often, celebrities feel compelled to say something, just to be part of the conversation. Unfortunately, too often they are clueless about the situation, haven't properly gathered their thoughts, or simply don't care. It would be wiser to simply keep quiet, but the hunger for attention is too strong. To illustrate this point, we can turn to a post written by Cher on Twitter in 2016, reacting to the terrorist attack on the airport in Istanbul, Turkey, in June of that year. In her post, she tweeted, "We all pray for innocent ppl in turkey airport". This sentence was simple and decent enough, but Cher added some emojis to the post that made the comment incredible insensitive. The emojis that she brilliantly used were a bomb emoji, and an explosion icon. She later apologized, claiming that she used emojis to "tell more than the 140-character limit permits." If that were the case, perhaps she could have held back saying something on Twitter and waited until she found a forum where she could properly communicate what was on her mind. However, the addiction to social media and being part of the conversation was simply too strong.

The second repercussion of this never-ending stream of celebrity content is the impact created on consumers. The most noticeable manifestation of this is that people emulate their celebrities. Unfortunately, many celebrities (especially the socialite or reality show celebrities) are no role models. Many will kick-off catchphrases—just think of Paris Hilton's "that's hot". Others will kick-off plastic surgery trends—just think of Kylie Jenner's lip surgery mystery. Some will do attention-grabbing stunts that others replicate—just think of Paris Hilton's sex tape, and the many copycat tapes that came thereafter. Still others will start "primitive" styling trends—just think of Kim Kardashian's "cleavage contouring". Each of these trends are superficial. None push healthy values. As such, they are really teaching those who admire them to live a superficial life to not put importance on promoting the healthy human values that most of us grow up with.

Corporations compound the problem by aggressively endorsing these celebrities, and thus supporting their "values void" antics. As an example, Kim Kardashian has been linked with everything from OPI nail polishes, to Charmin paper towels, to Sears department stores, to Midori liqueur, to QuickTrim diet pills, and to Silly Bandz accessories. It appears that brands in almost any category want a piece of Kim. Their greed encourages Kim to continue doing what she does, always notching up the ante, to attract more followers and thus more corporate money. There are absolutely no moral checks and balances in these types of relationships. It is truly concerning.

However, the main impact of this never-ending stream of celebrity content, is that consumers become addicted to celebrity culture. Since there is no downtime from their obsession, consumers get completely engulfed by the world of their celebrity. There is actually a medical condition for this. It is known as Celebrity Worship Syndrome (or CWS). According to Wikipedia, there are six classifications of CWS:

- *Simple obsessional* (the most common type of worship linked with stalking. Most sufferers have had previous personal relationships with their victims),
- *Love obsessional* (the type of worship where stalking turns into love. These sufferers have no previous relationship with their victims),
- *Erotomanic* (the type of worship where the sufferers are convinced that the victims are in love with them),
- *Entertainment-social* (the lowest type of worship, where the "sufferer" regularly creates conversation about his/her admired celebrity),
- *Intense-personal* (a type of worship associated with neuroticism and psychoticism. The "sufferer" may believe that they are soulmates with their celebrity), and

- *Borderline-pathological* (the most severe type of worship. "Sufferers" are willing to do extremely perverse things to be connected with their celebrity, such as buying a used napkin).

Researchers state that the main trigger for any of the classifications of this illness are either depression, anxiety, or stress. Interestingly, as was discussed in the previous chapter, depression, anxiety and stress are also associated with a life torn by opposing value systems. As such, the corporate world is impacting people in two separate ways via celebrity culture—through direct push (feeding celebrity culture) and pull (creating tension in life where people turn to celebrity for escape).

The most troubling aspect of the cult of celebrity is that the definition of "accomplishment" is being redefined. A fundamental human value, as described earlier in this book, is based on hard work and the reward that comes from it. Too many celebrities today are not hard workers. There are exceptions, and some get involved in entrepreneurial ventures as their fame grows (although the degree to which they are actually involved (versus their staff) is debatable depending on the celebrity). However, a large number of celebrities become popular because of social antics, extravagant shopping, and so forth. As their star ascends, and media attention and corporate endorsements pile up, they are inadvertently teaching their followers that fame can come without having to accomplish all that much. Pure self-indulgent and self-consuming behaviour is enough to become popular, as long as you use social media in the right way. Beyond promoting extremely unhealthy values, they are creating a false sense of hope. Sharon Osbourne, wife of iconic heavy-metal frontman Ozzy Osbourne, famously commented on people's unrealistic celebrity aspirations, saying "today, though, young people regard fame as a birth right. They have a sense of entitlement the size of one my houses." This is quite delusional and, if left unmanaged, it can lead to depression.

In summary, the total interdependence between the cult of celebrity and the corporate world is fuelling a decay in people's value systems. Consequently, the cult of celebrity and the corporations that encourage it are playing a big part in pushing people towards a split-personality way of living. Neither are holding the other responsible for merchandising constructive values, because they are blinded by their own greed and are completely self-centered (so they have no time to think of others!). The ubiquity of social media has only aggravated this dynamic. In addition to facilitating a constant stream of celebrity content, it also has somehow legitimized this content, turning it into "news". As a consequence, the news has also begun to pursue questionable values.

Chapter 6

The News' Influence in Encouraging Unhealthy Values

At its core, news is a central part of a healthy, and well-functioning democracy. A publication by the New Zealand Law Commission wrote about "What distinguishes the news media and why it matters". A passage beautifully describes the role of news:

> An independent and free press, unfettered by political interference, was seen to be a necessary embodiment of an individual's right to free expression and an essential condition for democracy. Put simply, unless citizens were able to freely access and exchange information and opinions about what was happening in society, they were not able to self-govern.

As a consequence, the tenets that are sacrosanct to news are truthfulness, accuracy, and the expectation that journalists maintain an objective stance and source different perspectives to understand the full story. Yet, somehow the commercial influence in news media has corrupted these tenets over the years. Television played a central role in this shift.

As the volume of stations grew off the back of cable and satellite television, competition for advertising dollars also grew. Since the revenue that was generated from news-driven advertising was significant, stations sought ways to lure viewers to their news coverage. Consequently, stations introduced entertainment into news reporting. A quote by the former White House press secretary, Bill Moyers, highlights the risk of blending news with entertainment: "When you mix fiction and news, you diminish the distinction between truth and fiction, and you wear down the audience's own discriminating power to judge."

The proliferation of the internet has only aggravated this reality. Not only is there further competition for consumer attention, but consumers themselves have become increasingly impatient and easily distracted. As a result, the "entertainment" levers used by the news have become stronger and more extreme—to shock and force viewers to choose one media choice over the other. Naturally, morality suffered. Honesty, trustworthiness, and loyalty to the viewer, have eroded. The situation has gotten so bad, and the news industry so unreliable, that we now have a global "fake news" epidemic.

Television's Role in Corrupting the News Media

Over the decades, the television has become the main distribution vehicle for news. While the internet now plays a significant role in information dissemination, the television news remains a staple source of information consumption. However, the proliferation of channels means that "the evening news" no longer is the sole source of "credible" information consumption. There are countless specialized programs that give their viewers news updates within that specialty. With the introduction of cable and satellite television systems, the number of channels across the world has risen to unthinkable levels. Today it is possible to access hundreds of different channels, when as recently as the 1980s, there were still only a handful of television networks that consumers could access in the various European countries. Prior to cable and satellite television, there were three big networks in the United States, and across Europe each country had its slim pickings of government managed stations. In other countries, the pattern was similar. This meant that the sheer volume of "news" exploded. There is now ruthless competition among the countless news programs. Meanwhile, the available hours of daily feasible watching time are limited.

Fortunately for the television networks, people in countries around the world have chosen to consume more and more television over the decades. The International Communications Market Report collects the data about daily television viewing time from countries on all continents. The numbers are surprising. The average time spent watching television in countries as diverse as the United States, Brazil, Russia, France, Germany, Japan, Korea, Poland, Australia, Spain, and the United Kingdom, is at least two hundred minutes per day, so three hours and twenty minutes. Some countries are a lot higher. In the United States, the average amount of time spent watching TV is four hours and forty-two minutes. In Russia, it is three hours and fifty-nine minutes. Clearly, the world is currently watching a lot of television. However, viewership growth rates seem to have plateaued, and we are seeing declines among younger audiences. This is very concerning for networks because they are seeing serious revenue troubles in the not-so-distant future.

The situation for networks is troubling. They have increasing competition from other networks, and the "watching time universe" is beginning to shrink with newer consumer cohorts. As a result, they have been forced to dial-up the entertainment power of their programming, and to produce programming more cheaply. The news programming has not become shielded from this dynamic. It is very common to see news segments that feel like scenes from reality shows.

The film *Anchorman* starring Will Ferrell parodies this dynamic beautifully. Particularly funny is a scene where the news crew jump into a bear pit. This scene is clearly over-the-top, but how many times have we seen weather reporters placed in the most absurd storms. People watch because there is a good chance that something bad or funny will happen to the weather anchor.

In some countries, regulations have effectively encouraged networks to pursue less quality programming. In the United States, for example, the FCC dismantled much of the regulatory framework that was imposed on the television industry to provide some minimum amount of serious public affairs programming. Networks were therefore encouraged to be creative and had no real accountability. To be fair, there remain many state-run or state-subsidized channels that are not subject to the same competitive ruthlessness as private stations, and their news programming remains of a high standard. A good example of this would be the BBC. However, the fact that a large number of stations are actively pursuing "infotainment" in their news coverage is subconsciously educating viewers that "this is what they want". Consequently, even the serious news programs have indulged, even if very slightly, in entertainment content.

Aggravating this change towards "infotainment" news is how viewers are now consuming news. Growing television network competition, combined with newly-learned social media behaviours, and the rise in news dailies (free newspapers that commuters grab on public transportation in bigger cities), means that people are increasingly looking for bite-sized news stories. In-depth news reporting is now riskier. While the journalistic work might be brilliant, viewers may tune out because their attention span is too short. If they do that, advertising revenue will suffer, which could have deadly repercussions for networks.

What are the news programs at television networks to do? They seek out storytelling techniques that work for other types of television programs. Taking inspiration from reality television, themes portrayed in some of the most popular shows of the time, and videos that have a huge number of views on social media, the news content has become about provoking emotions rather than telling meaningful news stories. Therefore, television has been a main force behind sensationalism in news media.

Sensationalism in News Media

The definition of sensationalism, according to Google, is "the presentation of stories in a way that is intended to provoke public interest or excitement, at the expense of accuracy." The last part of the definition is what is important— "at the expense of accuracy". Sensationalism is a threat to the values that govern proper news. It opposes the core tenets of truthfulness and honesty. However, sensationalism sells. The tabloid industry was built on this reality. When I was younger, I remember reading headlines in the German *Bild Zeitung* or the American *National Inquirer* magazine that were so misleading that they completed grabbed my attention. A famous *National Inquirer* headline from the 1960s illustrates my point: In big bold letters, it read "I came back from the dead" (referring to a quote by Rita Hayworth), and right underneath in smaller letters was written "for two years I was a zombie". These types of headlines trigger a strong emotion, making us naturally awake from our routine and focus. The problem is that "distorted journalistic reports can generate both false hopes and unwarranted fears", according to a paper written by David Ransohoff MD, and Richard Ransohoff MD, in a 2001 edition of the *Effective Clinical Practice* magazine. Therefore, sensationalism pulls us into the domain of unhealthy values: fear, protectionism, anger and distrust.

The news media was lured into sensationalism by pop culture and its growing appetite for intense emotions and distraction. Younger people have always looked for new experiences to shape the identity of their generation. Therefore, pop culture offerings seem to dial up in intensity over the years. Music and sport provide great examples. Think of the progression from David Bowie, to Madonna, to Lady Gaga. Each pushed boundaries that little bit further. Think of the rebel sports of the 1970s and those that exist today. The craziness has been dialled up to eleven. Motocross in the seventies was viewed as pretty intense. Now they are doing multiple backflips on motocross bikes! I use both of these references to illustrate the point that people are now conditioned to consume outrageous content. Therefore, news reporting has to adjust to this new reality or else many people will tune out.

Sensationalism has also gained importance as the stress of the real world has made people crave distraction. The working world has played a big part in this dynamic. Since the "thinking economy" has become a large part of the workforce, along with unhealthy dynamics and values that are increasingly part of this aspect of our lives, having the ability to shut down our brains is not just a "nice to have", but is actually needed. This yearning to "not have to think" or to reflect on one's own existence, is reinforced by people's fear of solitude. A 2015 article in Fast Company on the importance of solitude, mentioned a research study that "found that people can be so uncomfortable by solitude and quiet time for thinking, that they'd rather administer electric shocks to themselves than be left alone with their thoughts". In other words, the increasing extravagance of sensational content distracts from their uninspired reality and assures that they don't have to spend a moment reflecting about their true state of affairs. A further problem stemming from this behaviour is that people are increasingly struggling to pay attention.

People's Inability to Pay Attention and its Effect on News Reporting

John Cassidy, a writer for *The New Yorker*, published an article in February 2015 that started like this:

> I was as going to finish up this post earlier, but I got diverted on the Internet. First, there were those amazing videos of people snow-diving in Boston. Then I did an interactive quiz on Buzzfeed called "What Would Your Puritan Name Be?" Next, I got caught up in a story on Vice's Motherboard site about extra-terrestrial supercomputer robots, which was actually pretty educational, or so I told myself as I tweeted it to other people who should have been working.

The ubiquity of the internet, and significant smartphone penetration, is enabling this "distraction addiction". The FOMO phenomenon, or Fear of Missing Out phenomenon, is very real. You are in a constant state of catch-up, meaning you can't really focus on one thing because, if you do, you may fall too far behind on your updates that provide you with that all-important social currency. The pressure these dynamics put on the ability of news reporting to keep people's attention is enormous. The real goal of news is to report stories that will inform citizens so that they can help society progress by learning from the successes, failures, as well as the positive and evil actions of others. The FOMO phenomenon, however, is not encouraging a desire for learning or improvement. David Shaw from *The Los Angeles Times* highlighted this issue in an article he wrote on the rise of entertainment in news, saying:

> Thanks to MTV, and instant messaging and other rapid-fire features of the Internet, most young people today want everything in quick, small bites. They get their news, to the extent that they get any, inadvertently, almost by osmosis, absorbing bits of it on various websites or between the radio play of their favourite songs or while clicking the television remote control.

There is no importance put on news. Instead, people want to be kept emotionally energized. Therefore, news reporting is forced to implement less-than-healthy storytelling practices.

Society is becoming addicted to social information that triggers a vivid emotion. Studies have proven that with every "info hit" the body releases serotonin, generating pleasure. Therefore, in a way, our constant distraction behaviour is simply our "addict self" looking for that next serotonin fix. What is concerning about this behaviour is that it is making us immune to pleasure from little things. Our bodies are so used to constant stimulus that in order to trigger a proper serotonin hit, we are needing either more stimulus or greater stimulus.

News reporting editors and producers know this human reality very well, and thus they are not just creating more bite size reports to consume but are voluntarily leaning into sensationalism, or "dramatic storytelling", to make those short reports as memorable as possible. Aside from the occasional "feel good" stories that lean into the powerful emotion of love and caring, most stories tend to lean into the other strong emotions such as fear, shock, or anger. Clearly, most of these are not promoting healthy values. In addition, the danger with this "addiction" to stories that are rooted in highly intense emotions, is that information inaccuracy or blatant fibs are multiplying within the world or news.

The News Media's Role in Merchandising Inaccurate Information

Since the various news media are aggressively pursuing viewers, readers, and so forth, sacrifices will most certainly be made in reporting scrutiny. Subsequently, inaccurate information will be rife.

The most potent means by which news can skew information is through interest groups that build relationships with journalists or networks. There are soft influences and hard influences. A way that interest groups softly influence news reporting was nicely summed up by the Association of Accredited Public Policy Advocates to the European Union (AALEP) in 2016. They wrote:

> "Despite popular press accusations of partisan bias in the media, any such bias is not the result of the intentional slanting of stories, but rather results from a much subtler process in which journalists seek to obtain information with minimal costs and tell a clear and concise story. Interest group representatives who understand this provide factual and timely information to journalists, while perhaps focusing on information that support their group's viewpoint. If groups can develop goodwill with journalists in this way, they are more likely to have their information used by journalists and, thereby, to have stories reported in a way that benefits

their interests. In this sense, a lobbyist's relationship with the news media parallels his or her relationships with legislators. Providing services leads to goodwill and favourable treatment in subtle but important ways."

A harder influence that interest groups can have is by defining the debate around a topic and filling it with highly-biased, and even inaccurate, information. An example of this behaviour can be seen in the American public debate on climate change. An article written by Asher Schechter, from the University of Chicago, described the issue of misinformation given by interest groups, who have vested interest in curbing policies that have been brought about through research on the realities of climate change. Schechter writes, "while climate change sceptics are largely relegated to the margins of the scientific community, in American media they have been given roughly equal attention based on a paper by Maxwell T. Boykoff and J. Timmons Roberts, long after the formation of scientific consensus, thereby giving a sense of false balance to a debate that, scientifically speaking, has long been resolved." The media, looking to produce a regular stream of content in order to avoid losing audiences, can sometimes embrace this "debate" to maximize the entertainment value around specific topics. As such, in the pursuit of advertising revenue, they misinform the general public.

In rare cases, misinformation can get really out of hand. Adam Curtis, a reporter for the BBC, produced a documentary called *HyperNormalization* where he shed light on the staggering media manipulation taking place in Russia. He spoke about the political theatre that was set in motion by Vladislav Surkov, the personal adviser to Vladimir Putin and former First Deputy Chief of the Russian Presidential Administration, who completely manipulated the Russian electorate by blending theatre with politics, so that the people no longer knew real from fake. Countless stories of anti-government rallies, concerts, popular events, were distributed through the news, and after they had made an impact, the Kremlin would announce that it was behind these stories. As such, people became numb to news reporting, and eventually just "digested the information without thinking". In other words, the news media in these extreme cases has completely shattered the values of trust and honesty.

The dissemination of inaccurate information by the news media, be it slight or enormous, can be linked to a change in the journalist's role as a gatekeeper (in countries where there is a more-or-less free press). When time and space were limiting factors in news reporting, the journalist and editor were the true gatekeepers of information. However, as the internet has created a reality of infinite time and space, the journalist and editor no longer have control. Instead, they are playing catch-up with to the torrent of information. Relying on news aggregators for inspiration and information, who are filled with content written by readers, journalists become more dependent on the desires of readers versus leading the charge of the information that gets shared. The problem with this shift in the gatekeeper is that the public is not trained to source accurate information (nor does it likely care) and does not mind championing its various thoughts or causes.

How Technology is Furthering News Media's Influence of Unhealthy Human Values

The pressure to pump out content continuously in order to sustain your "fair share" of viewers, readers, and so forth, has clearly impacted reporting quality, and honesty. The time required for proper reporting has seriously been affected, at the expense of the time required to edit, package, and pump out story after story.

As we have discussed in this chapter, story accuracy is frequently sacrificed. While this is not great, it would be less concerning if there was a system in place to ensure that people were getting different perspectives, and different stories on a similar topic. If this were the case, inaccuracy would not be as damaging as it is today. The problem is that social media has undermined this. Social media platforms have algorithms that continually optimize the content you see based on your likes, previous views, and so forth. The reason they do this is to provide the most relevant information for you. We all are aware of the fact that many of our friends on Facebook never appear on our newsfeed. This is not because they aren't active, it is because you haven't engaged with any of their posts in a while, so the Facebook algorithm assumes you are no longer interested in them. The problem with this type of automation, is that you have a tendency to watch the same type of content repeatedly. If you tend to watch content by a select few publishers, bloggers, or writers that is inaccurate, the chance that you will get more of the same is large. Consequently, social media will feed your own ignorance. The reality is that these social media platforms plunge us into thought bubbles.

Interestingly, the motivation for social media firms to funnel users into thought bubbles is driven by the unhealthy corporate values that dictate these firms' behaviour. At the end of the day, these companies are driven by investor or shareholder performance expectations. Therefore, these firms are motivated by greed and selfishness. You'd think that with the enormous responsibility that they have in creating community and connection, in sharing real stories, and in fostering healthy human values, that they would do more to ensure that false information is not allowed to flow unchecked. The industry is taking this issue seriously and has made promises to introduce systems to offset this. However, it feels like there needs to be a lot greater integration between the news media and social media. In isolation, it feels that neither will have the ability, or true will, to fully shed the negative values that guide their decision-making.

Summarizing How News Media has Been Influencing Unhealthy Human Values

The news media has been a victim of society's shift towards darker values, as the separation of church and state has blurred, as interest groups have increasingly played greater influence, as advertising revenue has grown in importance, and as technology has democratized news, putting unrealistic pressure on journalists. However, the news media are now compounding the problem as they lean ever more into reporting practices that follow the morally-unhealthy rules of entertainment. Many journalists even have their hands tied by compensation structures that force them to pursue sensational, sometimes untrue, and mostly morally corrupt stories. A report by the BBC in 2015 highlighted the fact that select magazines pay their journalists by the clicks that their stories get online. How on earth does that encourage constructive journalism?

The fact that social media is forcing us into thought bubbles, allowing certain people to solely consume content with unhealthy values, encourages news media to produce more of this type of content. It is a vicious cycle with deadly consequences. Just look at the firm beliefs of supporters of the various nationalist movements around the world. They do not show compassion or caring for others. They seem to have dropped their inherent moral compass. Hearing the rhetoric of the leaders of these movements makes many shake their heads because the arguments are so flawed, but swaths of people totally buy into their words. This is totally understandable once you realize that their worldview only has these stories. To them, nothing else exists.

News media has a big responsibility to provide truthful information. Having a point of view is fine, but it needs to be expressed with accurate support. News media should pursue justice. They are there to keep gatekeepers in check, and to champion healthy human values. They should be the ones that expose the powers that further a split-personality way of living. However, they are increasingly powered by and dependent on the advertising revenue generated by the companies that are the main culprits in this unhealthy values existence. Consequently, the news media has increasingly replaced its healthy practices with ones that encourage the values of deceit, fear, anger, isolation, and selfishness.

As social media companies have become the new leaders of the news media, the decay in healthy news practices has further accelerated because they have historically viewed themselves as conduits for information versus the guardians of it. However, this has now changed, and therefore they have to take responsibility, and introduce ways to pursue justice, to pursue the truth, and ultimately to champion healthy human values. Unfortunately, they are increasingly motivated by their stock performance, which has little correlation with the advancement of healthy human values.

Chapter 7

Social Media's Role in Deepening the Adoption of Unhealthy Human Values

Social media has become a daily part of life for billions of people in all corners of the world. It has completely redefined the idea of connection. For this reason, its adoption has been staggering in the short time that it has been in existence. An article by the World Economic Forum spoke about the key positive changes that this technology has brought to the world. It described how social media was shaking up the healthcare and public care industry, providing access to professional help with greater ease than ever before. The article also said that social media is changing how we govern and are governed, stating that there is greater pressure on accountability since everyone has a voice, and information can quickly circulate that forces debate about topics meaningful to the people. It also wrote that social media allows us to better react to natural disasters, by having access to critical information with greater speed and accuracy, and by being able to interact with affected people on the ground in real time. The piece mentioned that social media is allowing us to tackle human rights, using the Arab Spring as the main example of how the technology can allow people to mobilize and speak out. Clearly, social media has integrated into our lives and profoundly impacted culture. In some circumstances, social media has even encouraged healthy human values to prosper, such as freedom (through borderless communication), and compassion (by allowing cultural immersion through your smartphone or computer).

There are a handful of companies that dominate the world's social media usage—Facebook (including Instagram), Twitter, Google (including YouTube), and Snapchat. All of these companies are listed on the stock exchange and are guided by the pressures of investors. As a result, the vicious pursuit of quarterly financial performance dominates these companies. Consequently, the true mission to help people connect and create a more transparent world, is difficult to perfectly and constantly live up to. Instead, the values of greed and selfishness seep into decision-making. In other words, the negative influences of the corporate world are increasingly dictating the allowed behaviours on these platforms.

This is very apparent in how the Facebook algorithm quickly removes updates from people, groups and brands that you haven't engaged with. The belief is that if you do not engage, their relevance to you is weak. Thus, the goal is to expose the most relevant information, the information that you are most likely to engage with. The problem is that this shoves you unwillingly into "friend and information funnels". For Facebook, and other social media platforms that apply similar algorithmic directives, this is very beneficial because they are able to serve up content and advertising that has a strong ability to initiate a reaction from you. However, it also creates several dynamics that are furthering unhealthy human values. First, it weakens connections because you are not being allowed to connect with your total network of friends. Second, it can contribute to greater anxiety by compelling you to be active to sustain your "popularity", or relevance, to those that you follow (and want to keep following). Third, it encourages vanity through the many apps and tools that enhance or "improve" your presentation on their platforms. Finally, it may even promote insecurity by constantly reinforcing unachievable perfection in high interest, and life-guiding, categories such as beauty or fitness.

How Social Media Actually Weakens Connection

Creating connections is what social media is all about. The first-recognized social media sites, such as Six Degrees in 1997 and Friendster in 2002, aimed to truly connect friends, and friends of friends, using the degrees of separation principle. The early manifestations of Facebook were also engineered to connect friends and communities. People jumped onto to these platforms, which equally attracted investment. With investment came performance pressures. Depending on the level of autonomy negotiated by the founders of these platforms, these performance pressures could be intense, and they quickly introduced mechanisms, apps, and content that would focus on making money rather than furthering connections.

This was most noticeable with MySpace. Firstly, it was never a pure social media company to begin with, being a type of e-commerce company that saw the massive user growth of Friendster and said, "we need to tap into that." MySpace actually grew its initial user base by inviting Friendster users who were kicked off the platform for not encouraging healthy human connections. A famous example was a woman called Tila Tequila, who was too racy for Friendster. MySpace had monetization as its core driver early on, even facing legal challenges when they wanted to charge bands to set up and grow their accounts on the platform. However, the main corporate influence came when NewsCorp purchased MySpace, introducing the unhealthy values of greed and deceit into the fabric of the social media site.

Facebook would also become victim to the pressures of demonstrating financial performance. Some early efforts had pretty harsh reactions from its community. An example of this was an advertising product called Beacon. It faced a vicious backlash from Facebook consumers, when it was revealed that the feature shared data about its users' information on third party sites in Facebook news feeds. A class action lawsuit was filed regarding privacy protection forcing Facebook to publicly apologize. However, the company kept pursuing greater relevance in its news feed, deploying EdgeRank, and now using machine learning that considers 100,000 factors in deciding the people, brands, and content that get prioritized for each person on its platform. Consequently, Facebook isn't really furthering connection because it dramatically reduces the number of people from whom you see updates. Many users feel compelled to "like" or "comment" so that people and brands don't disappear from their news feeds. As Facebook continues to focus on delivering content that ensures the most engagement (because this automated functionality seduces people into spending more time on the platform and buying more stuff through ads on the platform), it is creating both anxiety (to keep up) and addiction (to not miss out) among its users. That is a far cry from building connections to make life more meaningful.

Feeding the Need for Popularity

The constant need to stay connected within your social media community has created the very selfish need to sustain and grow your own popularity. Ultimately, the sheer volume of connections that many people have on social media aren't their real connections, they are their collections. How many of our "friends" do we truly consider actual friends, people that we'd want to go for a drink or coffee with? An article by *The Telegraph* in January 2016 quoted research that found that Facebook users only consider 28 percent of their "social media friends", true friends. This also reflected how they acted on the platform. Nonetheless, people continue to amass friends. The average friend count on Facebook as of 2016 was 338 friends, while it was 200 friends only a few years ago. Meanwhile, universally accepted psychological research states that it is only possible to keep up with 150 friendships, period. So, what about all those "extra friends"? Well, they are a collection, just like Star Wars figurines, coins, comic books, cards, and vinyl records. What do collections bring us? They help us stand out from the crowd, they showcase our "strength" on that topic. In the realm of social media, our collection of friends showcases our "strength" in popularity.

The "friend counter syndrome" exploded when celebrities began to aggressively use social media sites to promote themselves. Quantity versus quality was important. There were several well-publicized examples of celebrities hiring companies to create fake friends. One of the biggest "outings" came in 2014, when Instagram deleted millions of fake accounts in an effort to combat spam. The initiative exposed many celebrities' accounts, showing that they were clearly not as popular as they would want the public to believe. For example, Kim Kardashian lost 1.3 million followers, rapper Akon lost close to 56 percent of his following, and Justin Bieber lost 3.5 million followers. Platforms were trying to tackle the problem because advertisers were raising concerns that their money was being wasted on ghost accounts.

Certainly, social media platforms have become more committed to removing fake accounts. Nonetheless, anyone who has invested in fan growth knows it is incredibly easy and inexpensive to buy followers, who are then surprisingly uninterested in engaging with any content in a group or community that they showed interest in. In other words, it is not about creating meaningful human connections. Instead, social media has become a public forum for showcasing social currency. This affects brands, celebrities, and also everyday people. As such, regular social media users feel somehow compelled to collect people in the same was as they have collected sneakers or purses. Subsequently, people have become commodities on social media.

When brands began to get very involved in social media, they fuelled this "collection obsession". Arguably, the milestone moment when brands started to significantly impact social media user behaviour, was when Facebook opened up their API to app developers. The flood of cool apps created an environment where you could assemble a huge array of apps that showed your "fellow followers" all of your interests. Users hunted for all the cool apps that reflected their personality and showed how on top of things they were. The early site architecture of Facebook, when these apps were being developed en masse, allowed users to organize these apps exactly how you wanted—pure personalization. Therefore, the arrangement was just as important as the content. The environment became externally oriented and about accumulating stuff, not about personal human connections.

Subsequently, through the actions and investments of brands on social media, they were contributing to the growth of the unhealthy human values of self-obsession and anxiety. The interaction with others on social media became more about "contributing to the dialogue" rather than showing appreciation for one another. It was about promoting your knowledge and "hipness" through the brands, products, advertisements, and so forth that you knew about. It was as though, brands were helping social media users become more obsessed about themselves versus building bonds with the people with whom they are supposed to have a "healthy human connection". Therefore, brands helped fuel people's constant desire to one-up their "friends". This one-upmanship also creates anxiety because people can never rest from the "required information knowledge" that allows them to keep promoting their coolness to others.

Encouraging Vanity

As social media has become more image and video driven, the obsession with looking your best has grown. In an article in *The Guardian* in 2015, people were interviewed about their image obsession on social media. One 22-year old respondent provided this answer:

"Sometimes when I post a photo of myself, I end up taking 20 different pictures and choosing the best one."

Vanity has truly taken on an absurd dimension thanks to social media. This was most pronounced with the introduction of the selfie. While the selfie has been around for a while and was already extensively used on MySpace and Flickr in its early years, the popularity of this photo format exploded in the 2010s. It was rated by *Time* magazine as one of the top buzzwords of 2012 and became truly ubiquitous at that time. This was reinforced by a 2013 study from Australia, that claimed a whopping two thirds of Australian women took selfies (I suspect the number today to be a lot higher). What is so amusing about the rise of the selfie, is the pose culture that has evolved around it. According to *Seventeen* magazine there are eight core poses: Duck Face, Fish Gape, Sparrow Face, and so on. Their legitimacy is reinforced by being referenced in respectable fashion magazines such as *Elle*. Honestly, the poses look quite similar to me, but many people take them quite seriously. Celebrities work hard on mastering them, creating a perfection obsession among everyday girls. Men are just as fascinated by the selfie, showing off their abs and muscles. Celebrity talk-show host Geraldo took a famous selfie in-front of a mirror, showing off his physique and almost a lot more.

According to Wikipedia, there was "a study that examined the relationship between personality and selfie-posting behaviours that suggested that extroversion and social exhibitionism positively predicts the frequency of selfie posting". Since the volume of selfie picture-taking has risen to such enormous levels that the term was officially introduced into the Oxford Dictionary in 2013, vanity is very much being reinforced by this phenomenon. The entire feeder industry is only furthering this reality. Selfie sticks, selfie filters, and so on encourage us to "Duck Face" and "Fish Gape" all over the place.

It is not just the selfie that is promoting vanity on social media, it is the entire photo-taking culture being propelled by Instagram, Snapchat, Tinder, and so forth. Many of these platforms have introduced mechanisms that allow pictures to be quickly removed from the gaze of viewers. Snapchat was built on content that disappears. Tinder allows you to swipe away photos that don't interest you. With these functionalities, it is not surprising that social media users are so consumed by taking amazing pictures. They cannot help becoming increasingly vain, because the image ecosystem in social media forces them to be that way.

Perfection is further encouraged by the countless filters built into social media sites. The recent explosion of the filter universe on Snapchat has even added an entertainment angle to photo-editing that has grown users' hunger for more "beautification" tools for their photos.

The corporate world has played a key part in fuelling this cult of vanity by financing the growth of, among other things, influencers. Influencer marketing has become a huge part of many business plans. Many influencers are the pure embodiment of vanity. They are admired for their seemingly great lives. However, many of their lives are staged. The content is purposefully provocative and overly beautified to create envy. Agencies and corporations have learned to play the game and have been able to do so with surprising effect. A very recent example was the creation of Louise Delage by Paris agency BETC. This "influencer" was able to assemble 650,000 followers in a short amount of time by constantly being at cool places, having delicious drinks, looking beautiful and happy. Her followers were all surprised when it was revealed that the entire thing was a stunt to educate young people about the dangers of excessive alcohol use. This campaign was brilliant, and for a good cause, but most are not. They simply borrow interest in glamorous people and lifestyles.

The money that has gone into this business is significant, prompting influencers to up their game in order to get more marketing money from corporations. As such, these influencers showcase even more glamorous and shocking lives so that they attract even more followers. This, in turn, elevates the vanity threshold for the average social media user. Therefore, brands are indirectly encouraging the values of dishonesty and deceit.

Brands, Social Media, and Growing Insecurity

A *Forbes* article in 2017 listed several factors that lead to insecurity caused by social media. Many of the factors have already been listed in this chapter. However, the most fascinating factor mentioned in the article was that even the ads in social media make you feel inferior. Social media advertising algorithms are highly sophisticated, using all your historical information and behaviours to serve up, what it thinks, are ads for products that you would be interested in. The problem is that you may be heavily consuming content about topics that you admire, but where you don't feel that you live up to societal standards. As such, advertisements promoted by the likes of Facebook actually fuel your insecurity.

Noteworthy examples are within the beauty and fitness categories. If you are constantly posting photos of yourself showing your beautiful body, liking photos of fitness models, and using the word "beauty" and "fitness" and so forth, chances are that you will be served up ads that cater to beauty and fitness. These ads tend to show people who are in top form or are unbelievably beautiful. Therefore, they raise the bar even higher, feeding your insecurity.

Summarizing How Social Media Through Corporate Influence Push Unhealthy Values

Motivated by investor and stock market demands for financial growth, social media platforms are increasingly partnering with brands to promote products and services that these platforms believe are highly relevant to their users. In doing so, these platforms have distanced themselves from their core purpose: to create greater connection among people around the world. Instead, these platforms, through the influence of the corporate ills that have consumed their existence, have begun to promote very unhealthy human values such as greed, deceit, self-obsession, vanity, and dishonesty. Greater encouragement to pursue these unhealthy human values has, in turn, led to rises in anxiety, addiction, insecurity and narcissism.

The ubiquity of social media is only aggravating this dynamic. The responsibility for change sits with the social media platforms themselves. The problem is that they are blinded by their own ambitions to outperform financial expectations. As such, their efforts are concentrated on improvements and innovations that accelerate financial performance. Certainly, there are initiatives to remove fake news and promote honesty; to allow you to discover more and create broader connections; to share real and constructive content to encourage personal confidence, and so forth. However, the priority of the big social media firms is advertising revenue, and their most capable resources are allocated accordingly. This is further propelled by the fact that penetration and usage of the mobile phone is accelerating globally, creating enormous opportunities for social media companies to grow platform usage, and thus advertising revenue. Consequently, it is difficult to imagine that the social media industry will pivot anytime soon in order to remove the values that create the unhealthy addictions that make them so strong to begin with.

Chapter 8

How Mobile Living is Making it Easy to Indulge in Unhealthy Human Values

The explosion of mobile phone usage is jaw-dropping. According to We Are Social, global mobile data growth has skyrocketed from under half an Exabyte (billions of Gigabytes) in the third quarter of 2011, to over 7 Exabytes in the third quarter of 2016. That is a growth of over 1300 percent in five years! The growth doesn't look like it will stop anytime soon. In many countries the actual cell phone penetration is well over 100 percent, yet usage continues to grow. Do people have that much to say? Are we becoming a lot more communicative? No. Actual conversations have been going down for years.

Several reports outlined in a 2015 *Forbes* article show that phone minute usage has been going down, replaced by text usage. The situation is so pronounced that many large corporations are removing voicemails services for their employees. One such company is JP Morgan Chase, a financial services firm. They asked their employees who would be willing to part with their voicemail service. A staggering 65 percent opted to part with their voicemail service, resulting in a US$3 million in annual savings for the company. This shift in communication behaviour is affecting human interactions in ways that are concerning. Addictive and obsessive behaviour is growing, people are beginning to have difficulties reading emotions, creating healthy relationships can be challenging, the ability to have deep emotional connection can be impeded, and spontaneity can be stymied. Fuelling parts of this shift, is the corporate world with its insatiable hunger to make money.

Mobile Addiction and the Rise of Anxiety & Undesirable Social Skills

In the previous chapter, we discussed the growth of social media-influenced addiction. The mobile phone plays a key part in this. The simple reason is that it allows access to social media channels at all times. However, phone addiction is not simply related to social media. The phone itself is causing addiction. In fact, according to a report on the investigative news program *60 Minutes*, tech companies are engineering smartphones and apps to make you check them more and more. Tristan Harris, a former Google product manager, spoke about how psychology was being used by product developers to create greater engagement and usage with new products. Tristan shared an example that he experienced at Google. He said that when he was working on the Gmail team, there were discussions to create a buzz on your phone each time people received an email. The intentions weren't to create addiction, just to keep people more connected to their devices (which ultimately provides an opportunity for these tech companies to make money). However, by using psychological insights to draw people towards their phones, the likelihood that they are creating addiction is considerable.

The reality is that people are becoming glued to their phones and cannot seem to ignore them for longer periods of time. This is creating internal and external harm to people. Internally, there is growing anxiety. Externally, social skills are being harmed.

In the *60 Minutes* report, psychologist Larry Rosen, from California State University, says that mobile technology is "wreaking havoc on anxiety levels." His team found that when people spend time away from their phones, their brains signalled the adrenal gland to produce bursts of the hormone cortisol, which triggers the flight-or-fight response to danger.

Another study by James A. Roberts, PhD, from the Baylor University Hankamer School of Business, suggests that people will actually generate fear if separated from their phone. In the study, Roberts found that 68 percent of all adults have "an irrational fear of losing their cell phones". The knock-on effect of increased anxiety is that the human value of trustworthiness is weakened. A 2013 study conducted by Megan Willis, Helen Dodd, and Romina Palermo proved that there was a clear relationship between anxiety and the social judgment of trustworthiness. When thinking about the anxiety inducing constant checking of the cell phone throughout the day (an average person checks their phone 110 times per day), it is not surprising that trustworthiness would be affected. After all, if you are expecting answers from people and they are not coming, are expecting comments from friends on Facebook and they are not providing them, and so on, your willingness to trust people will decrease. Therefore, you will turn to yourself, becoming more self-consumed since others are not delivering to your emotional expectations.

Cell phone addiction is also harming social skills. If people check their phones on average 110 times per day, and true addicts can check their cell phone as much as 900 times per day, chances are that most people will be pulling out their cell phone during conversations, meetings, lunches, dinners, and so forth. Consequently, the people that are with these "addicts" while they pull out their phones, will be affected by this disrespectful behaviour.

Granted, if both parties are pulling out their phones, they may not feel disrespected, but they also won't be having focused interactions. So how meaningful and deep can the conversations and interactions really be? This lack of depth further impacts the ability to nurture the healthy human values of caring and reciprocal kindness. Picture a situation where two people are sitting face to face at a lunch and are engaging in conversations that frequently get interrupted by phone beeps, and quick glances to cell phones. It is impossible to feel that the person in-front of you really cares because a text, update, or "like" is more important that the live conversation right in front of them. Some research suggests that having communicated extensively via texts, posts and so forth, prior to meeting a friend "in the flesh" allows for conversations to be more meaningful because you are already "caught up". Sure, you may be caught up on information, but not on emotional energy that can only come from face-to-face interaction. If this interaction is not focused, due to constant distraction, your ability be emotionally caught up weakens enormously.

The ridiculousness of this phone-gazing behaviour is that it is not solely driven by updates from friends, but also push notifications from brands, app updates, and so forth. Companies now simply do not respect your alone time. With so many new tools to get a message in-front of a person, companies are jumping in head-first, and often do not think of the impact that they are having on things like addiction.

The Inability to Read Emotions

When people are spending more time looking at their cell phone screen, and not observing the people around them, the ability to read emotions can be impaired. A 2014 study by the University of California Los Angeles (UCLA) concluded that excessive exposure to smart-phones can stunt a child's ability to read emotions. The study used two groups of students aged 11 and 12 years old. One of the groups was deprived of all mobile-related activity, such as social media, texting, video watching, etc. The other was allowed to proceed as normal. The "deprived group" was able to recognize emotions significantly better within five days, compared to those that continued texting, constantly checking their social media profiles, etc. These findings are not sur-prising. Real time is increasingly competing with virtual time, and thus time to practice reading emotions is decreasing.

Aside from the fact that live time is increasingly competing with virtual time, an entire new system of emotional expression has taken over—emoticons. The culture of emoticons has begun to express very specific facial reactions that define somewhat broad emotions. Let's take being sceptical as an example. There seems to be only one emoticon for this. Does that mean that every person's expression of scepticism has them holding their chin and having their eyebrows in opposite directions? Likely not. To be fair, developers at Apple, Facebook, Google, Tencent, and so forth are constantly creating more elaborate emoticon options. Brands are also jumping into this world with gusto, creating even more animations to broaden and deepen this artificial world. Regardless of the volume of emoticons and emojis, the nuances that only the human body can create are simply not replicable, at least not yet.

Another important factor in being able to read emotions is understanding audio cues associated with select visual expressions. Since the interactions between people on phones are mostly visual, this critical ingredient is not observed. Even as technologies such as FaceTime, Skype and others grow, their audio quality will not be able to pick up the complexities of people's audio cues—tone, deep breaths, light groans, and so forth. Further aggravating this issue is that people tend to look at their own video reflection when using virtual conferencing tools (see Miller & Sinanan, 2014, on people's Skype behaviours). As such, people are not learning to pick up important attitudinal cues made up of the complex interaction between sound and visual human reactions that shape a person's emotional state.

Propagating this trend is the corporate world, through the extensive use of video conferencing tools. As remote working and inter-office working becomes ubiquitous, video conferencing meetings have become commonplace. In select companies, depending on your role, it is not uncommon to spend a large part of your day in back-to-back meetings that take place through video conferencing platforms. I have first-hand experience with this, and the research mentioned above is very much true. You tend to look at yourself when speaking. Worse even, you tend to also mute and freeze your video, and work on other things, when your part in the meeting is over. Clearly, neither of these behaviours contribute to being able to better read emotions.

A potential problem associated with a weaker ability to read emotions is that deep connection to another person becomes more difficult. There is difficulty feeling empathy, compassion, and so forth, because the totality of the emotional display of the person

standing in front of you passes right over your head.

The Damage Being Done to Relationships

The impact that mobile phone behaviour is having on relationships is profound. The weakening ability to read emotions suggests that physical bonding is more difficult. This is incredibly pertinent during the mating game.

The ritual of seduction is already a challenging social engagement for many people. You are putting yourself out there, trying to pick up cues to determine whether the person likes you, whether the person is enjoying what you are saying, or whether there is a chemistry that is being created. I can recall a very uncomfortable moment when I was in university and thought that I was connecting with this girl. When I tried to give her a kiss, I realized that I was way off! Now add cell phone checking behaviour to the mix, and I cannot imagine how hard it is to read a situation and then make a bold move where rejection is a very real possibility. When you are young, and lack self-confidence, this can be terrifying.

Even for those already in relationships, phone checking can be damaging to the couple. A study by Baylor University concluded that "phone snubbing" (the term used in the *Time* magazine article that summarized the study), had a negative impact on relationship satisfaction, going so far as to harm overall happiness. The co-author of the study, James Roberts, was quoted in *Time* magazine saying, "these lower levels of relationship satisfaction, in turn, led to lower levels of life satisfaction and, ultimately, higher levels of depression." It is frightening to think that couples readily admit that when their partners check their phones, it makes them feel unhappy and even depressed, and yet they continue to do the same behaviour themselves. That is true addiction.

Another damaging repercussion of phone checking on the health of relationships is that impatience is rising. The fact that mobile phones are constantly feeding the desire for instant gratification means that expectations in other parts of life are being distorted. Aside from the expectation of having a text answered almost in real time, the expectation of quickly "completing actions" is also growing. If you make plans to go out to dinner with your partner, there is a growing expectation that the reservation is made quickly. If you are explaining something to your partner about what you went through at work today, and he or she doesn't get you right away, then you feel frustrated because your partner should "get you" more quickly. After all, you did text him all day about the issues with your boss!

Deep Emotional Connections are Challenging

There have been countless examples of absurd behaviours done through the mobile phone, that are leaving emotional scars, and are becoming commonplace. The most universally known example would be breaking up with someone via text. This phenomenon is so widespread that there are articles written about how to do this properly. Here are actual article titles: "How to break up with someone over text message" (*GQ*), and "3 Rules of breaking up with someone over text" (*Refinery29*). It is alarming that publications, and the corporations that support them are encouraging this behaviour by helping people execute these actions. For me, breaking up over text is insane, but for many it is just normal. What this behaviour underscores is the ease with which difficult social topics and actions can be executed. It also highlights the fact that those taking the "easy way out" are also not learning to cope with deep emotional issues.

Ultimately, it is difficult to feel empathy for another person when you do not sense their emotional state; when you cannot see their physical reaction to a piece of information that you are sharing with them. Cell phones allow people to do this. Countless other difficult topics are now communicated via "shielded" methods—texts, social media updates, etc. Managing conflict, apologizing, forgiving, explaining a misunderstanding, highlighting a problem, and so on, require some real back and forth connection, so that the emotions and gravity of the situation can be felt and understood. When this is all done through the mobile phone, it is very difficult to meaningfully connect.

Since we are less able to comprehend or appreciate the emotional state of those with whom we are sharing emotionally-charged news, the focus turns inward. Instead of thinking about the feelings of others, we become consumed by our own feelings. They take absolute priority. In other words, we become very self-consumed. An article in *The Washington Times* in 2015 highlighted this issue, claiming that cell phones are creating a "Narcissist Generation". The article wrote "the Narcissist Generation truly believes that they are so important and popular with their thoughts, that they make themselves available to whomever needs them." With such a mentality, there is little room for compassion, true caring, and selflessness. Instead we find egoism and selfishness.

Spontaneity is Dissolving

The fact that dialogue is migrating to text and social media means that spontaneity of thought will be less exercised. The ritual of being spoken to, perhaps being caught off-guard, and having to think quickly to respond, is being replaced by the ritual of receiving a text or messenger, then having a moment to regroup, collect your thoughts, and then respond. With automated response technologies advancing in all facets of digital communication, it will not be long before the tech becomes so intelligent that it replaces the human act of responding, instead only calling on you when it is thrown off-guard, or decisions need to be made.

We may face a reality where the rush of reacting on the phone to that girl or boy you have a crush on, no longer exists. Those painful yet character-building moments where you are quickly searching for things to say, trying to be natural, but playing it cool, may be a thing of the past. The art of being quick on your feet—an important trait in many aspects of life, especially work life—may fade. All those sales-people will be replaced by a handful of "master texters" backed up by ultra-powerful machines that handle most of the work.

This is saddening because spontaneity is also a vehicle for honesty. After all, when you have to think fast, you tend to display elements of truth because you don't have the time to formulate a convincing made-up story. For example, I have been told many times by several different people throughout my career that people tend to lower their guards just a little during a first interview because the interaction tends to be quite spontaneous. As such, you can unearth the truth on key matters during those interactions, as opposed to later in the interview process when things are a bit more structured and planned. In other words, spontaneous phone conversations, help us to naturally display honest and trustworthy information and emotions. No matter how fast you text, there is still an element preparedness that dulls the benefits of spontaneity.

In Conclusion, Mobile Living is Stripping Away Behaviours that Fuel Healthy Human Values

The rapid proliferation of the mobile phone and smartphone has made it easier than ever to keep in touch with people. As these devices become the central portal to all interactions—friends, family, work, leisure, shopping, and so forth—there are two dynamics that are shaping the impact of this new ecosystem on human values. The first is that human contact is becoming filtered, and as a consequence learned biological behaviours are being affected and changed. The second is that the unhealthy tentacles of the corporate world have taken hold

141

of this new ecosystem, introducing "sticking" mechanisms to create addiction to cell phones (which in turn allows greater opportunities to find ways of extracting revenue from that added spent time).

The most glaring example of changing human behaviour is that conversations over the phone are decreasing, replaced by texting. This is having a profound effect on communication because you are removing critical components that make dialogue comprehensible. There are countless stories of misunderstood emails, texts, posts, and so forth. Some are banal and make for great laughs during after-work drinks. Others are a bit more concerning, such as the now famous middle-of-the-night Tweet by Donald Trump where he was complaining about negative press, ended with the obscure word "covfefe". It was a clear texting slip-up that caused an avalanche of press. Granted, it was a bit funny, but a texting error from the most powerful politician on earth can have dire consequences. This example simply illustrates that writing communication in bite-sized snippets will never have the clarity of live conversation.

By communicating emotions more simplistically, our sensory dynamism, which aids us in decoding millions of inputs and differences around us, such as sound, colour, sensations, etc., is being stripped down. Looking through a phone screen automatically removes a handful of these inputs and thus the richness of our senses are not being exercised. As with any human capability, if it is not practiced, mastery cannot be achieved.

We then choose to compensate for our growing inability to read emotions by utilizing over-the-top artificial emojis or emoticons. These "cute" icons may actually be somewhat trivializing emotional displays, turning communication into entertainment. This is truly concerning, since the pursuit of entertainment when communicating will negatively affect the ability to exercise the very powerful human values of honesty and caring.

Another example of changing human behaviour is how we are harming our relationships by not nurturing quality time with those that matter. Our phone cannot be left alone. We even pull it out during dates! This has become so problematic, that advertisers are using the subject-matter in their commercials. Vivo (part of Telefonica) produced a touching video that showed a young couple sitting at home, where the girl was glued to her phone even when the boyfriend tried to communicate, making the man feel unappreciated. Finally, he was so fed up that he stormed out of the apartment. Only a few minutes later, she realized that he was gone after he sent her a text. It had no words, just an image of the front door left open. As she made her way to the door, another picture was sent via text. She followed these visual clues until she ended up in-front of a café where her boyfriend was sitting near the front window. The story ended with him taking her phone and placing it face down on the table so that they could spend some quality time together. Gosh, if mobile companies are saying put down your phones, we know we have a problem. The story outlines the harm to healthy human values that this new behaviour is creating—her selfishness was superseding maintaining the health of her relationship, which provides love and companionship.

Fuelling these changes in human behaviour, is the corporate world. As companies aggressively try to financially benefit from a mobile-driven lifestyle, they latch onto any and all trends, regardless of their impact on society. Constant push notifications, the avalanche of new applications, an emoji for everything, more and more picture filters, and countless other pursuits deepen the addiction to mobile phones. All these efforts satiate an ever-growing expectation for instant gratification, which in turn impacts the way we interact in our relationships, how we communicate, how we absorb information, and how we see the world around us.

In addition to accelerating the behavioural changes outlined above, corporations are also contributing to a growing anxiety in society. There is simply so much information to keep track of, and by adding to this mountain of content and introducing mechanisms to glue people to their phones, corporations are heightening people's fear of missing out. People focus on digesting all the "necessary" information around them, rather than taking a moment to think and care for those

around them, the community and the world around them. As a consequence, people are becoming a lot more self-consumed and selfish.
Fortunately, new generations are somewhat awakening from the de-
structiveness of this new way of living. However, this new generation
is facing an uphill battle unless corporations shift their ways.

Chapter 9

Millennials and Gen Z are Fed up With the Split Personality World

I t is a warm summer night in Berlin. Three friends sit at the Odessa Bar on Torstrasse in Mitte, sipping drinks and engulfed in conversation. Thomas, originally from Munich, works at an Internet start-up as a programmer. Justine, from Bordeaux in France, works at a hotel. Darryl, who is from Chicago, is a musician. They are all new to the city, and new to the workforce. None of them are well off, but were drawn to Berlin by its authenticity, and its culture of collaboration. Their conversation focuses on a very controversial topic: the recently introduced travel ban by Donald Trump. Each has their opinion. They speak about the threat to democracy, racism, and of the decline of America. However, two passion points of discussion consume their discussion: The first is how such an isolationist mentality, if it were to spread among other governments, could have a detrimental impact on employment. The second is how negative values are consuming the world, and that something needs to be done to halt and reverse this trend. These are typical preoccupying thoughts of young millennials, or the younger Gen Z.

These two generations have grown up seeing first-hand what the current split-personality values world does to families, and communities. Defined as the group of people born after the early 1980s, they have seen how security in the world seems to have deteriorated. They have seen how profound hatred has consumed entire communities and created real rifts in society. They have seen their parents experience struggle, face work exhaustion, and even be subject to layoffs. They have seen their hope for financial independence seriously weaken, as the expected life-stage ritual of getting a job after graduation is no more. It is therefore not surprising that millennials believe that there is a profound decay in the values leading important forces in society. In turn, this has led to incredibly low levels of trust.

Millennials and Trust

A *Washington Post* article in August 2015 had the title "Millennials don't trust anyone". The article discussed some concerning facts uncovered in a Harvard Study about the depth and breadth of distrust among millennials. Not one societal pillar was unaffected. The main "villains" outlined in the study were the institutions that are part of the bedrock of democracy, such as the media, government, the global financial market, and legal institutions. Millennials are questioning the motivations of societal institutions since these institutions let them down time and time again. A poignant example is the corporate world and financial markets. The financial crisis rocked this generation. While the actual crisis may be over, its impact on youth is still felt. Youth unemployment in early 2017 sat at 13 percent, which was still higher than the pre-crisis level of 11.7 percent (according to the International Labour Organization).

The inability for these institutions to evolve quickly enough will result in their demise and re-definition. The main reason is that millennials are the biggest generation since the baby boomers and will make up 50 percent of the working population by 2020. Therefore, their opinions on the types of institutions that should guide society and how they should behave will hold serious weight. A strong indicator that the demise of these institutions is underway is that these young people are turning to themselves for their future well-being, not to the institutions that the previous generations did.

Millennials aspire to be the catalysts of their own destinies. They are acutely aware that the corporate world cannot be counted on for employment. They know that governments are self-serving and not aligned with the aspirations of the people. After all, they have seen it with Brexit, the bureaucracy of the European Union, the incompetence of the Republican Party in the face of a dangerous and dividing president Trump, the reluctance of the Hong Kong government to assure its uniqueness in the face of the forces in Beijing, and so forth. They know that the financial system is unpredictable. After all, many have seen the impact of the 2008 financial crisis on the well-being of their families, or friends. To them, it is very clear that these institutions cannot be trusted, and that the values that govern them are in conflict with theirs. These institutions seem self-serving, greedy, dishonest, disloyal, calculating, and unwilling to change. So, millennials turn to trusted entities—themselves, and their networks—to find solutions.

The 2016 BNP Paribas Global Entrepreneur Report confirms that millennials have launched twice as many businesses as baby boomers and are starting these businesses at a younger age. A 2017 *Forbes* article by Larry Alton writes "over 62 percent of millennials have considered starting their own business, with 72 percent feeling that start-ups and entrepreneurs are a necessary economic force for creating jobs and driving innovation". This suggests that independence from "typical" corporate world institutions is not just an aspiration but is being readily acted upon (and done so at the start of their careers). A 2014 survey done by Bentley University confirms that millennials feel that they have to be more nimble, independent, and entrepreneurial than other generations.

Clearly, not all of these undertakings will bear fruit. This generation is very aware of this reality. As such, they are fine walking back into the corporate world to earn money. However, they do so with the aspiration to find their next idea, passion, and opportunity. A 2016 Gallup report states that millennials are three times more likely to switch jobs compared to any other generation, and that a whopping 60 percent are open to a new job opportunity. This should be a serious wake-up call for the corporate world. Stability is critical for productivity and controlling overhead costs. Therefore, companies need to find ways to keep this generation around. Establishing trust, aligning with their values, and acting upon this alignment, is the way to go. However, corporations need to do so with authenticity, since this generation can sniff out posturing with ease.

Millennials and Authenticity

A 2015 article by Matthew Tyson in *The Huffington Post* wrote that millennials "are not moved by flashy ads, big promises, and 'wow' factor. They want authentic messages, authentic brands, and authentic interactions." There are a few dynamics that are driving this attitude.

First, this generation is experiential. They have grown up in a world where instant gratification, facilitated through technology, is a part of daily life. Texts are answered immediately, pictures are liked, commented and "emoticoned" with short delay, and questions can be quickly answered with a few thumb-strokes on their phone. As a result, there is a reactive, and perceived "pure" communication reality that they live in. Also, they have grown up with so much "stuff", and the world around them has become so commoditized (just think of the insane acceleration of fashion cycles brought on by the likes of H&M and Zara), that the marginal added value of one more garment is a lot less than it used to be. Consequently, happiness is now measured by one's collection of experiences versus one's collection of things.

Research conducted by the San Francisco State University in 2014 concluded that people who spent money on experiences instead of physical objects felt not only happier but also felt that their money was better spent. Big millennial brands such as Airbnb are very aware of this, creating new services such as "Local Tours" and "Experiences".

In the travel business in general, there has been an enormous growth of unique travel offerings - adventure travel, sport travel, cooking travel, and so forth. Even outside of the travel industry, the appetite for interesting experiences has grown. Walking tours have become more popular, even birthing a dedicated ecommerce destination called Detour (created by Groupon founder Andrew Mason). Online beauty platforms that facilitate finding massages, spas, treatments, and so forth have exploded in popularity. The examples are endless. There is a perceived sense of life being lived more authentically when consuming novel experiences.

The second facet of this drive for authenticity is millennials' increasingly seeking out uniqueness and craft. The fashion industry has been hit hard by this trend. Thrift stores and buying used goods has become very popular. This is not solely because of the desire to save money (because that certainly is a factor), but because of the desire for authenticity. This generation wants to have something unique, not an H&M outfit available to anyone. According to a 2017 *Forbes* article, "second-hand apparel, offline and online, is an $18 billion-dollar industry and is forecast to grow by 11 percent per year".

Many industries have been hit by this shift towards authentic tastes. Craft beers and spirits are thriving the world over. The commoditization of design has given way to the uniqueness that can be found on platforms like Etsy. DIY within home ownership has grown, where the thrill of shaping your home to your unique tastes is replacing the cookie-cutter sameness that was part of the homeownership reality during the "move to the suburbs" baby-boomer era. The hunger for greater uniqueness and craft is not surprising when considering the backdrop of how millennials live. They have grown-up with greater access to all the world has to offer, through globalization and the ubiquity of technology. Meanwhile, the desire to shape your identity through experiences and knowledge that are relatively unique, remains the same. As such, the expectation of what is unique has become more demanding, and seeking out authentic experiences and things has become more important.

The pursuit of authenticity naturally applies to the workplace. They want a meaningful experience at work, and don't want to be just another robot in the assembly line. They want their work to count, to be unique, to be special. This is why many seek a lot of responsibility early

149

on in their careers, often to the frustration of older colleagues who know that they need a bit more experience to be able to take on higher degrees of responsibility. Prince Charles famously wrote a letter to a staff member 2003 saying, "What is wrong with everyone nowadays? Why do they all seem to think they are qualified to do things far beyond their technical capabilities?"

Millennials also seek out work environments where managers care about their progress, development, and success. A 2017 article in *Fortune* that analysed the research conducted by Great Places to Work for "Great Workplaces for Millennials", found that work environments where managers "linked millennials' work and contribution to a broader purpose, providing access to a diverse array of learning and development opportunities, and demonstrating fairness in promotion and advancement decisions", made this cohort feel that they were getting a unique and special experience—in other words, a truly authentic work experience.

The importance of meaningfulness in the employee-employer relationship is not surprising, given how accustomed millennials have become to the more intimate and "meaningful" approach to living facilitated through social media. Although there are concerns about this level of transparency and relentless exposure of oneself to the world at large, there are also examples that suggest that these constant connections are creating more meaningful bonds between friends. A piece in *The Huffington Post* about a mom's observation of how her daughter's friends "stepped up" when she was ill, illustrates this point. This mother, like many others, couldn't wrap her head around the constant flow of selfies and superficial interactions among school friends. This all changed when her daughter was bedridden with a serious cold. The level of support from friends blew her away. Everyday her daughter would get some "get well" gesture. First, a friend came over with her favourite drink. Then the boyfriend of a friend was sent over to bring her a pizza. Then a delivery was sent over to make her feel good. The flow of kindness was ongoing. The mother compared this behaviour to how she would have experienced the same situation when she was young—no one would have cared until she was back at school. This was a true eureka moment for the mom. All this social media back and forth was actually creating more meaningful bonds for her daughter. There was greater depth in their relationship. It is therefore not surprising that millennials also wish for greater depth in the companies that they choose to work for.

Millennials and Purpose

"We believe that it is our duty to make the world a better place."

A staggering 84 percent of millennials agree with this statement, according to a 2017 report by Deloitte. They see the demise of many parts of society and a painfully slow reaction by the institutions charged with dealing with these ills. Instead of rebelling by plunging into pure indulgence and escapism, as would have been the case with many Gen Xers, they are more pragmatic and solutions-oriented. Confident and motivated by their mastery of technology, they believe that they can bring about change. They rally friends and communities towards ideas and actions that they have passion for, that give them a sense of purpose. Some of these efforts may be as small and localized as starting a crowdfunding campaign to raise money for a school friend who is down on her luck, or as significant as developing a water purification technology that can help displaced communities have access to healthy drinking water in overcrowded refugee camps.

Doing good is not just something that they do occasionally—doing good is a part of their lifestyle. In the same way that music plays a foundational role in shaping the identity of younger people, millennials now include purpose-led actions as fundamental to growing up and expressing yourself to the world at large. They see the world through a different lens than previous cohorts, and truly want to change it. It is very important that the people who they chose to associate with are aligned with their values. As a consequence, the "badges" that they want to show to the world have to reflect this commitment to purpose.

Therefore, products that they buy should be purpose-driven versus superficial, but also the groups and organizations, both professional and personal, that they engage with should have purpose.

A 2017 article in *Science Daily* wrote about a study by the University of Missouri-Columbia that confirmed that the core reason young workers decide to leave a company is that there is a "disconnect between their beliefs and the culture they observe in the workplace of that company." Since their passions and inspirations define what they do personally and professionally, they will have no issue departing if a company does not live up to their expectations. This is unlike other generations who believe that they have to grind through, that they are at the mercy of the company for which they work. Clearly, this new mindset is forcing companies to rethink their ways of working. However, far too many corporations have entrenched processes and still view the workforce as an expendable lever to cut and grow depending on their performance. This is creating a tension that is not sustainable.

Not all is lost. This generation believes that their pursuit of purpose should be done through corporations. Millennials would rather work through the system to initiate change versus fight it. After all, they are the collaborative generation, and are accustomed to change through the collective (facilitated through their intimacy with social media). This is a huge opportunity for corporations to keep millennials jumping elsewhere or venturing out on their own. Clearly, companies need to change their ways, but this generation is willing to give them a chance. The previously mentioned Deloitte study found that over 90 percent of millennials believe that business is the way to solve problems like unemployment and the like. Employers, therefore, have the opportunity to do good and make money.

Clearly, there are many details that need to be addressed in order for companies to fully pursue this new consumer expectation. Especially problematic for the corporate world is the aggressive revenue expectations that the financial system has ingrained in the business community. For most companies, especially the established ones, these demands are not sustainable. Consumerism is not what it once was, money is shorter, options are more readily available, and this generation is buying differently and less. Therefore, living in this new world without curbing old world expectations often leads to a hiring-and-firing workforce reality, which certainly isn't a good signal to the world at large that a company has good values and is credibly pursuing a noble purpose.

A big challenge for corporations who pursue a strong purpose is showing commitment both in terms of people and time. They have to be all in or they are not viewed as being credible and authentic in your beliefs. Meanwhile, consumers don't have to make the same level of sacrifice. Certainly, many among this generation are "all in" when it comes to the purpose or cause that they hold near. However, they can pivot to another one with relative ease, should a new purpose be more popular. Fortunately, meaningful purposes such environmental care, tackling inequality, and the like, are not fads. However, it is not uncommon for some to be trendy. The #IceBucketChallenge is an example. Raising awareness and driving donations for ALS is a worthy cause that captured the attention of millions in 2014. Today, the popularity of this cause seems to have faded. Companies should not get caught up in this up-and-down. There is a big chance that they can be viewed as not committed, and more interested in PR than actually doing good. Therefore, corporations need to pick a cause and pursue it unabashedly.

Through their passion for purpose, millennials are creating a social reality that is shaking up existing paradigms more so than other generations. Certainly, every generation brings with it change that the society at large needs to deal with. However, never before has a generation wielded so much power. As mentioned earlier on in this chapter, millennials' mastery of technology has given them an unprecedented level of societal power.

Millennials and Power

A 2015 *Forbes* article titled "Millennials and the Power of Influence", states that this generation has been more written about and more researched, than any other generation. The main reason is that the corporate world and governments do not understand this generation yet are at their total mercy. They wield enormous power because of their ability to influence large groups of people. The *Forbes* article mentions that millennials have been called "alpha-influencers" because they "shape the behaviour and purchasing decisions of their larger social circles" and do so with great velocity through the technology tools at their disposal.

In addition to their digital-savviness, Millennials are also more educated and diverse than previous generations. This gives them the courage and motivation to take action. There is also a sense of urgency to act, since they can see how the shrinking of the middle class is making their future more challenging. Consequently, they will make themselves heard and will not cower to big brother. The many demonstrations for countless causes such as Black Lives Matter or Occupy Wall Street or The People's Climate March are a testament to this. This generation believes that it is important to take calculated risks because they want to live on their terms, to enjoy life now, and to create a future that they will enjoy. Such a bold attitude and belief-system likely instills fear in the institutions that have enjoyed being in control of society largely unchallenged.

The corporate world needs to quickly realize that it must be much more flexible, transparent, open-minded, and caring. These are foundational values for millennials and they have the power to demand them with the companies and institutions that affect their lives. Interestingly, these are also values that have weakened, even evaporated in some cases, within companies the world over, creating this split-personality reality that has consumed society in the past decades. Millennials and Gen Z are set to reverse this unhealthy state. Whether we evolve to a workplace values reality similar to that of the 1950s, or birth something completely new is yet to be seen. One thing is for certain—we are on the cusp of significant change.

Chapter 10

Bringing Healthy Values Back into the Workplace

There is much talk about the fourth industrial revolution that we are currently experiencing. The speed of change has reached an inflection point where fundamental disruption to current ways of working is unavoidable. There are few, if any, industries that are unaffected by the technological advancements in everything from sourcing, to manufacturing, to distribution, to sales, and to marketing. The term being frequently batted around is "digital transformation".

There are even roles being created solely to help bring companies up-to-date in all things digital that are pertinent to their business. The most common of these new roles is the Chief Transformation Officer. I find this title amusing because it suggests that this role is utterly temporary, and that once the "transformation" is complete, the person is probably not much wanted anymore. This is clearly an oversimplification of these types of roles because the fact that the pace of change is so fast today, and is accelerating, means that any company truly being "totally digitally transformed" is doubtful. What this new workplace role underscores is an old-world problem that the corporate world seems unwilling to shake: they view their workforce as a commodity. However, since this "fourth industrial revolution" is bringing about change in seemingly all corners of the corporate and business world, it seems fitting that it should do so as well in human resources, or employment.

The fickleness of millennials and Gen Z in choosing and staying in their workplace should be motivation enough for the corporate world to heavily focus on looking at what needs to change in order to attract and keep employees. The fact that this generation will soon make up a majority of the workforce means that they will be able to act on their aspirations in the very near future. Those companies that accept this in advance and make proactive changes to address it, will have the advantage of attracting the strongest talent now (who in turn will recruit even stronger millennials or Gen Zers in the years ahead). In turn, such companies will be setting themselves up for success. Therefore, it is important to first understand where companies need to focus in order to bring about the healthy change that will genuinely attract this enormous new workforce.

As the previous chapter discussed, millennials and Gen Z want companies to focus more on them. They want companies to truly address their needs. If companies ignore this, or do so insincerely, the repercussions will be swift and serious—writing off the company and telling all their friends about it. Just look at the almighty Uber. It was the darling company among the investment community and the population at large. However, it operated with very unhealthy values. Deceit, manipulation, gender inequality and the like reigned supreme. It may be a technologically progressive company, but it behaved like the most established and poisoned companies. It actually behaved like a company in the most disliked and broken industry, finance. Therefore, it was simply a matter of time before someone internally would burst the bubble and expose them for who they really are.

That person was Susan Fowler, an engineer who simply could no longer accept the harassment and shameful behaviour that the company seemed to encourage. Her 2910-word blog post titled "Reflecting on one very, very strange year at Uber" exposed the horrible workplace culture, led the way for other stories to emerge, and ultimately was the spark that brought about the firing of twenty employees as well as the resignation of founder Travis Kalanick. The knock-on effect is that the company's valuation has also hit a bump. According to an article in Techcrunch in June 2017, "the value of Uber's shares has been falling on the secondary market, hammered by a barrage of press attention paid to its real and perceived misdeeds". Even their popularity has slipped. According to TXN Solutions, Uber's share of rides has dropped to 75 percent from 90 percent. Meanwhile, the share of rides of Lyft, a key competitor, are up to 24.7 percent from 21.2 percent as of June 2017. To top it all off, "the number of people globally viewing and applying for open roles at Uber has dropped by about 15 percent" based on an article by LinkedIn. Therefore, companies have to take employee needs very seriously.

The Uber fiasco exposed another point: this new work generation wants companies to have stronger values. No longer is it acceptable to adhere to the corporate workplace philosophy propagated in the 1980s. Millennials and Gen Z do not want the workplace reality of their parents, one where unhealthy values brought about a split-personality type existence that was destructive and exhausting.

This generation will act hard and publicly to expose culprits. If we look at the ten worst companies to work for according to Glassdoor, among them are giants such as Kraft Heinz. Employees complain that the company's cost-cutting has led to a horrible impact on work-life balance, and that that company acts deceitfully. Recently, the company launched a campaign in the United States that claimed that they would forego Superbowl advertising to give all employees the Monday off from work instead. This turned out to be more of a PR stunt than a legitimate effort to care for employees, as the free day only applied to select people. According to *The Huffington Post*, one former employee from Pennsylvania had no problem publicly saying "Kraft Heinz corporate leaders don't truly respect or care about their employees. They only care about making money off them." This attitude may have been tolerated a decade ago, but now people take action against it.

Another example is the Wall Street giant Goldman Sachs. According to the reputation scores documented in a 2016 Harris Poll, Goldman Sachs was the sixth worst company. The level of deceit, greed and dishonesty has gotten so bad that a former executive decided to write an article in *The New York Times* shunning his past employer for an environment where "the interests of clients continue to be side-lines in the way the firm operates and thinks about making money. The environment is so toxic and destructive." Clearly, workers no longer see the purpose in what they are doing and are not simply deciding to leave, but also telling the world about the real goings-on inside the polished walls.

Even Amazon, that seems to grow endlessly with exciting new products and services, is admired by many people around the world, and is a desired employer of many around the world, can face the wrath of employees because they feel that their work environment is toxic. A scathing *New York Times* article from 2015 by a former employee titled "Inside Amazon: Wrestling Big Ideas in a Bruising Workplace" exposed how "workers are encouraged to tear apart one another's ideas in meetings, toil long and late (emails arrive past midnight, followed by text messages asking why they were not answered), and held to standards that the company boasts are 'unreasonably high.' Even the internal phone directory instructs colleagues on how to send secret feedback to one another's bosses." The company is literally forcing people to behave in unnatural ways that bring out their worst characteristics. It is not surprising that, as the article stated, everyone breaks down crying at least once while working at Amazon. It is equally not surprising that people will come forward and challenge the company's ways. By doing so, they can bring about change.

Each of these examples illustrates that the demands on companies are changing, and due to a more confident and expressive generation of workers, they will be forced into action sooner rather than later. As was detailed in Chapter 9, millennials and Gen Z will not cower to Big Brother, and their lack of trust of the corporate world means that the spotlight is constantly on companies. This is an unprecedented reality. It is also a reality that will bring about a much-needed change. Those institutions and companies that continue to champion "greed is good" culture along with all the corresponding values associated with it, will be challenged. We see it with the examples stated above, and we see it in how governments are currently being challenged in all corners of the world.

So, what are the values that many millennials and Gen Z find important in the workplace? Project Aristotle, an initiative undertaken by Google to identify, through data, the ingredients that make good teams and work environments, concluded that there are five. They are dependability, structure and clarity, meaning, impact, and psychological safety. In other words, these are manifestations of the core human values that have been discussed throughout this book. This should not be all that surprising given that the values of trustworthiness (dependability), fairness and honesty (structure & clarity), purpose (meaning), caring (impact), and security (psychological safety) are hardwired into humans from birth, as discussed in Chapter 2. Since this generation is the most educated, connected, and global generation ever, the fact that they are more self-aware can be expected.

If we look at the lists of the most admired companies, those that millennials most want to work for, and pick out those known to have great cultures such as Etsy, Airbnb, Southwest Airlines, Zappos, Google, REI, Publix, Disney, Intuit, and so forth, and we also examine the conclusions from Google's Project Aristotle, there are two values that seem to play a more pronounced role for Millennials and Gen Z in the decision-making process to choose an employer: security and purpose.

The fact that these two values bubble to the top is not that surprising since they represent two of our most powerful existential needs. The first is self-preservation. At the end of the day, we are animals. And while we may be high up in the food chain, we still face a serious predator whose numbers are growing at a notable rate—other humans. Therefore, our primate-drive for survival is very active. Over the years, the way that we have exercised this drive has evolved to become very unhealthy. Deceit, manipulation, selfishness, have become common levers. However, as the economy has become less stable, especially in the last twenty years, these levers have been executed with greater vigour and have created an environment of less security. Therefore, millennials and Gen Z are looking for new approaches since the old ones seem to compound the feeling of insecurity.

The second most existential need is having meaning. People need meaning to propel them through life. It gives them drive beyond simply surviving. This is what has fuelled global religions and why core values have never shifted. But, with mass consumerism, meaning has evolved to be less purposeful. To many people it has simply become about "having more than my neighbour". The accumulation of "stuff" has distracted us from higher-order drives. Instead, we are fuelled by greed. However, this pursuit of "stuff" has reached a tipping point. As people's lives have become saturated with stuff, many people have fallen into debt. Millennials and Gen Z are realising that this dynamic is not only unhealthy, it is also unsustainable. As such, they are looking for authenticity and a means to replenish their soul with causes that have true purpose.

There has been extensive literature written about the importance of the above values, how they have evolved, which companies are implementing them well, and what needs to be done by the corporate world to begin addressing them more broadly. What is interesting, is that most companies focus solely on one area—either overtly ensuring security for their employees or being strongly focused on addressing a higher-order purpose. By looking at the companies in several "best companies to work for" lists across multiple countries (i.e. Glassdoor's "Best Places to Work 2017", *Fortune* magazine's 2017 "Millennials Favourite Places to Work", *Forbes* magazine's 2017 "Millennials Best Places to Work" Survey Monkey study, Morning Consult's 2017 "Millennials Best Places to Work" report, and Universum's 2016 "World's Most Attractive Employers"), and analysing each company's vision and mission, as well as their Indeed.com score on Job Security/Advancement, only 10 percent of companies had both a strong purpose and provided a superior sense of job security. The remaining companies either had a strong purpose or have a culture that provides a strong sense of job security, and a greater percentage tend to focus on the latter. Given the existential importance of both security and purpose, it seems logical that equal attention should be paid to both.

The Soil & Sun Strategy

A way to look at tackling the desire for greater purpose at work, while also having a very tangible sense of being taken care of to assure security, is to take inspiration from plants. Yes really!

Much like plants require soil to stay firmly grounded and to stay alive, employees today want corporations to provide a level of security that will keep them firmly grounded in their organization and allow them to grow. Plants also need sun for energy in order for them to thrive, which can be a way of looking at how employees need purpose in their jobs to allow them to grow and thrive as professionals and individuals. Most importantly, it is not enough to have great soil, but no sun, or plentiful sun and no soil. Plants need both to prosper. Humans need the same because we are also living entities and require the same basic elements to grow. Therefore, a way to ensure that both security and purpose are firmly embedded in a corporation, is to apply a "soil & sun" strategy.

This does not mean to simply review and implement the actions currently being taken by the companies that are known to be purpose-driven or known to be focused on providing a strong sense of job security. Certainly, this is an important first step. Many of these companies have generated enormous praise from their employees, have stability in their workforce, and have seen the productivity and innovation upside from a motivated team. Nonetheless, it is important to dig deeper into these two values and see how they can be brought to life more thoroughly and holistically to provide the same level of value to humans as sun and soil provide to healthy plants. In doing so, not only will corporations see even further value in the forms of productivity, creativity, and performance, but they will also inhibit unhealthy values from germinating. In other words, these companies will become healthy contributors to their respective communities and the society at large

Chapter 11

Soil: Providing Greater
Security in the Workplace

In a recent survey of 1,000 of its users who are looking for a job, Indeed.com discovered that more than 40 percent said job security was one of the most important factors they take into account when searching. Another study, by the Society of Human Resource Management in 2011, highlighted that only 28 percent of respondents reported being satisfied with their feeling of job security. Meanwhile, the study also concluded that job security is the most important aspect of job satisfaction.

The importance of security in the workplace is obvious. Job security provides stability, and stability allows us to plan for the future. Humans like to feel settled. We are not nomadic by nature and would rather plant roots. Doing so gives us a sense of belonging, which drives confidence and comfort. This same existential drive can be directly translated to the workplace, since the time spent in our work life represents a large percentage of our total time living. Consequently, the people and corresponding communities of our places of work are important anchors in our broader lives.

The workplace culture in the 1950s and 1960s nurtured this unabashedly. Unfortunately, the corporate world has evolved in a way that completely discards this innate human need, favouring the ability to hire-and-fire to help sustain healthy financial performances. Those that have chosen to follow a more employee-centric culture and have put job security high up on their corporate agenda, are greatly admired and tend to make the various "most-liked places to work" lists. According to neuroscience expert Christine Comaford, these companies are also more likely to have increased revenues since their workforce has greater alignment, collaboration, and communication.

Companies that Integrate Security Brilliantly

The companies that are renowned for a culture that provides security tend to focus on a handful of policies and behaviours. Southwest Airlines, one of America's largest carriers, is well-known for its great culture and job security. It proudly has one of the highest scores on job security and advancement on Indeed.com.

To ensure that security is embedded into its culture, it has made it part of the company mission. The second sentence of the Southwest Airlines mission reads, "We are committed to provide our employees a stable work environment with equal opportunity for learning and personal growth". This is brought to life through two simple behaviours—recognition and reward. The company has local as well as companywide culture committees, and it spends notable time recognizing employees through formal and informal ways. These include awards, programs, and milestone anniversary celebrations. In doing all this, employees feel appreciated, nurtured, and taken care of. Consequently, their feeling of job security is exceptionally high. This has translated into a company performance that rivals would die for. They have grown top line revenue and have operated profitably for 44 consecutive years, and have outperformed, in relative terms, the leading carriers since 2015.

Another company that ranks among the best places to work in several lists and is known to have a strong culture centered on job security, is the American grocery chain Publix. Its commitment to security has resulted in an amazing voluntary turnover rate of just 5 percent among full time employees, according to *Fortune* magazine. There are two behaviours that help drive this amazing culture of stability—guidance and giving. Company management focuses on communication and transparency to make sure that every employee knows what they have to do and is shown how to do it.

The company website illustrates this attitude by providing many resources which ensure that current and new employees find the career path at Publix that is right for them. Employees are also given regular reviews for performance feedback and are eligible for salary increases every six months. In addition, employees are given "skin in the game" in the form of equity. All full-time and part-time workers who average twenty hours per week receive company stock after one year of service, and additional stock each year. Lastly, employees are even named in a way that signals belonging; they are called "associates". Naturally, this attention to inclusion and betterment makes the associates feel very secure. As a result, Publix has achieved industry-beating performance. According to Business Insider, Publix became America's favourite grocery chain in 2017, beating giants such as Trader Joe's and Krogers. The chain also boasts a healthy 3.1 percent net profit growth, exceeding the industry average.

Ernst & Young (EY), a professional services company, is also known for a culture where employees feel secure. The company is loved across many countries and has made the best places to work lists in most regions across the globe. According to a survey of over 800 EY employees, a staggering 94 percent said that they had great pride in working for the company. This "love affair" is likely influenced by two behaviours that are readily exercised—community and care. An EY employee was quoted in *Fortune* magazine in 2016 stating, "I am proud of the community we have created within our offices and across the world. We have a significant focus on diversity and inclusiveness and develop high performing, inclusive, and sustainable teams. I believe we are truly measured on how we build a better working world".

Another employee mentioned, "I love the people culture. I feel that people come first, and it's not always about making a buck for them." This sense of caring is supported by extensive perks and programs that go well beyond those of other companies. Examples include corporate responsibility sabbaticals, reproductive technology assistance, and so forth. Consequently, employees feel that the company truly has their best interests at heart, which results in strong feelings of security. Financially, this focus on employee security has contributed to consistent revenue growth; EY consistently sits among the top three companies in the accounting firm global revenue ranking.

A final example is SAP, a global technology company. To understand how employee-centric their workplace is, we need only visit their website career section and read the copy. It reads: "SAPers usually stay at the company for quite some time, and we're all about developing deep and lasting relationships with our employees". The company accomplishes this by focusing on two behaviours—personalization and communication. Another quote from their website speaks to how they cater to the needs and aspirations of each employee. The company writes that, "we know that success means different things to different people: from climbing the leadership ladder to striking the perfect work-life balance and everything in between. So, we go to great lengths to ensure you have every opportunity to succeed in your own way."

The company also creates forums to ensure that communication across the organization is encouraged and realized, instituting coffee corners where open conversations about all topics across departments can be had, mentoring and fellowships to ensure that thoughts and concerns are never allowed to fester, and so forth. The individual focus makes each employee feel special, listened to, and clearly heard, which translates into a strong sense of security. As of the second quarter of 2017, SAP saw a revenue growth of 10 percent due to its momentum in cloud subscriptions, a business that they entered late and where they faced sizeable competition.

Security Feeds Happiness

The importance of job security to overall productivity and health cannot be underestimated. The few examples above are micro illustrations of this. Much bigger proof points are the countries who have elaborate job security and protection schemes. Many tend to rank among the world's "happiest places to live". Among the top five countries listed in the 2017 World Happiness Report, four have world-renowned employee protection legislation and robust unemployment services.

In Norway, number one on the list, it is quite difficult for an employer to fire an employee after the initial three-month trial period, and it is also uncommon for employees to be fired for underperforming.

In Denmark, number two on the list, the state provides up to nine-tenths of a person's last wage after being laid off. This is the highest in Europe. Furthermore, according to the Wall Street Journal, only 10 percent of Danes are concerned with job security, compared to nearly 40 percent in Germany and 60 percent in Spain.

In Switzerland, number four on the list, they have a very strong unemployment system in place, where up to 80 percent of a person's previous salary is granted to those who are unemployed, and the government provides a myriad of services and courses to help a person quickly re-enter the workforce.

Finally, there is Finland, number five on the list, where one of the most significant underlying principle of employment legislation is the protection of employees. In short, employee security is woven into the fabric of society in these countries which gives citizens less existential fears, and subsequently encourages an environment where healthy human values reign. There are lower levels of crime (greater fairness and honesty), they are family friendly (caring), and they are reputable (trustworthy).

Overall, what seems to be driving the strong sense of security among both the companies and countries that have programs and policies that focus on this area, is that there is a sense that a robust infrastructure is in place that will never allow someone to fall through the cracks. There is also a sense that you always have a back-up, regardless of your predicament. It is a little bit like having the ability to "go back and live with the parents for a while". Using the soil analogy, there is a permanent resource of nutrients that ensures that a plant will always stay in that ground and will always survive.

Going deeper, how can companies fortify these nutrients? How can companies build an even stronger infrastructure? By exploring the eight behaviours outlined above (reward, recognition, guidance, personalization, communication, community, giving, and care).

Building Security Through Reward

Most companies grant rewards based on an employee's contribution to key performance indicators that are usually tied to that person's job, her team, her new ideas, her demonstration of the company values, and so forth. Few companies look beyond the four walls to tie important company rewards to actions taken by an employee to help the broader communities and environments in which the company operates and affects. In other words, few companies look at how volunteering can play a more pronounced role in reward schemes.

Some companies make volunteering a strong part of the company culture, such Deloitte, Novo Nordisk, NetApp, and VMWare. These more progressive companies provide paid time off, even grant donations to favoured employee charities if that employee has gone beyond the company volunteering norm. Few, however, bake it into job descriptions. Salesforce is one of the best illustrations of how to think differently about volunteering. They use a unique 1-1-1 model, where 1 percent of employee time, company technology, and resources is used to help communities around the world. It is a brilliant approach that signals to the staff that the company is not just committed to ensuring personal security for employees, but that they are committed to ensuring a broader security.

This gives confidence to an employee that the company is concerned about the more existential security concerns that employees think about, especially when it comes to the future of their children. Taking the Salesforce model even further, companies could tie bonuses to exceptional employee engagement in the 1-1-1 scheme. This ensures that employees don't just do the minimum but engage more actively in volunteering.

Building Security Through Recognition

Companies with a culture of recognition show employees that they truly care about their efforts and thus make them feel like they are a desired and appreciated part of the organization. However, there is a school of thought that suggests that it is more important to focus on group recognition versus individual recognition. The reason is that group recognition creates unity, which translates into trust. If there is trust, there is security.

A *Harvard Business Review* article from December 2016 titled "The Problem with Rewarding Individual Performers", argues that human beings have evolved in groups and that we are unique among primates in that we "readily cooperate with in-group members even if they are completely unknown to us". Research suggests that when a person begins to identify with a group there is a notable shift in their goals. The more selfish mind-set ("what's in it for me?") changes to a group mind-set ("what does this mean for us?). The HBR article also confirms that "even otherwise selfish individuals often become cooperative, and even altruistic, when they identify with a group."

In order for companies to nourish this positive dynamic, they need to explore different approaches to recognition. Therefore, a combination between group recognition and individual recognition (when that individual furthers the goals of the group), should be explored. Sports teams do this well. One example is how Jim Tressel turned around the performance of the Ohio State Buckeyes (an American college football team), by shifting reward schemes from individual recognition to group recognition. If a certain part of the team accomplished set goals, they all were recognised. This forced the group to find ways of tackling the task together.

Many companies look to sport for business inspiration, and the tech start-up BuddyTruk (a moving delivery service) has taken the team reward philosophy to a next level. Individual teams set the goals and metrics and get group bonuses if they achieve them. There is total ownership and accountability. It forces everyone to step up, and avoids people simply riding coat-tails. When it comes to individual performance, it remains important to create a bit of competition to motivate people to perform at their peak. However, how this is done is critical. Competition can create a situation where people undermine others. Therefore, ensuring that individual performance helps the broader group can make backstabbing less common. The challenge is to keep the group goals relatable enough so that the employee sees her role in attaining it. If the goal is overall company performance, especially among larger companies, the individual's sense of contribution is limited.

It is important to find the right context to create relevance. Zappos, an online retailer, does this brilliantly by aligning employee raises with helping grow their ten core values and delivering team targets.

One of the more innovative ways to create greater team-driven recognition, to feel full trust in the system that allocates rewards, and to make each individual employee see their role in achieving bigger goals that impact their annual rewards, is instituting a steward ownership model.

A simple explanation of this model is that companies can own, in whole or in part via a trust, a club, or a foundation (more on this in the following chapter). The British retailer John Lewis has done this very well. Their mission is to further the happiness of their employees, who they have named "partners" (a similar employee naming approach to Publix, as mentioned above). The company has created a Partnership, whose responsibility it is to share the responsibilities of ownership as well as its rewards. As such, it is responsible for distributing profits more evenly. Through this approach, the company "practices a blend of employee democracy and meritocracy." The employees are responsible for their own recognition. They can truly see themselves and their roles in company targets, and are encouraged to act as a team, and to further that team. There is a very strong sense of security that is fostered in this system because the workers have control, which is not the case in most other systems.

Building Security Through Employee Guidance

The changes we are currently seeing in all industries, in all departments, is staggering. Not only are new capabilities being introduced more frequently, thanks to technology and a rapidly changing consumer behavioural reality, but entire job sectors are being threatened by automation. Many companies are grappling with this new world order by exploring new ways of working. The result is that reorgs are becoming commonplace.

The corporate world is actually being encouraged to reorganize more frequently. A McKinsey study from 2017 states that the success rate for organization redesign efforts is less than 25 percent, suggesting that reorgs should be viewed as an ongoing discipline; "as a living, breathing organism, your organization must be continually redefining and improving."

Fuelling this fire, the media readily jumps on stories of corporate layoffs. They are looking for sensational stories after all. While writing this section of the book, Microsoft announced it would lay off thousands of employees in a reorg. All major news outlets such as Forbes, Fortune, CNBC, BBC, CNN, and so forth, quickly distributed this announcement. Naturally, this new employment reality creates enormous anxiety for employees, often resulting in unhealthy survival behaviours flourishing. In such a turbulent environment, companies that provide guidance to their employees to help them progress through these changing times will be loved and admired.

Fortunately, companies are increasingly doing this. In a global Manpower Group report in 2017, 60 percent of employers are looking to invest in internal training to keep skills fresh.

The most inspiring example comes from an unexpected company, the American telecom giant AT&T. It made the "*Fortune* 100 Best Companies to Work For" list for the first time in 2017, thanks to their newly introduced initiative called "Workforce 2020". This is likely one of the boldest company retraining initiatives in corporate history and could be a blueprint for other companies once completed.

Instead of planning on replacing just under 50 percent of its work-force due to the realities of the rapidly changing industry, AT&T has decided to retrain them. The number of employees needing retraining is 100,000. To tackle this mammoth task, the company is embarking on a radical redesign of everything from job classifications (stream-lining the volume of job types to create greater clarity and housing several disciplines under a new name to prepare the workforce for the "org reality" of the future), to the online job portal (now called Career Intelligence that allows employees to explore new jobs that would interest them and be informed about the training that they can take to attain these jobs). The system also recommends (a) jobs that can be attained more readily with an employee's current skill set, (b) training (where the company has partnered with Udacity to create the teaching programs), and (c) internship programs (where employees can "test run" new roles to see whether they are right for them).

This monumental program is challenging, but brilliant. It completely goes against the corporate paradigm of a disposable workforce, and in-stead shows that it is possible to keep employees by helping them evolve and pivot as professionals to create a win-win scenario (for company and employee). Above all, the initiative shows loyalty and caring. Therefore, it injects humanity into the culture which will most likely translate into much greater productivity (especially once the training is complete).

Building Security Through Greater Personalization

Greater personalization assures employees that their unique abil-ities are not just appreciated, but proudly utilized. There is no better example of where this is best exercised, than in sports teams. Using football (or soccer), it is very common to see teams that have the best individual players but seem to perform well below their potential. More often than not, a core reason is that the individual players are not being put in positions where they perform best, where their individual skills can really shine.

Whereas the teams that play at another level have found collective excellence in the marriage of all the individual brilliance. Each player recognizes and proudly showcases his or her unique ability, all the while being wed to the broader team goal. As a result, there is drive, confidence, and joy.

A study by Professor Dan Cable from the London Business School, found that nurturing individuality in the workplace translated into greater dedication by the employee, higher performance, and a willingness to lend a helping hand to peers. According to the research, these behaviours were consistently demonstrated regardless of race, gender, age, intellectual diversity, or personal eccentricities.

Most likely, this dynamic will only grow in importance as these behavioural traits, readily exercised in social media (as discussed in Chapter 8), become universal. Ultimately, millennial behaviour in social media is about manifesting individualism that adds to the strength of the groups to which they belong. That is not to say that conflict and debate is absent. Quite the contrary is often the case since a collection of different people and perspective will naturally create friction. However, it is the role of the company to harness this conflict constructively. When Island Records was at its peak, it did this brilliantly, according to Rob Goffee and Gareth Jones in *Why Should Anyone Work Here?* As a result, they were able to attract such diverse artists such as U2, Bob Marley, Anthrax, and Tricky.

As is the case in great football teams, such as the legendary Manchester United teams of Sir Alex Ferguson, they are often moulded by on-field disagreements, contrition and confrontation, but the bigger common goal ultimately overrides individual tensions. Consequently, these football teams have strived forward, accomplishing unimaginable feats.

Many companies encourage individual interests and prowess. IDPs (or Individual Development Programs) are a common tool used in companies the world over. Additionally, the 70 20 10 philosophy, which is championed by Google to encourage employees to work on things that interest them, regardless of whether they are directly linked to that person's job description, has been embraced by many companies across industries as a means to spark innovation.

Certainly, these initiatives help to create a culture where individualism is encouraged, but it may not go far enough to really champion people's strengths in the same way as is done in high-performing football teams. One way to accomplish this, is to allow all "coaches" (people managers) to create new opportunities that cater to their team members' individual strengths, helping the broader organization.

Kat Cole, the president of Cinnabon, illustrated this while on the reality show "Undercover Boss". She realized the individual potential of some of her front-line managers and created roles for them so that they could exercise that potential more overtly for the benefit of the company. In one case, she put a cashier into a trainer program after seeing her leadership abilities, and in the other she created a breast cancer fundraiser and put a young girl in charge after seeing her organizational acumen. These types of actions don't just create a sense of belonging and security, they build loyalty and excitement for a company.

The most radical way of acknowledging and championing individualism in a company is through the introduction of self-management. In his book *Reinventing Organizations*, Frederic Laloux, identifies that those companies leading the charge in reshaping the paradigms of the corporate world are big proponents of self-management. What is exciting about the findings in his book, is that those companies that have successfully implemented a self-management philosophy range in size, are from all types of industries, and come from a wide variety of different countries and cultures.

One such company is Morning Star, a big agribusiness and food processing company in the United States. To illustrate their scale, if you've ever eaten ketchup or tomato sauce in the U.S., chances are that you've consumed a Morning Star product. For a company of this size, it seems incomprehensible that they could have "no bosses". However, they are fully self-managed. They successfully implement this process through adhering to a few coordinating principles. These include, negotiating responsibilities with peers, the agreement that any-one can spend company money, the understanding that compensation decisions are peer-based, and that it is each employee's responsibility to acquire tools as they need them. At the heart of these rules is their "Colleague Letter of Understanding" (or CLOU). Essentially, it is a simple contract that Morning Star employees adhere to whereby any actions need to seek the advice of both experts (to assure actions are properly informed), and of people who will be affected (so that imple-mentation realities are understood). Consequently, employees have the perspective to take decisions for which they take full responsibility.

This bold approach to management takes individual empowerment to the extreme, creating a strong sense of security because employees believe that they are part of the fabric of the company, and therefore are not easily disposable.

Building Security Through Greater Communication

In a very dynamic working world, paying great attention to commu-nication in the workplace is critical to alleviate fears and stop misin-formation from spreading. Employees need to understand where their company is heading, and where they stand in the current and future organization.

It is very easy for conversations to spin out of control and for fake news to rapidly spread through news media looking for a catchy story, as well as through social media publishers that do not have robust fact-checking systems in place (as was discussed in Chapters 6 and 7). Therefore, companies need to do several things.

First, they need to encourage collective communication inter-nally. This can be done very easily by facilitating existing "grouping" behaviours and utilizing these forums to discuss topics on people's minds, to expose the elephants in the room. The most common is the coffee break. In most companies today, there are no official breaks. Instead, there are pantries where employees can freely go at all times of the day. However, this does not encourage broader discussion because you either go alone or with another colleague versus as a group. Beyond improving productivity (an *HBR* article in April 2012 suggested that efficiency improved at a call center by 8 percent due to instituted coffee breaks), having teams or groups "break" together, bigger and broader conversations naturally occur.

A new workplace trend is the introduction of the Swedish coffee-break ritual called "fika", which is essentially a regularly scheduled coffee break to encourage re-energizing through food and drink, and to relax by tuning out of the task you've been working on. Some companies use this forum to discuss broader questions that are on the mind of employees. Due to the casual nature of the break, freedom to express one's thoughts flows more easily. As a consequence, issues that may be on the minds of many are brought into the open and addressed.

The second thing that companies need to do to ensure that communication clarity reigns, inside and outside of the organization, is take control of the dialogue. Therefore, they must have strong customer service and community management teams in place to make sure that the right conversations are taking place, and to quickly discredit those that are false. In 2017, GE embarked on a radical new corporate strategy that aims to foster and promote a "start-up-like" mentality. To seize control of the dialogue and ensure that employees are getting readily and clearly informed, they aligned internal and external communications to leverage key social media platforms extensively (knowing that their employees were already there), and empowered/encouraged managers from multiple levels to be the spokespeople of the changes. This ensured that there was little opportunity for secrecy, which would create feelings of distrust.

The third thing that companies need to do is to hold publishers accountable for the dissemination of correct information. The scandal around Russia meddling in the U.S. election and data manipulation by Cambridge Analytica that brought Donald Trump into power underscored that not enough attention has been paid by today's leading publishers, notably Facebook and Google, to fact-checking.

Certainly, they have dialled up their efforts, and have legal hurdles that they need to figure out, but at the end of the day their algorithms are circulating information that isn't always correct and is causing masses of people to react. Therefore, they are gatekeepers and have the corresponding responsibility to be sure that false information isn't allowed to spread like wildfire on their platforms. If the corporate world wants to truly champion greater and better communication, it has to hold these big publishers accountable and force them to change.

Public pressure is one way to do so, as is to support fact-checking organizations. Companies such as Correctiv and Full Fact are doing fantastic work to combat misinformation and will continue to scale their efforts with investment. The corporations that hold publishers to account and invest in fact-checking organizations, will signal to their employees that they take transparency and communication very seriously and are championing it in the world at large. Ultimately, this behaviour will make employees feel more secure because they feel that their companies are authentic in their desire to openly communicate.

Taking the commitment to authentic communication and transparency a little further, companies should also revisit their advertising practices to ensure that they are truthful. Honesty and ethics in advertising have been seriously debated for many years. At the end of the day, advertisers are trying to sell a product or service, so they will do their very best to convince potential customers that their brand is best. In doing so, the tendency to distort reality through a myriad of storytelling techniques is alluring.

There are government bodies across the world charged with keeping advertisers in check, but there are always grey areas. Therefore, if companies want to champion healthy communication, they have to be exceptionally critical of themselves in their advertising. If they truly champion transparency, they must reflect this in how they merchandize their product or service to the world at large. This sends a very powerful message to their employees, creating stronger trust and thus security.

One of the most widely known examples of this, is by Dove. The beauty business is renowned to be a disseminator of distorted, and unhealthy, realities. Dove publicly fought this via their "Real Beauty" campaign that championed natural, everyday beauty, not the overly manufactured emblems of perfection. It was a powerful message that fuelled confidence, belief, and therefore a sense of security. Other companies can take inspiration from Unilever (the parent company of Dove) in how they can use their advertising to reinforce to their own employees that they want honest communication.

Building Security Through Community-Building

Most companies engage in team-building events such as company outings or events, pizza Fridays (or something to that effect), and other common schemes. However, too many of these initiatives feel forced. I've often attended offsite team-building events and felt that it was strange that a bunch of adults were being asked to take part in treasure hunts, or egg and spoon races. The games reminded me of the kind of things we did at camp when I was young. Sure, these "silly" games break down people's guards, but there is a level of authenticity that is missing. After all, what on earth do potato sack races have to do with creating a leading-edge online retail company? Therefore, there may be an opportunity to explore two areas to truly build a community: internally explore family versus team thinking, and externally rethink the company's consumer community-building approach.

The true "workplace-as-extension-of-home" dynamic that was common in the 1950s and 60s, is now very rare. The paternal role that a company played, the loyalty of employees, and the community created among employee families is generally unimaginable. The world is simply very different today, so certain things are more difficult.

Lifetime employment is one of them. There are examples where this still exists, and the connection that the employees have to the company is unparalleled. One such company is NextJump, a New York City based

177

start-up. Their "Lifetime Employment Policy" states, "we don't hire employees, we adopt family members." This has created a proud culture of consistency, not intensity. Boiling down the ingredients that encourage a family culture to thrive, while allowing the unique personality of a company to be uninhibited; it is simply respecting the people, listening to them, and supporting them. There is less emphasis on company events and outings (unless they are connected to an authentic reason to celebrate, such as the completion of a company-wide project, a festive holiday, etc.), and more on communication, addressing needs through a wide variety of employee programs, and encouragement in the form of manager support, mentoring, and a "failure is fine" mentality.

This breeds confidence, a willingness to try new things, and a sense of comfort that the person is protected. In companies that follow a Steward Ownership model, this is readily exercised because the employees either guide the company directly or have a strong voice in the direction the company and its policies should take. However, public companies can also institute more authentic community-building initiatives because the key is to simply develop initiatives that are honest, consistent, and connected to company goals and to the company purpose. This way, employees see the value—see that the company is really trying to find ways to make them better connect to themselves and to the ambitions of the company, and thus feel greater security in their role within their companies.

Another way to reinforce a true sense of community, is to demonstrate healthy "tribe" behaviours with consumers. By doing this, employees will feel much more connected to the company because they buy-into the way that the company bonds with its consumers.

As was discussed in Chapters 7 and 8, brands are increasingly taking advantage of the growing FOMO dynamic among people, especially among millennials. One of the main levers utilized, especially in retail, is urgency. Utilizing email marketing, many brands push sales or promotions readily to trigger a behaviour from potential buyers. These obviously work, or they would not be so actively used. However, what do they say about a company and the community it is trying to build, especially if a company is leveraging this marketing tactic too aggressively? It certainly says that the brand is pushy, and it also says that the brand is not being respectful or listening to your needs. If you don't respond to an email after three attempts, there is little need to send a few more out in the days that follow. Some coupon selling websites do this extensively.

Ultimately, it is like that person who always talks about himself in social settings, even after his girlfriend kicked him under the table to make him shut up. Eventually, the group just wants him to leave. Instead, it would be more constructive and useful to the group if this person would share stories that would pique their curiosity, that would be useful or of interest to them.

Looking at two competing travel ecommerce brands, Airbnb and Wimdu, we can see the stark difference in their approach to building community. Airbnb wants to spark your curiosity about local destinations and the lovely things that you can discover there. Their email reminder campaigns do this beautifully, and don't hard sell. They are truly living up to their promise of encouraging everyone to belong anywhere. Wimdu on the other hand, a German me-too competitor, sends emails that use urgency messaging to "force" consumers to take notice. Furthermore, they do not listen to their consumers since they make it enormously difficult to unsubscribe to their emails (I've tried countless times and continue to get their emails). The result is that the Airbnb community is a lot stronger, and the bond to the brand is more robust. Additionally, the security that you feel with Airbnb, is surprisingly high (especially when considering that you are staying at someone's house, and not a professional holiday accommodation). This outward image has a knock-on effect internally. Airbnb rates above norm on security on Indeed.com, and the overall culture is readily praised by employees.

Building Security Through Giving and Care

The final behaviours that reinforce security are giving and care. Many companies attempt to address these points through benefits packages that often include stock options and protection schemes (health insurance, retirement plans, and so forth), as well as incentive schemes. These are great, but they may not go far enough to demonstrate to employees that their company truly cares about them and wants to go beyond the norm to show an authentic willingness to give to its fellow workers.

The power of caring and giving cannot be underestimated. As was discussed in Chapter 2, caring is a value that is fundamental to children, therefore to our "base self". We look to our parents to feed this base need when we are young, because it gives us stability and confidence to explore the world unknown.

As we grow up, the dependence on our parents weakens and therefore the absolute power that parental nurturing, or caring, plays in our lives also weakens. However, deep down there remains a longing for that unquestioned love and protection. It is remarkable to see how people become more spiritually and emotionally healthy with just little doses of caring and giving. The global "pay it forward" movement (there is even an official "pay it forward" day), or "random acts of kindness" movement have shown that not only does a little caring create a feeling of happiness and strength to the person receiving the act, but the person doing it is also lifted. The net result is a stronger sense of community, compassion, and security.

Companies can leverage this cultural trend by introducing a reciprocal kindness mind-set in the workplace. In doing so, they go beyond a generic stock option scheme to show that the company cares about its employees' well-being. The impact on the individual worker is more immediate, therefore more tangible.

Some companies have done this to great effect. Coca-Cola conducted an experiment, documented in a *Forbes* article, where workers were encouraged to surprise colleagues with a coffee. The initiative not only created better happiness at work, there was also an increase in productivity. The one example where the "random acts of kindness" philosophy was properly inserted into company policy, is the American bank BBVA Compass. They have introduced a "Bank It Forward Day", where employees (or "associates", as they call themselves, similar to the approach taken by Publix) are encouraged to bring the brand to life through random acts of kindness in the community. The company equips all associates with a $25 gift card, and in teams of between five and ten, they head out into the community. Some examples of what the BBVA Compass associates have done are as significant as paying off the debt of a family member who was in the hospital, or as "everyday" as helping a mother repair her car's flat tire to allow her to get on with her day.

The idea of labelling is another way to demonstrate true caring. Much research has been done on how labelling by teachers has a negative effect on students' academic performance, or how labels carry a stigmatizing effect on those individuals who have been identified as criminals. The same thinking can be applied to employment, especially in an environment where what it means to be an "employee" no longer means stability and longevity, but rather a short term, and easily terminated, contract.

For this reason, many strong-cultured companies have created unique labels for their employees. Google has googlers, Publix has associates, Starbucks has partners, and so forth. The last two examples are worth pointing out because these labels aren't simple "branding" elements, they are "belonging" descriptors that have been set in stone into the vernacular of the company to send a clear message to their organization about how people inside the four walls are viewed by the company.

Speaking to Jez Frampton, the CEO of the global brand consulting company Interbrand, he mentioned that he pays special attention to labelling. He has chosen to avoid calling business units "divisions" because it suggests differences and splits versus encouraging a sense of team and togetherness. His thinking can be an inspiration to other companies looking to create a sense of caring and belonging within their organization.

Whether it is labelling your employees to reflect how you see them (such as "associates" or "partners"), or whether it is labelling your

181

groups or teams to reflect the relationship dynamics that you want to encourage (such as "Asian Arm" versus "Asian Division"), a label that is well thought through can encourage a union that will make people feel more secure within their organization.

While the institution of a giving policy within a company can promote a caring and giving behaviour to people working at a company, the ultimate means to accomplish this is through a wholehearted pursuit of a strong purpose.

Chapter 12

Sun: Providing Greater Purpose in the Workplace

In the chapter that analysed millennials and Gen Z, the importance of purpose in their lives was clearly articulated. Nigel Vaz, EMEA and APAC CEO of Publicis.Sapient, beautifully described this generation as "more motivated by impact, versus being solely motivated by achievement."

The need for meaning in a world that seems to have strayed away from some basic ethics and societal "unwritten rules", is understandable. People need meaning to propel them through life. This is what has fuelled global religions and why core values have never shifted. As a consequence, Millennials and Gen Z have made doing good a part of their lifestyle, in same way as music and fashion. They feel that they have a duty to right current wrongs, and they have the confidence that they can actually create change through their mastery of technology and social media.

Since purpose is a lifestyle choice by millennials, it is sought after in the workplace as well as privately. According to the 2016 Global Report: Purpose at Work by LinkedIn:

> People are increasingly looking for jobs that give them personal fulfilment; and companies are seeing that purpose-oriented employees are more productive and

successful. As the economy evolves, purpose and re-cruiting purpose-oriented talent will be a competitive differentiator. Companies of all sizes and industries are realizing the power of inspiring employees with a strong social mission and creating an environment that fosters purpose.

The literature on the topic of purpose in business is extensive. Consequently, whether or not to implement it is readily debated in the corporate world at large. At the end of the day, unless there is a tangible impact on company performance that will allow business leaders to better deliver to their promised targets, few companies will truly embrace a purpose-led company ethos. Instead, they may try to "distract" their millennial and Gen Z workers with free food, funky fur-niture, and games areas. I have seen this first hand countless times. Therefore, it is important to look at some compelling data that shows that purpose drives profits. In the same LinkedIn report mentioned above, their research concluded that between 2013 and 2016, "58 per-cent of companies with a clearly articulated and understood purpose experienced growth of plus 10 percent", and a striking 85 percent of purpose-led companies showed positive revenue growth.

The top companies that are readily written about when it comes to purpose-driven organizations and are admired by Millennials and Gen Z are Google, Airbnb, Unilever, Adobe, LinkedIn, Patagonia, Danone, Disney, and Purina (Mars). Interestingly, these companies have been driving very strong business performances. Google's stock price has tripled in five years, Airbnb's valuation continues to climb along a hockey stick curve, Unilever's stock price has gone up by just under US$20 in five years, Adobe's five-year CAGR is 36.6 percent, and so forth. Naturally, it is not credible to suggest that their purpose-led attitude is the reason for their success, but it certainly is a factor.

A core reason for this performance superiority is employee motiva-tion and loyalty. The same LinkedIn report also concluded that 73 per-cent of people in purpose-led companies, compared to 63 percent at others, are satisfied in their jobs. These same people are also over 10 percent more likely to stay at their jobs than other people. Therefore, there is stability. Naturally, this creates better productivity which will positively impact the bottom line.

Implementing a strong purpose to galvanize employees is not simple and is not something that can be achieved through "add-on" company efforts, such as CSR programs. It makes sense to look at a handful of companies that have successfully integrated purpose into all parts of their business, in order to pinpoint key table-stake actions that are paramount to a strong, purpose-led organization. In doing so, it will also be possible to see deeper ways of reinforcing the value of caring and thus create an organization where meaning or purpose takes on an even more profound role.

How the Best Purpose-led Companies Do It

Companies that are renowned as purpose-led are successful because they do two things very well. Firstly, they have an authentic desire to pursue their chosen purpose. Secondly, they integrate the cause across all aspects of the business.

To accomplish the first point, a company must be honest and have clarity, play the long game, and be very bold in what they pursue. It makes little sense to pursue a purpose if it is not intrinsically linked to your product or service. Otherwise, it becomes a throw-away exercise; something executed on the side.

One of the more brilliant recent examples of this is Airbnb. From early in the company's life, they realized that their unique business model didn't just revolutionize the travel accommodation industry, it revolutionized how people could think about travel. By staying at someone's home instead of a hotel, your experience in a new city or country could be a lot more genuine. You could feel like a local. As such, it was very important that their inventory was equally genuine, and that they helped those that rented out their homes become true hosts (which ultimately became what they were called—"hosts"). Airbnb could have just as easily pursued a price strategy, but they chose a purpose-driven direction because it was more powerful, more ownable.

Airbnb's vision of a world with greater belonging was born. It was a big space, it was relevant, and it was firmly anchored to their unique offering. The fact that "belonging" is so big was what gave it such power. In a global study by Universum in 2016, the importance of going big when it comes to purpose was confirmed by a pool of more than a million career-seekers. The top two criteria that attract young workers to companies, across a large majority of their researched countries, were "changing the world" and "making an impact".

That is exactly what Airbnb set out to do—to change the world by encouraging belonging. Speaking to Jonathan Mildenhall, the company's Chief Marketing Officer responsible for spearheading Airbnb's bold and ambitious vision, he confirmed that it was not simply about advertising the purpose, it was about internalizing it. Certainly, the company pushed advertising boundaries in the pursuit of belonging, championing gender equality and diversity in powerful pieces of creative work. However, it was how senior management constantly reinforced the vision to staff during all-hands meetings and internal memos; it was how hiring practices evolved to embed the idea of belonging so that people being brought in truly embodied the values, and it was how product development fundamentally believed and championed the vision to create experiences that would further a feeling of belonging. As a result, every part of the experience with the brand fortified the idea of belonging. Naturally, employees feel this, are proud of it, and do that extra bit more work because they buy-into what their company is doing.

The importance of integrating the purpose in all aspects of the business in paramount. The Airbnb example reinforces this. However, there are many other purpose-led companies that do it just as vigorously. One example is Purina. They are truly passionate about pets. On the "about" section of their main website it states that Purina is a company of pet lovers, and that their belief is that "nourishing pets enriches lives, because pets and people are better together." That is very powerful. Dig a bit further into their culture, and it becomes clear that all aspects of their business feed this purpose.

When it comes to hiring, candidates must be pet lovers, and ideally pet owners, or they aren't considered. When it comes to office living, they encourage people to bring their pets. When it comes to benefits, they take care of employees as well as their pets. When it comes to loving pets in the world at large, they actively fund, push, and support bringing pets to work because they have proven that doing so creates better productivity, less anxiety, and greater harmony. They even launched an official campaign called Pets at Work (or PAW), to promote more pet-friendly work cultures. In other words, they make all aspects of their day-to-day business about bringing pets and people together. As a result, Purina has very strong employee satisfaction scores. As part of Nestle, they regularly rank among the top fifty of the world's most admired companies. Glassdoor gives them a 4.2 across countries, which is well above norm, while Indeed gives them a 3.9.

Maintaining an authentic purpose-driven culture that has its cause fully integrated across the organization, requires protection. Some companies go as far as changing their operating model in order to be protected from the "poisoning effects" of relentless external profit and performance demands. One such company is Waschbär, the German online retailer whose purpose is to help people live and act in an environmentally sustainable way in their everyday life. They have implemented this purpose in the types of ecologically responsible items they sell, all the way to the CO_2 neutral shipping service they provide. To ensure that Waschbär's commitment and resolve towards its purpose is protected, they introduced a steward-ownership operating model. Consequently, their employees hold full control of the company and its pursuit of its purpose (more on steward-owned company structures later in this chapter).

Don't Get Distracted by the Mixed Signals Sometimes Sent by Millennials

It is very easy for companies to get a bit confused by the priorities of millennials. Somehow this cohort is fine with a good dose of superficial tech company bells and whistles, while also wanting serious, purposeful, topics to pursue. On the surface they seem to be incompatible. However, this dichotomy reflects millennials' social media lifestyles. They indulge in frivolous distractions that allow them to live a "social" and "liberated" life, such as "selfying" every part of their day, following countless influencers who are simply known for doing silly things, getting lost in the exploration of hours of meaningless videos, and so forth. At the same time, they use social media to champion something more profound, such as causes they support or movements that want to further.

In other words, their superficial side is as strong as their purposeful side. This approach to life naturally applies to the workplace. There is the desire for a lot more play in the workplace, greater freedom, aesthetic appeal, originality, and the ability to be spontaneous. Simultaneously, there is the desire for the company to be serious about its purpose, to pursue it unabashedly, and to include its employees in the realization of the purpose.

Therefore, giving millennials "amusement-park-fun" with "NGO-meaning" is what needs figuring out. The key is to be authentic. Since there is an ingoing cautiousness by millennials towards the corporate world, companies need to be real.

Aligning Company Working-life with Company Purpose

There is a growing trend to introduce "tech-company playfulness" into company cultures. A plethora of amenities such as free food, a gym, laundry services, and so forth are entertained. Funky furniture that gives you many different ways to work are being explored, such as bean bag chairs, alien-like cubby holes, and café-style couches.

However, it has been well documented that many of these office perks have been designed to keep people focused on work, to keep people at work for longer, and to keep them preoccupied. They are "shiny objects" that keep their employees within the company's four walls. As such, these perks actually create a type of dependency. Millennials know this, and when the office redesign is done to distract, and not to honestly make employees working lives better, and without a strong connection to the purpose of the company, employees will feel that they are being tricked. The result can be a backlash on forums such as Glassdoor or Indeed.

It is paramount that the "amusement-park-fun" aspect of company life, is intricately linked to the company's purpose. Etsy is a good example. Their powerful purpose is to "keep commerce human". In 2016, they moved into an elaborate workplace in Dumbo, an area of Brooklyn. Before they did, they sent a survey around to employees asking them what would be important for the office to have, so that they would feel better. A very human gesture. They decorated all parts of the office and acquired the furniture from their marketplace. Therefore, employees would work inside a "mega-showroom" of their clients' products, making for a human immersion into their marketplace.

Lastly, Etsy also introduced monthly craft nights "where teachers are invited to host workshops on everything from sewing to weaving to printmaking." This is such a human way to make their employees feel the passion and effort that their sellers put into the products being sold on their platform. Therefore, while the Etsy office may look similar to many new "hip" interior designs and have perks that could easily be replicated at other companies, everything was chosen to reinforce the purpose of the company.

Companies truly need to be transparent in what they say and how they look. It is perfectly fine to want to create a fun office environment to ensure that you are appealing to today's talent, *but* you have to do it in a way that is true to your culture, and a culture grows from your purpose.

I recall when I first visited the Google HQ campus in Mountain View. This is the place that is commonly referred to when tech company

189

culture and workplace design is written about. The energy was noticeable, and I felt like I was at university again, where curiosity reigned. There was a blue-eyed optimism that galvanized my thoughts. Sure, there are a lot of seemingly unnecessary perks, and quirky office experiences that exist throughout the campus, but they come from an authentic place, and they stem from their culture of curiosity. As such, the Google environment keeps people in a state of youthful optimism and drive. These are important if the company is to wholeheartedly pursue its purpose to "organize the world's information and make it universally accessible and useful".

Creating Meaning that Matters

The quest for meaning in professional undertakings has never been more universally sought as in the present time. Employees seek it and are increasingly vocal about their demands. A growing number of entrepreneurs and investors are looking to build companies that create a positive social impact. Even family business owners are looking to leave a positive legacy for their children and communities. This is not surprising when considering that individuals have an inherent need for meaningful work, according to the findings of leading motivation theorists and humanistic psychologies.

In order to create profound meaning, one that galvanises an organization, that steers the direction of a company, it is worth considering both strategic and operational ways to do so.

A Strategic Approach to Creating Meaning that Matters

Creating meaning that matters requires utter clarity about who you are as an organization, your true motivations, and being able to honesty articulate this information to the world at large. Frequently, companies proudly showcase their values and cultural tenets on websites, company literature, and even plaques are emblazoned around the office.

However, these words and phrases do not reflect how the company actually behaves, how the employees interact with one another, and how the place hums. With such disconnect, it is impossible to create meaning that matters because there is a fundamental lack of self-awareness by the company, or worse, an absolute lack of honesty and straightforwardness.

It is therefore very important to anchor a company's purpose in a robust strategy rooted at the core product or service that the company and brand can provide. A nice example of this comes from LinkedIn. This job searching platform is one of the biggest social networking destinations online, and provides unparalleled tools, groups, and content to help employees become better informed, better networked, and ultimately helps job searchers connect with the right employers.

When I attended the WPP Stream event a few years ago, LinkedIn's founder Jeff Weiner spoke to the group. He shared the company's purpose, which beautifully anchored the platform's functionality and service offerings to something truly meaningful. He said that LinkedIn aimed to "rid the world of unemployment". Not only was this tightly connected to what the site could actually do, but it addressed one of the most important human values—security. Above all, it is immensely bold. People who work for LinkedIn feel that they are part of a very meaningful mission, a task that will truly help make the world a better place.

Not all companies can have a purpose that will fundamentally make the world a better place, but all companies can pursue a value that leaves an impact. Sweetgreen, an American fast casual food chain, aims "to inspire healthier communities by connecting people to real food." While this may not make the world a better place, it certainly will leave an impact for those people who find this important. Moreover, it is anchored to what the service provides, but clearly sets guardrails for how Sweetgreen will be different than other fast casual food chains.

This message will have strong appeal to a group of consumers and employees for whom healthy eating is important. There is a brilliant quote from Simon Sinek that says, "customers will never love a company until employees love it first." A meaningful purpose that is brought to life in everyday work activities, projects, and tasks, will achieve this—much like it does at Sweetgreen.

In addition to rooting a company's purpose in what it credibly does as a product, or provides as a service, and to lean into a universal human value, it is critical that the purpose is bold but achievable. This is what makes people connect with a company, it is what pulls them to work every day, and it is what allows the company's appeal to thrive. This "bold but achievable" purpose should also be something tangible.

Sweetgreen was driven by the desire to connect people with real food. This is something that employees could see, every day, when they prepared the various dishes. Consequently, the purpose is not just emotionally motivating, it is physically visible.

One of the strongest examples of a purpose that is bold, achievable, and tangible is TOMS. This shoe company has built its entire company on the human value of giving. For each shoe that they sell, one is given to a person who doesn't have the privilege of having access to constant, reliable footwear. Their "One for One" mantra, is the ultimate example of a tangible purpose. Shoes are physically sent to less fortunate communities around the world where locals will be outfitted with TOMS shoes. Therefore, everyone who works at TOMS will not just feel this purpose, they will see it in action. Additionally, everyone who buys a pair of TOMS doesn't solely contribute to a societal movement, it is actually monetarily helping people in other parts of the world have a better life. This makes TOMS not just a shoe company, but somewhat of an NGO as well. For millennials who want to bring about change, who want to re-write what a company should look like, who want real purpose, a company like TOMS is the gold standard.

Operational Approaches to Achieving Meaning that Matters

The idea of turning a company into an NGO-type commercial/ giving entity is ambitious, and far-fetched for many corporations.

However, there are two ways that this ideology can be translated into an operational reality that will ensure that a company stays focused on pursuing meaning that matters. The first is through Conscious Capitalism, and the second is via Steward Ownership.

Conscious Capitalism

Conscious Capitalism was coined by John Mackey and Rajendra Sisodia in their book of the same name. The book debunks the conventional wisdom that purpose is a tax on the bottom line. The company that Mr. Mackey led, Whole Foods, was a case in point, but so are many others such as Patagonia, Virgin, Starbucks, and Southwest Airlines. Each of these companies has shown that pursuing a meaning that matters is very desired by consumers and can have a "profit advantage giving them staying power". This is vitally important, since the relentless pursuit of short-term performance is distracting some organizations from their ultimate goal—creating a strong, long-lasting company.

This reality was beautifully exposed by Larry Fink, the CEO of BlackRock, the world's largest investor. He said, "Today's culture of quarterly earnings hysteria is totally contrary to the long-term approach we need." Furthermore, the relentless pursuit of profit maximization is impacting many facets of our lives in seriously unhealthy ways: the 2008 economic crisis, the challenging recovery, ignoring climate issues, accepting growing pollution rates, mushrooming income inequality, and so forth.

It is therefore important to bring greater variety to the types of "masters" that companies serve. Instead of solely serving the interests of shareholders, companies should also include the interests of customers, employees, suppliers, communities, society and the environment. The principles of Conscious Capitalism do just that. There are four tenets that should be adhered to in order to build strong businesses, and to create shared prosperity. They are: a higher purpose, stakeholder integration, conscious leadership, and a conscious culture. The true power of Conscious Capitalism comes when these four tenets are executed together with equal energy and passion.

The first principle is ensuring a clear higher purpose, which becomes the north star that guides everything. It is a line in the sand that states the company's intention, and that is strongly linked to what types of products or services that are offered by the enterprise. Much of this was already discussed in this chapter. To quote the Conscious Capitalist website, "by focusing on its deeper purpose, a conscious business inspires, engages, and energizes its stakeholders. Employees, customers, and others trust and even love companies that have an inspiring purpose."

The second principle is stakeholder integration. The definition of "stakeholder" is important to understand. It includes people from the entire business ecosystem, which includes employees, customers, suppliers, funders, and supportive communities. By creating a more inclusive stakeholder set, there are better checks and balances towards creating a thriving company that drives profits and purpose equally.

The unhealthy forces and values that creep into "profit or nothing" companies are never given a chance to put down roots. Therefore, it is important to take a systems approach to stakeholders. The company's higher purpose (the north star), guides the tone and intent of interactions with stakeholders, and decisions are based on how well the projected outcomes would support the broader, interdependent system of relationships. As quoted in the book, "any preference or favouritism towards a particular stakeholder would set in motion a dynamic that can destroy the harmony and sense of oneness in the system." Therefore, an inclusive and transparent process, with set gates among the broader stakeholder set, ensures a balanced agreement on company goals and strategies.

The third principle is conscious leadership. In very simple terms, this type of leadership is about "we" versus "me". It is a leadership that creates an environment where everyone wants to contribute, and one that activates constructive emotions among employees. An article in *The Ivy Business Journal* in 2011 analyses how the wrong management approach, one where individual pressure is reinforced, activates a part of the brain that negatively impacts economic decision-making. However, if a company focuses on the collective, and does so positively, there is notably greater trust. According to *The Ivy Business Journal*, high-trust organizations outperform low-trust organizations by 286 percent in total return to shareholders.

There are many different ways that a leader can instill great collaboration. Many of these ideas were discussed in the previous chapter. How teams are incentivized is one such way. How teams are structured is another way to encourage a true team mind-set and approach. Creating stretch assignments whilst shielding the group from distractions has also proven effective. Ultimately, the tactics used will depend on the leader, the industry, and the company. The bottom line is that the negative values of individualism are never given a chance to germinate. Instead, you work towards the common goals. When these goals are tied to a broader purpose, the bonding ability of a "we" approach is exponentially more powerful.

The final principle of Conscious Capitalism is conscious culture. The right culture can turn an average company into a gold star company because it galvanises the energies and abilities of employees, removing suffocating emotions, allowing each individual to thrive in the pursuit of the company's goals and ambitions.

This is all that more powerful with a company that has a strong purpose, one that is anchored in a healthy human value, and that has a tangible benefit to the community and world at large. Employees see the bigger picture, feel their role in pursuing this ambition thanks to the culture that fosters this inclusiveness, and thus the positive momentum is astounding.

An example is the Finnish mobile gaming company Supercell. The founders put a huge importance on culture and created a team-type approach to how they ran the company, where the game developers were the "star-players". This empowered the teams enormously. The result was that employees took it upon themselves to make company-defining decisions. A case in point was how one "cell" (team) decided to pull the plug on the live game Smash Land. Much was invested, it was close to meeting its targets, and it was a game that the company really loved. However, the team felt that it would not achieve what was planned, and thus they stopped the project, sent out a mail to the company, and didn't even consult the CEO. Ultimately, their decision was the right one. Through a great culture, individual employees have the bravery to take on huge responsibilities, and the belief to perform and act at their peak.

When all four principles of Conscious Capitalism work together, there is greater focus, clarity, transparency, and empowerment through trust. In order to achieve this, companies need to pay great attention to keeping communication flowing, introducing processes to ensure that this happens, and introducing feedback loops to learn and apply successes and failures. Once the four principles are running, and there is understanding and appreciation for a Conscious Capitalism way of working, there is a good likelihood that leadership oversight will be less necessary. Instead, employees will likely take the reins. This is the ultimate accomplishment when a more democratic and "full company" approach to leadership is achieved. In some cases, it can even go further where the employees become more than shared leaders of their company, they become shared owners.

Steward Ownership

Armin Steuernagel is a German serial entrepreneur who became consumed by corporate structures as he led his own companies and looked to create a culture that unlocked the true potential of people, where the interests of a few didn't dictate the efforts of the many. He was profoundly affected by the plight of his father's hospital, which went from a great local employer to a cost-cutting machine after being acquired by a publicly traded organization.

The hospital went from a place where doctors and nurses loved their jobs, and truly cared for their patients, to a place where the doctors were mandated to spend no more than ten minutes with patient admissions. When he dug a bit deeper into the key shareholders to these types of organizations, he realized that pension funds were consistently present. It was ridiculous that these insurance entities that are there to "protect" the future wellbeing of employees, are part of the problem that is costing employees their jobs, subjecting them to unhealthy environments, and even not allowing employees to do their jobs well (as was the case with the doctors at his father's hospital). As a result, Armin decided to explore a way where companies could fend off the pressures of acquisition, and assure control is kept in the hands of the employees.

The Purpose Foundation was founded to show company owners legal ways to turn themselves into self-owned businesses. This is particularly interesting for entrepreneurs and bold owners who want to build businesses that will leave a social impact that will go beyond generating profits to helping add value to the customers, communities, and employees that they are responsible for. Through this approach, company owners can fend off the acquisition attempts, and the resulting potentially destructive clutches of financial markets.

The legal approach the Purpose Foundation takes to help companies is called Steward Ownership. Much like Conscious Capitalism, Steward Ownership aligns the interests of owners, workers, investors, and society. It accomplishes this by having the company controlled by autonomous "steward-owners", who do not focus solely on financial performance but on the wellbeing of the company as well as every person and entity that the company interacts with.

According to the Purpose Foundation, there are two principles to steward ownership. The first is that ownership is internal. Rather than have investors or outside influences direct the decisions of the company, steward-ownership governance is executed by people directly involved in the day-to-day running of the firm. The second principle of steward-ownership is profit reinvestment. Profits should serve the company purpose, and therefore should be reinvested or donated accordingly. In their book, the Purpose Foundation writes that healthy reinvestment "is achieved through a separation of dividend rights from governance rights to eliminate financial incentives and bolsters purposeful, intrinsic motivation in the leadership."

For companies that are just starting out and need capital, steward-ownership may seem difficult. Capital is required, and fast. Consequently, the type of financial arrangements with investors, even socially-driven investors, often result in companies working towards aggressive growth curves, and legally-binding investor-driven decision-making. Fortunately, there are alternative ways in which early-stage companies can access capital and be steward-owned.

The Purpose Foundation outlines four ways that this can be achieved. The first is via equity loans. How these loans are structured can vary to create greater legal flexibility on repayment terms. The challenge is that the interest requirements will feel like a cost. The second financial option is through redeemable shares. As articulated in the Purpose Foundation book, "the advantage of such an agreement is that the valuation is flexible and yet determined beforehand to minimise the potential for conflict." The downside is that the shares become a liability. The third financial option is through phantom shares. This agreement works similarly to a redeemable share, but the entrepreneur has greater freedom to make changes to the shareholder structure. The final financial option is through non-voting shares. The benefit is that dividends can be paid back over time or through a share buyback. Additionally, the entrepreneur retains control. However, investors are not used to scenarios where they don't exercise some form of control, resulting in protective measures often being put in place.

While steward-ownership may be a great idea for younger companies, ones that have greater flexibility to pivot into a corporate direction that best suits them, larger and established companies can also successfully operate with this model.

The iconic British department store, John Lewis, is a case in point. Spedan Lewis, who was the son of John Lewis, took it upon himself to create a profit sharing scheme after he realized that his father and brother were earning the equivalent to what the entire workforce of two shops was earning. The discrepancy in earnings between shareholders and workers who "could hardly earn a bare living" was too stark in Spedan's eyes. As a result, he implemented an operating structure that more evenly "shared the wealth", ensured the company remain independent, and stayed committed to its purpose of "fostering the happiness of its employees."

Off the back of this operating model, John Lewis has thrived, and is a consistent performer today. The way that their model works is that the company is owned by a trust on the behalf of its employees. Leadership of the company is decided by a worker-elected council that is in agreement with the chairman. In other words, the company is truly operated by its employees, a true "eighty thousand people strong" family. The values of caring, compassion, and humanity can be seen in the way that they manifest themselves to the world today. The store designs, the items that they sell, are incredibly comforting with an eye for craft. Even their advertising embodies their values, where their annual Christmas ad is consistently heart-warming, embodies the value of caring, and is the envy of the marketing industry all around the world.

There are many other globally known companies that follow similar ownership models. Toy giant Playmobil (Germany), luxury watch company Rolex (Switzerland) and pharmaceutical behemoth Novo Nordisk (Denmark), all follow a charitable or trust ownership structure, so that all can adamantly pursue their higher order purpose. There is enormous stability in these companies, and employees have greater motivation since they feel that their efforts are for their own benefit, and for a cause that they buy into.

Some companies take the pursuit of purpose even further by making it more dynamic. Frederic Laloux, in his book *Reinventing Organizations* coined the term Evolutionary Purpose to define companies that allow their purpose to be altered, to evolve, based on the aspirations of its employees. Laloux says that employees of these types of companies listen to where the company wants to go and follow the appropriate purpose. This is a very difficult model to follow because it requires a process of collective intelligence where there is little hierarchy. Everyone is their own boss, but they follow advice-driven decision-making so that the best interest of the company, not the individual, is always exercised.

Dutch home care provider, Buurtzorg, does this incredibly well. They believe that their nurses are on the pulse of what patients need, and thus are empowered to pivot the direction of the company based on what the market is telling them. An example of this was the introduction of an education program to help their patients prevent issues, resulting in less required regular care time. The program was introduced by one group of nurses, proved out, then introduced by these same nurses to the broader Buurtzorg community, and later adopted. This shifted the purpose of the company to not simply being a carer but also an educator.

Summarizing the Power of Purpose

Purpose truly is the unparalleled growth source for an organization, in the same way as the sun is to plants. People crave it like never before; it unlocks immense productivity among employees, and it gives companies a focus that allows them to thrive.

Never before has there been such discussion around purpose. The next big generation is craving it, which has influenced the rise in discussion and debate. However, the generational relevance of purpose goes beyond millennials. The combination of better living standards, growing economies, and entertainment distractions over the past decades, has enabled late boomers and Gen Xers to become less connected to meaningful motivations. As hardship has become more widespread, inequality more pronounced, and evil more blatantly pursued and powerful, people across generations are seeking purpose to find happiness and counteract these negative societal trends.

Purpose creates clarity. Since there is so much uncertainty, ambiguity, even misinformation in the world at large, purpose is a north star that allows people to find their way, to weed through the clutter.

The most obvious place where people look, is at work, since it plays a monumental role in their lives. If they find a workplace that has a purpose that they believe in, they will be driven by healthier values; those of caring, hard work for a greater good, and honesty. Consequently, they will work a lot harder because they are less pre-occupied with selfishness and greed. As they see their contribution helping the greater good, they will be motivated to do a lot more.

Companies who truly integrate their purpose across all aspects of the organization have the chance to thrive. Beyond fuelling the motivation and productivity of its employees, they begin to evolve from a mere workplace, into a family or tribe. There is greater trust, greater reliability, and greater unspoken understanding. When compared to the chaos in other parts of life, such as government, the financial system, world affairs, and the environment, a truly purpose-driven and purpose-operated company provides a daily sanctuary for its fortunate employees. Since outside forces are becoming more unpredictable, the desire for refuge will only grow. As such, models like Conscious Capitalism and Steward Ownership will be more readily adopted.

Chapter 13

Conclusion

Human resources software company Workday is a high-performance organization that has grown vigorously off the back of hard working and capable employees. The company could have continued to pursue its operating model since it was generating results. Instead, it decided to undertake a significant pivot because employees, especially their growing millennial cohort, were looking for an environment that encouraged the types of values that created greater belonging, and ultimately drove a stronger sense of security.

Workday decided to move from a culture of "performance management", which focused on penalizing low performers, to a culture of "performance enhancement", which focused on boosting employee efforts. Workday's vice president of leadership and organizational effectiveness, Greg Pryor, stated that this was "an important shift" because it reframed high performance to be more inclusive, less fearful, and a lot more productive. Ultimately, this pivot changed the values of the organization to be less about intimidation and more about caring. Workday injected more humanity into its organization.

We seem to be at a point in time where corporate paradigms are changing. The split-personality living has reached its end point. People are looking for a way to create better balance, to nurture the healthy values that they are born with.

The decades of values decay at the hands of companies fuelled by relentless performance aspirations have worn people down. At a macro level, there are global illnesses that have grown in correlation with the increased values decline. At a micro level, the current number of people unhappy at work is staggering. Added to this dissatisfaction is a growing fear of job security, which will only get more intense as automation removes employment sectors, and as competition for open positions becomes more pronounced due to population growth from well-educated countries in Asia and Africa.

Continuing the status quo of corporate world behaviour is no longer an option. It is unhealthy, which ultimately impacts performance, creativity, and innovation. It is dangerous, because there are countless ways for frustrated workers to mobilize themselves and cause chaos (we need only take note of the revolutions in the Middle East). Above all, it is wrong, because it is forcing behaviour that is against our innate values.

Many cultural developments that have become integrated into our day-to-day lives can easily encourage the unhealthy values that are now part of the working world. Social media is a wonderful innovation that allows us to stay more connected, to make the world feel more like a community, and to create belonging. However, the giant social media companies are subject to the financial demands of their shareholders and thus need to continually grow their advertising revenue. As such, these companies are finding ways to keep users hooked on their platforms, feeding obsession, a "me me" user behaviour, and narrowing down the things we see in order to improve the likelihood of us clicking on paid content. In other words, these social media platforms can easily feed negative human values. Fortunately, governments and large groups of people are holding companies like Facebook more accountable.

The news media is also becoming potentially more harmful when it comes to nurturing unhealthy values. At its essence, the news media should inform the people, broadening your worldview in order for its readers and viewers to be able to keep governments, institutions, and corporations in check. However, as media consumption behaviours have evolved to become more bite-sized, and as news media options have proliferated thanks to the internet, news corporations have been forced to find ways to keep their readers and viewers hooked. As a result, sensationalism has grown, and news has become more about entertainment rather than about factual information.

Consequently, the bedrock value of the news media, trust, has seriously faded. Fortunately, there are independent news organizations that are fighting the "fake news" phenomenon by changing their revenue models so that they are only accountable to trustworthy reporting.

Even the convenience that our mobile phones provide us can encourage negative values. A device that has given us such freedom, such access, is also luring us into a state of living where we consume the world around us through a screen. It is not uncommon to see people together for dinner, and instead of speaking to each other, they are gazing at their phones. The convenience of hiding behind a device is very alluring.

Communication has changed. Live voice conversations have been replaced by text, photos, and emoticons. The artificiality of this is making it easier to weaken our ability to cultivate true human connection, because we are not learning the subtleties of body language, changes in voice volume and pitch. Fortunately, there are countless movements that encourage people to leave their phones at home, and recognition of the importance of face-to-face connection both socially and professionally is growing.

As we enter into a pivotal moment in human history, where there are many opportunities for negative values to flourish, the role that corporations play in championing a path that encourages healthy human values is meaningful. Fortunately, due to the demands of the biggest generation to hit the workforce since the boomers, millennials and Gen Z, there seems to be greater energy in finding ways to change business in order to foster healthier human values.

The two areas that are most important to today's employees when it comes to employment choices, and that have the biggest ability to allow healthy human values to blossom, are security and purpose. A Sun and Soil approach can help achieve these values. The nature-inspired name of this strategy reflects the authenticity and comforting aspects to employment that workers are craving today.

The underlying healthy human values guiding the demand for greater security and a more meaningful work culture, require that companies understand who they are, and who they truly serve, in order for them to be able to set up programs and operating principles that reflect these truths. For many companies, such changes may prove too difficult given the dependencies that they face. For others, they may have greater freedom or may have leadership with the strength and bravery to take on the status quo. Either way, there is greater debate around the topics of organizational change, and consequently a growing number of options for employees who want a change.

The "greed is good" mantra of the 80s that poisoned a large part of the corporate world is no longer the dominant force in today's employment landscape. This book serves to continue challenging the unhealthy philosophy that continues to plague companies the world over. The more it becomes obvious that the destruction caused is not just harming corporate productivity and innovation, but also harming humanity, the more change will be unavoidable. As the global population rises, and globalization continues, our ability to manage this strain on our planet can only happen if we become more grounded in our core healthy human values.

The Soil & Sun approach is by no means the only strategy, but it is one that has many proven effective tactics that can inspire action. As mentioned at the beginning of this book, I feel that I have a responsibility to add to this cultural conversation because I have a daughter who should not have to be subjected to the same toxic corporate environments that I have experienced. She should have the opportunity to find a workplace that aligns with who she is, with what is important to her, and where she can thrive. If I can contribute, even so slightly, in making this reality possible, I will feel that I am that one step closer in being the best dad that she deserves.

References

Introduction

- Illustrative stories
    - http://timesofindia.indiatimes.com/india/this-teenage r-raised-over-rs-10-lakh-to-build-libraries-in-leh/article-show/57673419.cms

Chapter 1

- Adult Role Models
    - http://time.com/collection/2016-time-100/
    - http://www.forbes.com/powerful-people/list/
    - http://uk.businessinsider.com/most-successful-celebritie s-2015-12?r=US&IR=T
    - http://www.bbc.co.uk/newsbeat/article/38179392/ selena-gomez-is-revealed-as-instagrams-mos t-popular-celebrity-in-2016
    - http://www.biographyonline.net/people/famous-100.html
- Universal human values
    - http://segr-did2.fmag.unict.it/allegati/convegno%20 7-8-10-05/schwartzpaper.pdf
- Psychopathy
    - https://www.psychologytoday.com/blog/mindmelding /201301/what-is-psychopath-0

- o http://www.forbes.com/sites/victorlipman/2013/04/25/the-disturbing-link-between-psychopathy-and-leadership/#7b8a5cb32740
- o http://www.inc.com/jessica-stillman/11-signs-you-re-working-with-a-psychopath.html
- Desire For Change
  - o http://www.theatlantic.com/national/archive/2012/06/21-charts-that-explain-american-values-today/258990/

Chapter 2

- Scientific Proof
  - o http://www.thepropelprinciples.com/2014/08/04/5-inherent-values-were-born-with/,
  - o http://edition.cnn.com/2014/02/12/us/baby-lab-morals-ac360/,
  - o http://www.lifenews.com/2014/02/26/are-babies-born-with-an-innate-sense-of-morality/
  - o http://www.smithsonianmag.com/science-nature/are-babies-born-good-165443013/?page=2
  - o https://www.theatlantic.com/health/archive/2015/12/evolution-of-morality-social-humans-and-apes/418371/
- Anthropology and Values.
  - o http://humanorigins.si.edu/education/introduction-human-evolution, http://humanorigins.si.edu/evidence/behavior/primate-behavior, https://www.ncbi.nlm.nih.gov/pmc/articles/PMC4174343/, http://www.livescience.com/26245-chimps-value-fairness.html, http://www.earthisland.org/journal/index.php/elist/eListRead/chimps_and_bonobos_prove_that_moral_behavior_is_a_product_of_evolution/, http://public.wsu.edu/~taflinge/socself.html

- Religion and Values
  - https://integralchurch.wordpress.com/2012/07/10/15-great-principles-shared-by-all-religions/
  - http://www.artofliving.org/human-values-common-ground-all-religions
  - http://bahai-library.com/pdf/b/buck_abc-clio_enduring_values.pdf
  - http://www.globethics.net/documents/4289936/13403256/Texts_1_online.pdf/1f335f4b-2ad8-43a4-87ff-bb651ac810fb
- Human Values and Our Hierarchy of Needs
  - https://www.psychologytoday.com/blog/the-main-ingredient/200912/pack-mentality
  - https://en.wikipedia.org/wiki/Jungian_archetypes
  - https://en.wikipedia.org/wiki/Maslow's_hierarchy_of_needs
  - https://www.washingtonpost.com/news/wonk/wp/2014/03/27/divorce-is-actually-on-the-rise-and-its-the-baby-boomers-fault/

Chapter 3

- Work life in the 1950s
  - http://www.thisismoney.co.uk/money/news/article-2094769/Workers-1950s-worked-longer-hours-tougher-conditions-holiday—happier-now.html
  - http://www.history.com/topics/1950s
  - http://study.com/academy/lesson/post-war-american-life-culture-of-the-late-1940s-1950s.html
  - https://en.wikipedia.org/wiki/I_Love_Lucy
  - http://www.let.rug.nl/usa/outlines/history-1994/postwar-america/the-culture-of-the-1950s.php
  - http://wps.prenhall.com/wps/media/objects/108/110999/ch_27.pdf

- https://prezi.com/fdkhvy08hgkx/culture-change-since-the-1950s/
- http://admin.bhbl.neric.org/~mmosall/ushistory/textbook/chapter%2027%20postwar%20america/ch%2027%20sect%203%20pop%20culture.pdf
- http://www.internationalschoolhistory.net/western_europe/europe/rebuilding_europe.htm
- https://en.wikipedia.org/wiki/Ed_Sullivan

- Work life in the 1960s
  - http://www.cam.ac.uk/research/news/ive-been-working-like-a-dog-revisiting-a-1960s-study-of-the-working-class
  - https://www.psychologytoday.com/blog/living-single/201409/7-stunning-ways-life-was-different-in-the-1960s
  - https://socialistworker.org/2011/08/26/workers-rebellion-of-the-1960s
  - http://news.bbc.co.uk/2/hi/uk_news/england/1584445.stm
  - https://en.wikipedia.org/wiki/1960s
  - http://www.hoover.org/sites/default/files/uploads/documents/0817939628_29.pdf
  - http://www.history.com/topics/1960s
  - https://europa.eu/european-union/about-eu/history/1960-1969_en
  - http://history.as.nyu.edu/docs/IO/38751/282.pdf
  - http://www.ranker.com/list/best-60s-tv-shows/ranker-tv
  - http://www.theatlantic.com/magazine/archive/1995/12/the-conservative-1960s/376506/
  - https://critiqueofcrisistheory.wordpress.com/the-five-industrial-cycles-since-1945/the-u-s-economy-in-the-wake-of-the-economic-crisis-of-1957-61/
  - http://www.tcm.com/this-month/article/24133%7c24138/Pop-Culture-101-Bonnie-and-Clyde.html

- o https://www.uspto.gov/web/offices/ac/ido/oeip/taf/h_counts.htm
- o https://www.ourdocuments.gov/doc.php?flash=true&doc=96#
- o https://books.google.ch/books?id=Ey4TCgAAQBAJ&pg=PA363&redir_esc=y#v=onepage&q&f=false
- o http://adage.com/article/75-years-of-ideas/1960s-creativity-breaking-rules/102704/
- Work life in the 1970s
  - o http://www.ranker.com/list/best-70s-tv-shows/ranker-tv
  - o http://socialwelfare.library.vcu.edu/war-on-poverty/american-social-policy-in-the-60s-and-70s/
  - o https://en.wikipedia.org/wiki/1970s
  - o http://www.history.com/topics/1970s
  - o http://news.bbc.co.uk/2/hi/talking_point/8680362.stm
  - o http://www.theatlantic.com/national/archive/2014/01/personal-history-life-in-the-1970s-as-2-women-lived-it/283357/
  - o http://inthesetimes.com/working/entry/6768/when_workers_fought_back_1970s_rebel_rank_and_file
  - o https://www.bls.gov/opub/mlr/1982/11/rpt1full.pdf
  - o https://www.bls.gov/opub/mlr/cwc/compensation-in-the-1970s.pdf
  - o http://www.thepeoplehistory.com/1970s.html
  - o https://data.bls.gov/timeseries/LNU04000000?years_option=all_years&periods_option=specific_periods&periods=Annual+Data
  - o https://www.bls.gov/fls/flscomparelf/lfcompendium.pdf
  - o https://en.wikipedia.org/wiki/Watergate_scandal
  - o https://en.wikipedia.org/wiki/New_York_City_blackout_of_1977
  - o https://en.wikipedia.org/wiki/Winter_of_Discontent
  - o https://en.wikipedia.org/wiki/List_of_strikes#1970s

- https://en.wikipedia.org/wiki/Cold_War#Confrontation_through_d.C3.A9tente_.281962.E2.80.9379.29
- https://newzoo.com/insights/articles/global-games-market-reaches-99-6-billion-2016-mobile-generating-37/
- http://www.npr.org/sections/alltechconsidered/2014/12/08/369405270/inventor-ralph-baer-the-father-of-video-games-dies-at-92
- http://www.bbc.com/news/technology-13260039
- http://www.telegraph.co.uk/news/obituaries/8339181/Nobutoshi-Kihara.html
- https://auroraprize.com/en/armenia/detail/6893/raymond-vahan-damadian-scientist-and-inventor
- https://en.wikipedia.org/wiki/List_of_aircraft_hijackings
- https://en.wikipedia.org/wiki/Kent_State_shootings
- https://www.wired.com/2013/06/skyjacking-gallery/
- https://en.wikipedia.org/wiki/Red_Army_Faction
- Work life in the 1980s
  - https://en.wikipedia.org/wiki/1980s
  - http://www.bbc.com/news/10613568
  - http://www.express.co.uk/life-style/life/605295/80s-office-pictures
  - http://www.ushistory.org/us/59d.asp
  - http://www.forbes.com/sites/johntamny/2013/04/21/a-blast-back-to-our-glorious-1980s-past-not-on-your-life/#4d3272672d4f
  - http://www.bates.edu/student-affairs/2015/09/16/80s-night/
  - http://www.history.com/topics/1980s
  - https://prezi.com/bdq2xv9vm74g/1980s-values-and-culture/
  - http://www.thepeoplehistory.com/1980s.html
  - http://www.shmoop.com/reagan-era/culture.html

- o http://www.the-numbers.com/movie/Crocodile-Dundee#tab=summary
- o http://www.rollingstone.com/music/news/12-thrilling-facts-about-michael-jacksons-thriller-20131029
- o https://en.wikipedia.org/wiki/We_are_the_99%25
- o https://en.wikipedia.org/wiki/Yuppie
- o http://www.telegraph.co.uk/news/politics/margaret-thatcher/9979915/Margaret-Thatcher-Seconds-from-death-at-the-hands-of-an-IRA-bomber.html
- o http://www.pepsi.com/PepsiLegacy_Book.pdf
- o http://content.time.com/time/nation/article/0,8599,1907884,00.html
- o https://en.wikipedia.org/wiki/Video_rental_shop
- o http://www.infoplease.com/ipa/A0762181.html
- o https://www.wto.org/english/res_e/booksp_e/wtr13-2b_e.pdf
- o https://www.washingtonpost.com/news/wonk/wp/2014/03/27/divorce-is-actually-on-the-rise-and-its-the-baby-boomers-fault/?utm_term=.f0c4878014a6
- o https://www.bls.gov/opub/mlr/1990/09/art1full.pdf
- o https://core.ac.uk/download/pdf/6852225.pdf
- Work life in the 1990s
  - o http://www.ranker.com/list/best-90s-tv-shows/ranker-tv
  - o https://en.wikipedia.org/wiki/1990s
  - o http://repettilab.psych.ucla.edu/perry-jenkins%20repetti%20crouter.pdf
  - o ftp://ftp.ukc.ac.uk/pub/ejr/RePEc/ukc/ukcedp/0205.pdf
  - o http://www.nytimes.com/2015/02/08/opinion/sunday/the-best-decade-ever-the-1990s-obviously.html?_r=0
  - o http://www.peopleproject.eu/wiki/PEOPLE%20WIKIS/Bestpractices/mainSpace/files/recon_5.pdf
  - o http://channel.nationalgeographic.com/the-90s-the-last-great-decade/articles/the-90s-arts-and-culture/
  - o http://www.thegreat90s.com/

- http://www.thepeoplehistory.com/1990s.html
- http://www.economics21.org/html/story-1990s-economy-276.html
- http://cultureby.com/2016/02/the-rise-of-a-celebrity-culture.html
- http://www.knowyourmobile.com/nokia/nokia-3310/19848/history-mobile-phones-1973-2008-handsets-made-it-all-happen
- https://www.itu.int/ITU-D/ict/publications/wtdr_99/material/wtdr99s.pdf
- http://www.marketplatforms.com/wp-content/uploads/Downloads/The-Growth-and-Diffusion-of-Credit-Cards-in-Society.pdf
- http://assets.cambridge.org/97805218/02413/sample/9780521802413ws.pdf
- https://www.americanprogress.org/issues/economy/reports/2011/10/28/10405/power-of-progressive-economics-the-clinton-years/
- http://data.worldbank.org/indicator/CM.MKT.LDOM.NO
- https://www.wired.com/2015/01/90s-startup-terrified-microsoft-got-americans-go-online/
- https://www.britannica.com/topic/feminism/The-third-wave-of-feminism
- http://www.pewsocialtrends.org/2015/01/14/chapter-1-women-in-leadership/
- http://time.com/3645828/y2k-look-back/
- Work life in the 2000s
  - https://en.wikipedia.org/wiki/2000s_(decade)
  - https://www.theguardian.com/world/2009/oct/17/decade-timeline-what-happened-when
  - http://www.ranker.com/list/best-shows-of-the-2000s/ranker-tv

- http://www.ilo.org/wcmsp5/groups/pub-lic/—-ed_norm/—-ipec/documents/publication/wcms_221881.pdf
- http://documents.worldbank.org/curated/en/486761468153862970/pdf/WPS5961.pdf
- http://channel.nationalgeographic.com/the-2000s-a-new-reality/
- https://www.bls.gov/opub/ted/2001/dec/wk1/art02.htm
- http://www.epi.org/publication/webfeatures_snapshots_20080827/
- http://money.cnn.com/2008/08/27/news/economy/state_of_working_america/index.htm?cnn=yes
- https://hbr.org/1991/03/global-work-force-2000-the-new-world-labor-market
- https://prezi.com/610cmr1ttnns/2000s-decade/
- https://en.wikipedia.org/wiki/Dot-com_bubble
- http://data.worldbank.org/indicator/NY.GDP.MKTP.KD.ZG
- http://www.epi.org/publication/webfeatures_snapshots_20080806/
- http://money.cnn.com/2016/03/29/news/economy/us-manufacturing-jobs/
- https://www.statista.com/statistics/192356/number-of-full-time-employees-in-the-usa-since-1990/
- http://ac360.blogs.cnn.com/2009/11/24/the-dot-com-bubble-how-to-lose-5-trillion/
- https://en.wikipedia.org/wiki/Coalition_casualties_in_Afghanistan
- http://thoughtcatalog.com/charlie-shaw/2013/11/32-military-veterans-share-their-craziest-war-stories/
- https://en.wikipedia.org/wiki/2004_Indian_Ocean_earthquake_and_tsunami

- http://www.stylist.co.uk/people/tsunami-thailand-I-feel-so-lucky-that-I-survived-real-life-story-survivor-honeymoon-koh-phi-phi-tidal-wave
- http://blogs.wsj.com/economics/2012/10/01/total-global-losses-from-financial-crisis-15-trillion/
- http://www.forbes.com/sites/steveschaefer/2011/08/10/the-great-recessions-biggest-bankruptcies-where-are-they-now/#378f705a68f2
- http://www.copypress.com/blog/the-rise-of-search-engines-a-brief-history-of-the-webs-most-essential-tool/
- https://en.wikipedia.org/wiki/Smartphone
- http://www.digitaltrends.com/features/the-history-of-social-networking/
- http://www.lse.ac.uk/IDEAS/publications/reports/pdf/SR012/li.pdf
- https://www.statista.com/statistics/203688/handset-penetration-per-capita-in-north-america-since-1996/
- Work life in the 2010s
  - http://www.addictiontips.net/phone-addiction/phone-addiction-symptoms/
  - https://en.wikipedia.org/wiki/2010s
  - http://www.ranker.com/tags/2010s-tv
  - https://www.bls.gov/fls/flscomparelf/lfcompendium.pdf
  - http://www.forbes.com/sites/sarwantsingh/2014/05/12/the-top-10-mega-trends-of-the-decade/#2ce63c66570a
  - https://www.dol.gov/oasam/programs/history/herman/reports/futurework/execsum.htm
  - https://wheniwork.com/blog/facts-about-work/
  - https://www.statista.com/statistics/264810/number-of-monthly-active-facebook-users-worldwide/
  - http://www.smartinsights.com/social-media-marketing/social-media-strategy/new-global-social-media-research/

- http://www.pewinternet.org/2016/11/11/social-media-update-2016/
- http://www.business2community.com/social-media/social-media-growth-statistics-01545217#IH5XWdo7dXyPulqO.97
- http://www.slideshare.net/wearesocialsg/digital-in-2017-global-overview
- https://en.wikipedia.org/wiki/History_of_the_electric_vehicle
- https://en.wikipedia.org/wiki/Uber_(company)
- http://www.cnbc.com/2016/06/07/2016-cnbcs-disruptor-50.html
- https://en.wikipedia.org/wiki/WeWork
- http://www.ibtimes.com/police-shooting-statistics-2016-are-more-black-people-killed-officers-other-races-2421634
- http://middleeast.about.com/od/humanrightsdemocracy/a/Definition-Of-The-Arab-Spring.htm
- http://www.bbc.com/news/world-middle-east-12813859
- https://en.wikipedia.org/wiki/Occupy_Wall_Street
- https://research.hks.harvard.edu/publications/getFile.aspx?Id=1401
- https://www.theguardian.com/world/2017/jan/21/marine-le-pen-leads-gathering-of-eu-far-right-leaders-in-koblenz
- https://en.wikipedia.org/wiki/Black_Lives_Matter
- https://mic.com/articles/166084/black-lives-matter-inaugurates-four-years-of-resistance-with-anti-trump-disruption-protest#.Le3r0dbWl
- https://en.wikipedia.org/wiki/2017_Women's_March
- http://www.trustologie.com.au/2016/02/28/does-your-company-fake-caring-about-the-community/
- https://www.linkedin.com/pulse/purpose-ask-vw-amazon-author-speaker-brand-activist-smu-fellow

- o https://www.theguardian.com/business/2015/sep/25/
  volkswagen-scandal-us-reputation-emissions
- o https://www.theguardian.com/business/2016/
  may/31/vw-volkswagen-profits-down-20-diesel-
  emissions-scandal
- o http://www.businessinsider.com/jobs-that
  -will-be-lost-to-robots-2014-1?IR=T
- o http://www.businessinsider.com/the-future-of-jobs-th
  e-onrushing-wave-2014-1?IR=T
- Summary of the evolution of values in work life across the decades
  - o http://www.forbes.com/sites/kathryndill/2015/12/14/th
    e-best-places-to-work-in-2016/

Chapter 4

- Health of society overview
  - o https://www.theguardian.com/science/head-quarters/
    2015/jan/16/declinism-is-the-world-actuall
    y-getting-worse
  - o http://blogs.reuters.com/great-debate/2015/04/28/th
    e-world-looks-like-its-getting-worse-heres-why-its-not/
  - o http://www.geekwire.com/2016/ray-kurzweil-world-isn
    t-getting-worse-information-getting-better/
  - o https://www.washingtonpost.com/news/in-theory/
    wp/2016/01/26/the-world-is-getting-better-wh
    y-dont-we-believe-it/?utm_term=.5a949ef4cb5a
  - o http://ec.europa.eu/eurostat/statistics-explained/index.
    php/Quality_of_life_indicators_-_measuring_quality
    _of_life
  - o http://www.oecd.org/statistics/measuring-well-being-an
    d-progress.htm
  - o http://time.com/4616866/barack-obama-administratio
    n-look-back-history-achievements/

- http://www.npr.org/2017/01/10/508606465/scorecard-for-a-departing-president-assessing-obamas-successes-and-shortcomings
- https://www.buzzfeed.com/jamesball/now-is-the-winter-of-our-discontent

- Split personality disorder and the health of society
  - https://www.psychologytoday.com/conditions/dissociative-identity-disorder-multiple-personality-disorder
  - http://www.healthyplace.com/abuse/dissociative-identity-disorder/dissociative-identity-disorder-did-signs-and-symptoms/
  - http://medical-dictionary.thefreedictionary.com/split+personality
- Depression in society
  - http://www.healthline.com/health/depression/facts-statistics-infographic
  - http://www.huffingtonpost.com/2015/01/20/depression-statistics_n_6480412.html
  - http://www.clinical-depression.co.uk/dlp/depression-information/major-depression-facts/
  - https://www.cdc.gov/nchs/fastats/depression.htm
  - http://www.suicide.org/international-suicide-statistics.html
  - www.suicide.org/suicide-causes.html
  - https://www.theatlantic.com/health/archive/2015/03/workplace-suicides-are-on-the-rise/387916/
  - https://www.ncbi.nlm.nih.gov/pmc/articles/PMC3330161/
  - http://nymag.com/scienceofus/2016/03/for-80-years-young-americans-have-been-getting-more-anxious-and-depressed.html
  - http://ajp.psychiatryonline.org/doi/10.1176/ajp.2006.163.12.2141

- Substance abuse in society
  - https://www.drugabuse.gov/publications/drugfacts/nationwide-trends
  - http://www.thehindu.com/news/national/kerala/alarming-rise-in-substance-abuse/article17388045.ece
  - http://drugabuse.com/library/drug-abuse-statistics/
  - https://www.drugabuse.gov/related-topics/trends-statistics/overdose-death-rates
  - https://www.unodc.org/doc/wdr2016/WORLD_DRUG_REPORT_2016_web.pdf
  - https://www.globaldrugsurvey.com/past-findings/the-global-drug-survey-2016-findings/
  - http://nypost.com/2013/10/05/female-alcohol-abuse-becoming-global-epidemic/
  - http://www.portmangroup.org.uk/research/trends-in-alcohol
  - http://www.gallup.com/poll/1582/alcohol-drinking.aspx
  - https://www.researchgate.net/publication/284826731_Alcohol_Consumption_An_Overview_of_International_Trends
  - https://www.usnews.com/news/blogs/data-mine/2015/01/06/6-americans-die-every-day-from-alcohol-poisoning
- Obesity in society
  - https://www.niddk.nih.gov/health-information/health-statistics/Pages/overweight-obesity-statistics.aspx
  - http://www.who.int/mediacentre/factsheets/fs311/en/
  - http://www.oecd.org/health/Obesity-Update-2014.pdf
  - http://www.medicinenet.com/obesity_weight_loss/page3.htm
  - http://www.apa.org/helpcenter/obesity.aspx

- o https://www.urmc.rochester.edu/news/story/2803/rochester-study-connects-workplace-turmoil-stress-and-obesity.aspx
- Rage in society
  - o https://www.psychologytoday.com/blog/fulfillment-any-age/201010/is-our-society-getting-increasingly-angry
  - o http://articles.chicagotribune.com/2001-03-19/news/0103190061_1_road-rage-incidents-aaa-foundation
  - o http://www.livescience.com/5333-evolution-human-aggression.html
  - o https://www.theguardian.com/society/joepublic/2008/mar/26/alltherage
  - o https://realtruth.org/articles/101228-001-society.html
- The health of marriage in society
  - o http://www.dailymail.co.uk/femail/article-2874475/One-four-married-couples-children-fifth-planning-split-final-family-Christmas.html
  - o https://familyinequality.wordpress.com/2013/06/12/marriage-is-declining/
  - o http://family.jrank.org/pages/1094/Marital-Quality-Trends-in-Reported-Marital-Happiness.html
  - o http://theconversation.com/why-are-fewer-people-getting-married-60301
  - o http://uk.businessinsider.com/fewer-millennial-marriages-are-ending-in-divorce-2015-9?r=US&IR=T
  - o https://www.theguardian.com/lifeandstyle/2013/jul/14/marriage-out-of-fashion-babies-statistics
  - o https://www.oecd.org/els/family/SF_3_1_Marriage_and_divorce_rates.pdf
  - o http://ec.europa.eu/eurostat/statistics-explained/index.php/Marriage_and_divorce_statistics

- Child abuse in society
    - http://americanspcc.org/child-abuse-statistics/
    - https://www.nspcc.org.uk/services-and-resources/research-and-resources/statistics/
    - http://www.japantimes.co.jp/opinion/2015/09/26/editorials/child-abuse-rate-record-high/
    - https://en.wikipedia.org/wiki/Child_abuse
    - http://www.who.int/violence_injury_prevention/violence/child/ispscan_report_june2013.pdf
    - https://academic.oup.com/ije/article/40/1/219/661252/Child-abuse-in-28-developing-and-transitional
    - http://arkofhopeforchildren.org/child-abuse/child-abuse-statistics-info
    - http://newsinfo.inquirer.net/798772/child-abuse-on-rise-dswd-report-shows

Chapter 5

- The bad side of the cult of celebrity
    - http://www.pitlanemagazine.com/lifestyles-and-subcultures/the-cult-of-celebrity-and-its-effects-on-society.html
    - http://www.telegraph.co.uk/news/uknews/1581658/Cult-of-celebrity-is-harming-children.html
    - http://www.huffingtonpost.co.uk/rae-mullins/the-cult-of-celebrity_b_5687656.html
    - http://www.dailymail.co.uk/tvshowbiz/article-1254209/SHARON-OSBOURNE-The-dark-fame—cult-celebrity-destroying-todays-children.html
    - https://medium.com/i-m-h-o/a-crying-shame-the-cult-of-celebrity-594adb33eb09#.q8o5rgron
    - https://www.westminster.ac.uk/file/75791/download

- http://www.independent.co.uk/news/uk/this-britain/celebrity-obsession-is-turning-nasty-academics-warn-311928.html
- Reality show culture
  - http://www.foxnews.com/entertainment/2014/10/28/11-most-scandalous-reality-show-moments-all-time.html
  - http://entertainment.time.com/2011/04/08/32-epic-moments-in-reality-tv-history/
  - http://www.today.com/id/18472845/ns/today-today_entertainment/t/paris-hilton-sentenced-days-jail/#.WODKLBKGNE4
  - http://www.wetpaint.com/paris-hilton-frenemy-feud-history-796865/
  - http://www.eonline.com/news/808221/8-of-the-most-memorable-quotes-from-the-simple-life
- Celebrity and social media
  - https://storify.com/jsavsss/celebrity-social-media-use
  - http://www.zimbio.com/The+50+Most+Influential+Celebrities+Online/articles/Ak5gydC99Qa/1+Rihanna
  - https://www.ubizarre.com/top-10-social-media-addicted-celebrities/
  - http://www.therichest.com/rich-list/most-shocking/10-celebrities-who-made-unforgettable-mistakes-on-social-media/
  - http://www.foxnews.com/entertainment/2016/12/20/biggest-celebrity-social-media-mistakes-2016.html
- Celebrity and corporate endorsements
  - http://observer.com/2014/10/a-brief-history-of-kim-kardashians-endorsement-deals/
  - http://www.celebrityendorsementads.com/celebrity-endorsements/celebrities/paris-hilton/

- Trends started by reality show celebrities
  - http://www.therichest.com/expensive-lifestyle/entertainment/15-disastrous-trends-made-popular-by-reality-stars/
- Addiction to celebrity
  - https://en.wikipedia.org/wiki/Celebrity_worship_syndrome

Chapter 6

- Evolution of news
  - http://www.huffingtonpost.com/hannah-loesch/the-evolution-of-technolo_1_b_5342964.html
  - http://ip27.publications.lawcom.govt.nz/chapter+4+-+what+distinguishes+the+news+media+and+why+it+matters/the+evolution+and+the+role+of+the+news+media
  - http://www.medialit.org/reading-room/whatever-happened-news
  - http://articles.latimes.com/2004/jul/11/entertainment/ca-shaw11
  - https://www.fastcompany.com/3052061/how-solitude-can-change-your-brain-in-profound-ways
- News & television
  - https://www.recode.net/2016/6/27/12041028/tv-hours-per-week-nielsen
  - http://www.statisticbrain.com/television-watching-statistics/
  - http://www.telegraph.co.uk/technology/news/12043330/Which-country-watches-the-most-TV-in-the-world.html
  - https://www.tomorrowsworld.org/magazines/2003/january-february/how-the-media-mold-the-world
  - https://www.nyu.edu/classes/stephens/History%20of%20Television%20page.htm

- o https://www.statista.com/study/17302/television-industry-worldwide-statista-dossier/
- Sensationalism
  - o http://kwhs.wharton.upenn.edu/2013/09/extra-extra-sensationalism-in-journalism/
  - o http://www.bbc.com/news/uk-wales-34213693
  - o https://www.upf.edu/pcstacademy/_docs/200108_ran-sohoff.pdf
- Inability to focus and influence on news media
  - o http://www.newyorker.com/news/john-cassidy/twitter-buzzfeed-hurting-economic-growth
  - o http://www.nytimes.com/2013/12/15/health/the-selling-of-attention-deficit-disorder.html?pagewanted=all&_r=0
  - o http://www.healthline.com/health/adhd/facts-statistics-infographic
  - o www.wsj.com/articles/SB10001424052702304360704579415752076737902
  - o http://www.telegraph.co.uk/technology/internet/7967894/How-the-Internet-is-making-us-stupid.html
  - o http://www.brainfacts.org/sensing-thinking-behaving/awareness-and-attention/articles/2013/the-multitasking-mind/
  - o http://www.huffingtonpost.in/entry/the-global-explosion-of-a_n_6186776
- Inaccurate info and news reporting
  - o http://www.aalep.eu/interest-groups-and-media
  - o http://www.mediacompolicy.org/2010/04/14/interest-groups-and-the-news-media/
  - o http://isites.harvard.edu/fs/docs/icb.topic248791.files/Petrova2.pdf
  - o http://www.nber.org/papers/w15865
  - o https://promarket.org/study-journalists-fear-of-appearing-biased-benefits-special-interests/

- News & Trust
  - http://www.aim.org/briefing/media-harm-nations-moral-values/
  - http://www.edelman.com/insights/intellectual-property/2016-edelman-trust-barometer/global-results/
- Tech influence on news
  - http://www.bbc.com/news/uk-wales-34213693

Chapter 7

- Social media & progress
  - https://www.weforum.org/agenda/2016/04/6-ways-social-media-is-changing-the-world/
- Social media statistics
  - https://smallbiztrends.com/2016/11/social-media-statistics-2016.html
  - https://www.statista.com/topics/1164/social-networks/
  - http://www.pewinternet.org/2016/11/11/social-media-update-2016/
  - http://www.slideshare.net/wearesocialsg/digital-in-2017-global-overview
  - http://www.telegraph.co.uk/news/science/science-news/12108412/Facebook-users-have-155-friends-but-would-trust-just-four-in-a-crisis.html
  - https://www.brandwatch.com/blog/47-facebook-statistics-2016/
  - http://www.smartinsights.com/social-media-marketing/social-media-strategy/new-global-social-media-research/
- History of social media
  - https://www.theguardian.com/technology/2015/mar/06/myspace-what-went-wrong-sean-percival-spotify
  - https://www.digitaltrends.com/features/the-history-of-social-networking/

- https://smallbiztrends.com/2013/05/the-complete-history-of-social-media-infographic.html
    - https://www.theguardian.com/technology/2015/mar/06/myspace-what-went-wrong-sean-percival-spotify
- Social Media & weakening community
    - https://www.cnet.com/pictures/facebooks-feature-wins-and-many-losses-pictures/6/
    - https://en.wikipedia.org/wiki/EdgeRank
- Feeding the need for popularity
    - http://www.socialmediatoday.com/social-business/adhutchinson/2015-07-17/celebrities-buy-social-media-followers-should-you-do-it-too
    - https://www.pri.org/stories/2015-12-13/maintaining-real-relationships-digital-world
    - https://www.psychologytoday.com/blog/media-spotlight/201609/when-social-media-sparks-depression
    - https://www.forbes.com/sites/amitchowdhry/2016/04/30/study-links-heavy-facebook-and-social-media-usage-to-depression/#27df53674b53
    - http://www.bbc.com/news/education-36824176
- Encouraging people to be more vain
    - https://en.wikipedia.org/wiki/Selfie
    - http://www.vulture.com/2014/01/history-of-the-selfie.html
    - http://www.huffingtonpost.com/2013/10/15/selfie-history-infographic_n_4101645.html
    - http://www.elle.com/culture/celebrities/news/a31216/the-evolution-of-the-selfie-face/
    - http://www.seventeen.com/beauty/a36410/types-of-selfie-faces-on-instagram/
- Insecurity
    - https://www.forbes.com/sites/jimmyrohampton/2017/02/21/5-ways-social-media-makes-millennials-feel-insecure/#468303e36271

- https://www.theguardian.com/media/2015/nov/04/instagram-young-women-self-esteem-essena-oneill
  - http://www.menshealth.com/guy-wisdom/instagram-self-esteem
- Social media & fear and depression
  - https://www.psychologytoday.com/blog/media-spotlight/201609/when-social-media-sparks-depression
  - http://psychnews.psychiatryonline.org/doi/full/10.1176/appi.pn.2017.1b16
  - https://www.forbes.com/sites/amitchowdhry/2016/04/30/study-links-heavy-facebook-and-social-media-usage-to-depression/#27df53674b53
  - http://www.livescience.com/51294-cyberbullying-social-media-teen-depression.html
  - http://cyberbullying.org/summary-of-our-cyberbullying-research

Chapter 8

- Phone usage
  - We are Social 2017 Global report
  - https://www.forbes.com/sites/neilhowe/2015/07/15/why-millennials-are-texting-more-and-talking-less/#4b3727e95975
- Phone & addiction
  - http://www.addictiontips.net/phone-addiction/phone-addiction-facts/
  - http://www.psychguides.com/guides/cell-phone-addiction/
  - https://www.entrepreneur.com/article/273682
  - http://www.washingtontimes.com/news/2014/dec/31/cell-phones-promote-serious-social-psychological-i/
  - https://www.youtube.com/watch?v=MacJ4p0vITM (60 Minutes with Anderson Cooper & Tristan Harris)

- o https://www.youtube.com/watch?v=MacJ4p0vITM (PBS with Tristan Harris)
- Phone & anxiety
  - o http://journals.plos.org/plosone/article?id=10.1371/journal.pone.0076825
  - o http://www.cbsnews.com/news/hooked-on-phones/
- Phone & reading emotions
  - o http://eagnews.org/study-smartphones-stunting-students-social-skills/
  - o https://en.wikipedia.org/wiki/List_of_emoticons
  - o https://www.ncbi.nlm.nih.gov/pmc/articles/PMC5318447/
- Phone & relationships
  - o http://time.com/4311202/smartphone-relationship-cell-phone/
  - o http://time.com/4057948/cell-phone-hurting-relationship/
  - o http://eagnews.org/study-smartphones-stunting-students-social-skills/
  - o http://greatergood.berkeley.edu/article/item/how_smartphones_are_killing_conversation
  - o http://www.livescience.com/46817-smartphones-lower-conversation-quality.html
  - o https://www.psychologytoday.com/blog/mental-mishaps/201401/cell-phones-are-changing-social-interaction
- Trouble with deep emotions
  - o http://www.refinery29.com/2017/04/152063/how-to-break-up-by-text
  - o http://www.gq.com/story/the-ultimate-breakup-text
  - o http://eagnews.org/study-smartphones-stunting-students-social-skills/

- Weakening spontaneity
  - http://greatergood.berkeley.edu/article/item/how_smartphones_are_killing_conversation
  - http://indianexpress.com/article/technology/social/artificial-intelligence-machines-gadgets-devices-smartphones-whatsapp-audio-messages-technology-innovationa/
  - https://www.psychologytoday.com/blog/psy-curious/201605/why-we-need-be-spontaneous

Chapter 9

- Millennials statistics
  - http://www.pewresearch.org/fact-tank/2016/04/25/millennials-overtake-baby-boomers/
- Millennials motivations
  - https://www.entrepreneur.com/article/206502
  - http://blog.archprofile.com/archinsights/motivation-generation
  - http://www.wmfc.org/uploads/GenerationalDifferencesChart.pdf
- Millennials and purpose
  - https://www.visioncritical.com/generation-z-statistics/, http://www.huffingtonpost.com/christine-horner/say-hello-to-the-worlds-transgeneration_b_8071528.html
  - https://retail.emarketer.com/article/just-how-much-of-millennial-behavior-really-unique/599c4002eb-d40003acdf2e21?ecid=NL1014
- Millennials and trust
  - https://www.washingtonpost.com/news/the-fix/wp/2015/04/30/millennials-dont-trust-anyone-what-else-is-new/?utm_term=.7ecd5a9e539e
  - http://adage.com/article/special-report-4as-conference/mccann-survey-finds-half-america-trust-brand/308544/

- https://ourworldindata.org/trust
  - https://qz.com/747595/millennials-are-smart-to-distrust-their-employers-and-their-schools/
  - http://fortune.com/2017/06/27/best-companies-millennials/
- Millennials and entrepreneurship
  - https://www.forbes.com/sites/robasghar/2014/11/11/study-millennials-are-the-true-entrepreneur-generation/#5dadaa4173dc
  - https://www.forbes.com/sites/larryalton/2017/02/15/are-millennials-more-or-less-likely-to-start-their-own-businesses/#226f14921301
  - http://www.gallup.com/businessjournal/191459/millennials-job-hopping-generation.aspx
- Millennials and authenticity
  - http://www.washingtontimes.com/news/2016/nov/9/millennials-prefer-authenticity/
  - http://www.campaignlive.co.uk/article/so-millennials-want-authenticity-give-them/1437265
  - https://www.linkedin.com/pulse/what-does-authenticity-really-mean-millennials-jean-mcdonnell
  - https://www.forbes.com/sites/ilyapozin/2016/03/03/the-secret-to-happiness-spend-money-on-experiences-not-things/#2ceb096239a6
  - https://www.forbes.com/sites/richardkestenbaum/2017/04/11/fashion-retailers-have-to-adapt-to-deal-with-secondhand-clothes-sold-online/#189167771a7f
  - http://www.defymedia.com/2016/12/12/half-millennials-diy-crafts/
  - http://www.hitwise.com/blog/2017/06/diy-market/?lang=1&bis_prd=1
  - http://www.goldmansachs.com/our-thinking/pages/millennials/

- o http://fortune.com/2017/06/27/best-companies-millennials/
  - o http://80-20agency.com/2017/06/12/millennial-values/
- Millennials and purpose
  - o https://www.visioncritical.com/generation-z-statistics/, http://www.huffingtonpost.com/christine-horner/say-hello-to-the-worlds-transgeneration_b_8071528.html
  - o https://retail.emarketer.com/article/just-how-much-of-millennial-behavior-really-unique/599c4002eb-d40003acdf2e21?ecid=NL1014
  - o http://www2.deloitte.com/global/en/pages/about-deloitte/articles/millennialsurvey.html
  - o https://www.theodysseyonline.com/problem-with-trendy-activism
- Millennials and power
  - o https://www.forbes.com/sites/jeancase/2015/06/24/millennials-influence/#1991eb775095
  - o http://www.nielsen.com/au/en/insights/news/2017/millennial-myth-busting-tapping-into-the-buying-power-of-the-connected-generation.html
  - o https://www.millerheimangroup.com/blog/2017/04/millennials-power-purpose/
  - o https://leaderonomics.com/personal/millennials-power-change

Chapter 10

- Fourth Industrial Revolution implications
  - o https://www.theverge.com/2017/6/21/15846014/uber-kalanick-resignation-fowler-blog-post
  - o https://www.cnbc.com/2017/08/15/whats-ubers-valuation-not-70-billion-dollars-roger-mcnamee-says.html
  - o https://techcrunch.com/2017/06/22/as-ubers-value-slips-on-the-secondary-market-lyfts-is-rising/

- https://www.usatoday.com/story/tech/news/2017/06/13/uber-market-share-customer-image-hit-string-scandals/102795024/
- https://www.linkedin.com/pulse/uber-terrible-place-work-why-does-everyone-want-caroline-fairchild/
- Horrible work cultures
  - https://www.huffingtonpost.com/entry/worst-companies-to-work-for_us_575b26b0e4b0e39a28ada793
  - https://www.cheatsheet.com/money-career/bad-places-to-work-4-of-the-most-toxic-company-cultures.html/
  - https://www.thestreet.com/story/13257755/1/6-companies-with-worse-workplaces-than-amazon.html
  - http://www.marketwatch.com/story/companies-with-the-best-and-worst-reputations-2016-05-12
- Companies Millennials want to work for
  - https://morningconsult.com/2017/06/12/millennials-admired-companies/
  - https://www.forbes.com/sites/kaytiezimmerman/2017/08/26/top-10-companies-millennials-want-to-work-for/#5641467a453c
  - http://fortune.com/best-workplaces-millennials/
  - http://universumglobal.com/worlds-attractive-employers-2016/
  - https://www.entrepreneur.com/article/249174
  - https://www.fastcompany.com/3048197/why-purpose-driven-companies-are-often-more-successful
  - https://www.entrepreneur.com/article/249174
  - http://www.businessinsider.com/top-100-millennial-brands-2017-5?IR=T/#100-dollar-tree-1
  - http://www.businessinsider.com/brands-millennials-love-think-do-good-2017-6?IR=T/#9-fitbit-1
- Important values in the workplace
  - https://www.inc.com/michael-schneider/google-thought-they-knew-how-to-create-the-perfect.html

- FM Excel analysis on top admired companies

Chapter 11

- Security in the workplace
  - https://www.forbes.com/sites/karstenstrauss/2017/01/11/20-companies-offering-great-job-security/#56e7b83b4cc1
  - http://blog.indeed.com/2016/09/21/build-great-organizational-culture/
  - https://books.google.it/books?id=Rk3F6wQ7eosC&pg=PA160&lpg=PA160&dq=companies+that+provide+-real+job+security+for+employees&source=bl&ots=7o-joLwG6RU&sig=VaQkpQANWEDwbmL6H-6IEiw8mXHY&hl=it&sa=X&ved=0ahUKEwjRv6XfgPDWAhXBHxoKHUhmA7w4ChDoAQhkMAc#v=onepage&q=companies%20that%20provide%20real%20job%20security%20for%20employees&f=false
  - http://www.mbahro.com/News/tabid/110/entryid/439/Promote-the-feeling-of-job-security-with-your-employees-to-retain-them.aspx
  - https://www.japantimes.co.jp/news/2017/07/21/business/japans-millennials-tend-sacrifice-higher-earnings-job-security-thwarting-bojs-economic-reforms/#.WeH4GxOCxE4
  - https://www.lifeinnorway.net/working-culture-norway/
  - https://www.justlanded.com/english/Denmark/Denmark-Guide/Jobs/Denmark-s-labor-market
  - https://seekingalpha.com/article/4052562-analyzing-big-4-u-s-airlines-buy-southwest-delta
  - http://fortune.com/2016/10/26/best-global-companies/
  - http://reviews.greatplacetowork.com/ernst-young-llp

- http://www.telegraph.co.uk/travel/galleries/worlds-happiest-countries/
- https://www.forbes.com/sites/karstenstrauss/2017/06/30/the-worlds-most-reputable-countries-in-2017
- http://careers.nextjump.com/about/culture
- https://www.theguardian.com/commentis-free/2016/dec/12/cult-compulsory-happiness-ruining-workplaces-office-fun
- http://fortune.com/2016/04/12/modern-work-culture/
- Security through volunteering
  - http://fortune.com/2015/03/21/companies-offer-incentives-for-volunteering/
  - http://www.rrgexec.com/rewarding-your-employees-15-examples-of-successful-incentives-in-the-corporate-world/
- Security through collective vs individual recognition
  - https://hbr.org/2015/06/reward-your-best-teams-not-just-star-players
  - https://hbr.org/2016/12/the-problem-with-rewarding-individual-performers
  - https://www.sesp.northwestern.edu/masters-learning-and-organizational-change/knowledge-lens/stories/2011/team-based-rewards.html
  - https://tech.co/41-startups-share-motivate-teams-2015-04
  - https://www.entrepreneur.com/article/249174
- Security through self-management
  - http://www.self-managementinstitute.org/about/what-is-self-management
  - http://morningstarco.com/index.cgi?Page=Self-Management
  - http://www.hbs.edu/faculty/Pages/item.aspx?num=45683

- https://www.youtube.com/watch?v=qqUBdX1d3ok
- https://www.slideshare.net/Ashuvyas2128/morning-star-case-study

- Security through in-house capability upgrading
  - https://hbr.org/2017/02/most-reorgs-arent-ambitious-enough
  - https://qz.com/885879/accenture-research-at-davos-fight-automation-by-making-a-companys-competitive-advantage-their-employees-not-their-technology/
  - https://www.thebalance.com/tap-the-power-of-internal-training-1919298
  - https://www.economist.com/news/special-report/21714171-companies-are-embracing-learning-core-skill-what-employers-can-do-encourage-their
  - http://www.hrdive.com/news/how-automation-will-impact-employee-training-and-company-leadership/434143/
  - http://fortune.com/att-hr-retrain-employees-jobs-best-companies/

- Security through the freedom & celebration of individuality
  - http://www.right.com/wps/wcm/connect/81f2dae6-54ff-4721-b132-c699ee43ac5d/Right-Management-Career-Management-Brochure.pdf?MOD=AJPERES
  - http://govleaders.org/idp.htm
  - https://emplo.com/blog/reasons-for-using-individual-development-plans
  - https://hbr.org/2013/05/creating-the-best-workplace-on-earth
  - https://www.hrzone.com/lead/culture/be-yourself-individualism-in-the-workplace
  - https://www.amazon.com/Why-Should-Anyone-Work-Here-ebook/dp/B00WDDOSKA/ref=sr_1_1?s=-books&ie=UTF8&qid=1509278072&sr=1-1&keywords=9781625275103

- Security through excellent communication
  - https://www.forbes.com/sites/forbescommunication-scouncil/2017/05/01/four-corporate-communications-best-practices-to-learn-from-ge/
  - https://axerosolutions.com/blogs/timeisenhauer/pulse/281/11-ted-talks-on-effective-communication-in-the-workplace
  - http://www.techradar.com/news/fighting-fake-news-how-google-facebook-and-more-are-working-to-stop-it
  - https://www.ft.com/content/afe1f902-82b6-11e7-94e2-c5b903247afd?mhq5j=e6
  - https://en.wikipedia.org/wiki/Dove_Campaign_for_Real_Beauty
  - http://digitalcommons.calpoly.edu/cgi/viewcontent.cgi?article=1107&context=joursp
  - https://hbr.org/2012/04/the-new-science-of-building-great-teams
  - http://europe-institute.com/training/effective-communication/importance-of-coffee-breaks/
  - https://www.entrepreneur.com/article/248031
  - https://inews.co.uk/essentials/lifestyle/wellbeing/fika-coffee-break-work-swedish-uk-companies/
- Security through community
  - https://www.huffingtonpost.com/robin-hardman/if-your-company-feels-lik_b_9465870.html
- Security through care & giving
  - https://www.theguardian.com/money/2012/apr/13/better-business-acts-of-kindness
  - http://socialmediaexplorer.com/content-sections/movers-and-makers/one-company-using-random-acts-kindness-build-brand/
  - http://opencommons.uconn.edu/cgi/viewcontent.cgi?article=1074&context=srhonors_theses

Chapter 12

- Purpose in the corporate world
    - http://fortune.com/2017/07/10/tech-employees-bosses/
    - https://www.theguardian.com/sustainable-business/2016/sep/14/millennials-work-purpose-linkedin-survey
    - https://business.linkedin.com/talent-solutions/job-trends/purpose-at-work?src=gua#
    - https://www.forbes.com/sites/danpontefract/2016/02/04/the-story-of-candice-and-her-quest-for-purpose-at-work/#2e8c1d9e7c16
- Companies with strong purpose
    - http://3blmedia.com/News/Purina-Calls-Organisations-Reap-Rewards-Bringing-Pets-Work
    - https://www.petfoodindustry.com/articles/6690-purina-supports-pets-at-work-policy-in-europe
    - https://www.bizjournals.com/stlouis/print-edition/2015/03/13/top-dogs-why-nestl-purina-petcare-is-consistently.html
    - https://www.prnewswire.com/news-releases/purina-is-searching-for-americas-most-pet-friendly-companies-182091261.html
    - https://www.purina.com/about-purina/better-with-pets/pets-at-work/5-steps-to-pet-friendly-workplace
- Aligning work life with company purpose
    - http://uk.businessinsider.com/inside-etsys-new-perk-filled-office-2016-6?r=US&IR=T/#in-fact-about-50-of-the-furnishings-in-the-entire-building-were-made-by-local-artists-and-etsy-sellers-16
    - http://moneyinc.com/cant-fake-corporate-culture/
- Meaning at work
    - motivation theorists and humanistic psychologists (Alderfer, 1972; Herzberg, Mausner, & Snyderman,

1959; Maslow, 1943; McClelland, 1965; McGregor, 1960; Rogers, 1961)

- o http://www.sesp.northwestern.edu/masters-learning-and-organizational-change/knowledge-lens/stories/2016/the-power-of-purpose-how-organizations-are-making-work-more-meaningful.html
- o https://blog.hubspot.com/marketing/inspiring-company-mission-statements
- Purpose-driven operational models
  - o http://www.wired.co.uk/article/julie-hannah-profit-purpose-startups
  - o Managing Social Purpose Driven Organizations (book) https://books.google.ch/books?isbn=1351997092
  - o http://causecapitalism.com/category/build-a-purpose-driven-business/
  - o https://theplatoproject.com/glossary-understanding-the-purpose-driven-business-sector/
  - o https://www.consciouscapitalism.org/
  - o Conscious Capitalism by John Mackey (book) https://books.google.ch/books/about/Conscious_Capitalism_With_a_New_Preface.html?id=BryKAgAAQBAJ&redir_esc=y
  - o https://iveybusinessjournal.com/publication/a-case-for-conscious-capitalism-conscious-leadership-through-the-lens-of-brain-science/
  - o http://blog.innoduel.com/amazing-employee-engagement-examples
- Steward ownership
  - o https://hbr.org/2003/05/gearing-up-at-rei
  - o http://purpose-economy.org/en/blog/interview-armin-steuernagel-co-founder-purpose/
  - o http://purpose-economy.org/en/blog/armin-steuernagel-on-different-types-of-steward-ownership/
  - o http://www.buurtzorgusa.org/about-us/

- http://accessh.org/wp-content/uploads/2016/04/
Buurtzorg.compressed.pdf

Chapter 13

- Companies pivoting away from bad values
  - http://fortune.com/2017/03/14/best-companies
  -to-work-for-culture/

About the Author

 Frank Mertens is a seasoned global marketing executive who has worked at The Coca-Cola Co., eBay, Bacardi, Groupon, and BBDO Worldwide. His professional journey has taken him to countries across North America, Europe, and Asia, where he was responsible for global, regional, and local teams. He's also worked closely with startups and has developed a training program for high school students to help them find their ideal careers.

Made in the USA
Columbia, SC
28 October 2018